Routledge Studies in the Modern World Economy

Economic Uncertainty in the Post-Pandemic Era
Policy Responses and the Way Forward
Edited by Shilpa Deo and Fatma Feyza Gündüz

Data Governance and the Digital Economy in Asia
Harmonising Cross-Border Data Flows
Edited by Paul Cheung, Liu Jingting and Ulrike Sengstschmid

Corporate Systems in Emerging Market Economies
A Comparison of China and Eastern Europe
Ichiro Iwasaki, Xinxin Ma and Satoshi Mizobata

Geoeconomics of the Israel-Palestine Conflict
Governance, Global Trade and Regional Dynamics
Edited by Rajesh Kumar, Debasis Neogi, Prasoon M. Tripathi and Dayanand Pandey

Free Market and Perfect Competition
Global Data Trends
Weshah Razzak

National Strategy and Global Competitiveness
Human Behaviour and Market Dynamics in the Age of Competition
Ihor Hurnyak and Oleksandra Werbowa

For more information about this series, please visit: www.routledge.com/Routledge-Studies-in-the-Modern-World-Economy/book-series/SE0432

National Strategy and Global Competitiveness

Human Behaviour and Market Dynamics in the Age of Competition

Ihor Hurnyak and Oleksandra Werbowa

Routledge
Taylor & Francis Group
LONDON AND NEW YORK

First published 2026
by Routledge
4 Park Square, Milton Park, Abingdon, Oxon OX14 4RN

and by Routledge
605 Third Avenue, New York, NY 10158

Routledge is an imprint of the Taylor & Francis Group, an informa business

British Library Cataloguing-in-Publication Data
A catalogue record for this book is available from the British Library

ISBN: 978-1-041-11484-0 (hbk)
ISBN: 978-1-041-11486-4 (pbk)
ISBN: 978-1-003-66019-4 (ebk)

DOI: 10.4324/9781003660194

Typeset in Sabon
by codeMantra

Contents

Figures

Tables

Preface

In the contemporary world, marked by volatile geopolitical realities, technological revolutions, and an ever-deepening interdependence among nations and regions, strategic thinking has evolved from a mere professional skill into a fundamental way of interpreting and navigating the forces that shape global power, competition, and influence. Today, strategy is no longer confined to boardrooms or corporate planning sessions. It has become an essential lens through which we examine shifts in international alliances, the economic consequences of geopolitical conflicts, and the fierce contests for technological, financial, and industrial leadership that increasingly define the global order.

Whether in diplomatic negotiations, national security deliberations, trade policymaking, or multilateral institutions, strategic decisions taken by states reverberate far beyond national borders. They ripple through global economic systems, redefine technological races, and influence the delicate architecture of international relations. The boundaries between economics, security, and technology have blurred, creating a new strategic landscape in which states and major institutions are simultaneously partners and rivals – engaged in an intense competition for resources, innovation, and sustainable competitive advantage.

This competitive dynamic lies at the heart of the modern age. National strategy and global competitiveness have become deeply entwined, as governments increasingly view economic performance not only as a matter of domestic prosperity but also as a crucial pillar of geopolitical strength. The contest for global influence now extends into domains such as artificial intelligence, quantum computing, green technologies, and advanced manufacturing, where leadership often translates directly into political leverage and national security advantages.

Strategic thinking, as understood in this book, transcends the narrow confines of tactical manoeuvring or short-term optimisation. It represents a structured way of perceiving the world – identifying patterns in apparent chaos, mapping interdependencies, and anticipating the cascading consequences of choices made under uncertainty. It is not merely about reacting to external events but about deliberately shaping the environment in which geopolitical and economic interactions unfold, and about securing competitive positions in a world increasingly defined by rival claims to markets, technologies, and spheres of influence.

Over recent decades, multiple disciplines – from classical economics and political science to physics and computational science – have contributed tools and models that allow for a more rigorous examination of strategic behaviour among nations, alliances, and economic blocs. Yet despite growing mathematical sophistication, a persistent gap remains between abstract theorising and the practical realities that define global strategic rivalry, economic competition, and institutional transformations. Bridging this gap is precisely the purpose of this book.

Central to our approach is the concept of **"econothinking"**. This mindset involves viewing decisions and phenomena through the prism of economic consequences, but not merely in terms of immediate profit or loss. It requires a strategic, long-term perspective that examines how choices made by states, corporations, and institutions aggregate into systemic outcomes – often in ways that defy linear expectations. To think economically, in this sense, is to recognise that geopolitics and competitiveness are deeply intertwined – and that economic power, technological capacity, and market leadership are increasingly the currencies of geopolitical influence.

This book rests upon several fundamental propositions:

1 **Strategic behaviour is intrinsic to states and institutions.** While strategic thinking is often associated with individual actors or private enterprises, it is nations, supranational bodies, and global economic blocs that most significantly engage in strategic behaviour on a scale that shapes world affairs. Whether through forging alliances, advancing technological frontiers, or orchestrating economic influence, states operate in a competitive environment where strategic calculations determine their global standing and capacity for resilience.
2 **Global competitiveness is a multidimensional contest.** It is not merely about GDP growth or export figures. Competitiveness encompasses technological leadership, innovation ecosystems, resource security, institutional adaptability, and even the ability to attract talent and investment. Nations today compete in a complex matrix where economic strength translates into strategic influence, and where lagging behind can quickly erode geopolitical relevance.
3 **Modern strategic contexts demand new analytical tools.** Classical models like the Prisoner's Dilemma provide lasting insights but cannot alone capture the emergent phenomena and nonlinear interactions that characterise today's interconnected world. New methods – from agent-based modelling and evolutionary game theory to neural networks, econophysical simulations, and multidimensional cluster analysis – are indispensable for understanding how strategic rivalries unfold among states, industries, and global institutions.

In the chapters that follow, we explore these themes through a multidisciplinary lens. We examine how **game theory**, originally focused on individual or corporate decision-making, has evolved into a powerful framework for modelling international rivalries, alliance dynamics, and competitive strategies among nations. We investigate how repeated games, evolutionary tournaments, and simulation-based methods – such as the **Axelrod Tournament framework** – can illuminate the logic of cooperation, betrayal, and strategic adaptation in the high-stakes arena of global markets.

We extend our analysis to **econophysics**, which brings insights from statistical physics into the modelling of systemic economic phenomena. This approach enables us to distinguish between fundamental forces driving global economic interactions and the "vibrational" forces introduced by institutional frictions, market volatility, and technological disruptions. At the same time, we reinterpret classical financial models – such as the **Fama–French framework** – not merely as instruments for predicting asset returns but as strategic maps of institutional behaviour. In a world where national champions, state-owned enterprises, and sovereign wealth funds play significant roles, understanding financial performance and market behaviour becomes inseparable from understanding geopolitical strategy and national competitiveness.

The impetus for this book arises from the profound transformations of our time. The **COVID-19 pandemic**, the resurgence of great-power competition, the **Russia–Ukraine war**, and the escalating race for technological supremacy have revealed the vulnerabilities of global interdependence. They have underscored that competitiveness and strategic resilience are now intertwined imperatives for states seeking not just economic prosperity but geopolitical security and influence.

In discussing national strategy and global competitiveness, we examine how governments deploy policy tools – from R&D investments to industrial alliances – to gain strategic advantage. Using multidimensional cluster analysis, we identify patterns that link national performance to technological capacity and geopolitical positioning. Yet, modern geopolitics remains full of paradoxes, where short-term competitive moves can undermine long-term global interests such as climate action or financial stability. The strategic behaviours modelled in game theory reflect this fragmentation, revealing that no universal blueprint exists for national strategy; instead, nations must adapt continuously to an evolving landscape of rivalry and cooperation. This book also pays particular attention to **regional dynamics**, notably in **Central and Eastern Europe** and emerging markets in **Latin America**. These regions are crucial arenas where national strategies intersect with global forces. In Central Europe, countries navigate between integration into larger blocs like the European Union and the desire to maintain strategic autonomy. In Latin America, economic actors face challenges from currency instability to political volatility, making strategic competitiveness both a survival necessity and an opportunity for global engagement.

Yet this book is not merely a catalogue of models and concepts. At its core lies the conviction that knowledge of strategic tools is insufficient unless paired with the capacity to **apply them contextually**. Our goal is to democratise advanced analytical methods, making them accessible not only to policymakers and strategists but also to scholars, economists, and practitioners seeking to understand and influence the dynamics of global competition. We believe that strategic insight is not the exclusive preserve of a small elite but a critical literacy for all who wish to comprehend – and shape – the rapidly evolving global order.

Accordingly, this book offers guidance for practical application, including references to computational tools and software implementations in Python and R. We avoid excessive technical detail likely to become outdated, focusing instead on principles and frameworks robust enough to remain relevant amid technological change. Our aim is to enable readers to adapt methods for their own strategic challenges – whether in policy analysis, institutional decision-making, or competitive intelligence.

Ultimately, our ambition is twofold:

- To examine the mechanisms underlying strategic decision-making and how entities across various domains – from individuals and corporations to national governments – adapt their strategies in the face of unpredictable challenges.
- To **equip readers with practical tools and conceptual frameworks** that empower them to assess strategic risks, anticipate competitive dynamics, and make informed decisions in a world characterised by volatility, uncertainty, complexity, and ambiguity.

Engaging with the ideas and methodologies presented here is not merely an intellectual exercise. It is a way to cultivate the foresight and resilience necessary to navigate – and influence – the turbulent geopolitics, economic transformations, and relentless competition that define the 21st century. We invite you to join us on this journey through the intellectual landscapes of modern strategy, where theory and practice converge, and where knowledge equips us not merely to survive, but to thrive in an era of global competition.

1 Evolving Strategic Tools and Models for the Modern Economy

1.1 Game Theory as a Strategic Framework: From Theory to Simulation

1.1.1 Foundations of Game Theory and Strategic Thought

Over the past century, the theory of strategic decision-making has undergone a fundamental transformation. Initially rooted in static models of equilibrium and rational choice, classical economic frameworks focused on assumptions such as perfect information, utility maximisation, and market-clearing behaviour. These early models – emerging from neoclassical economics – offered valuable mathematical clarity but struggled to account for the nuances of human behaviour, institutional rigidity, and dynamic interaction under uncertainty.

A paradigm shift began with the publication of *Theory of Games and Economic Behaviour* by John von Neumann and Oskar Morgenstern (1944). This foundational work introduced game theory as a rigorous, mathematical approach to modelling interdependent decision-making. Unlike prior frameworks that treated agents as isolated optimisers, game theory emphasised relational dynamics – how the payoff of one actor is shaped by the actions of others. The von Neumann–Morgenstern utility theorem formalised rational behaviour under uncertainty and paved the way for new ways of understanding competition, negotiation, and coalition-building.

The next decisive advance came from John Nash (1950), who introduced the concept of Nash equilibrium, which occurs in a game when each player's strategy is optimal, given the strategies of all other players. Thus, no player has anything to gain by changing only their own strategy unilaterally. This innovation allowed game theory to extend into a wide array of economic, political, and social domains. Importantly, Nash's equilibrium concept generalised strategic reasoning beyond zero-sum or strictly competitive settings, making it applicable to cooperation, mixed motives, and institutional design. Later refinements by Selten (1975) introduced the concept of subgame perfect equilibrium, strengthening the internal consistency of strategic reasoning in dynamic contexts.

DOI: 10.4324/9781003660194-1

Throughout the second half of the 20th century, game theory was further enriched by contributions such as repeated games, evolutionary models, and bounded rationality. For example, the work of Fudenberg and Tirole (1991) formalised strategic interaction across time, while Camerer (2003) introduced experimental insights into how real individuals behave in strategic settings. Binmore (2007) emphasised the real-world application of game theory to ethical, political, and economic dilemmas. These developments deepened the analytical lens through which economists could examine long-term incentives, signalling behaviour, trust dynamics, and strategic deception.

In the 21st century, the scope of strategic analysis has expanded dramatically in response to the increasing complexity of global markets. Digital platforms, financial interdependence, geopolitical fragmentation, and network externalities have all challenged the assumptions of traditional economic models. As Gintis (2009) argues, modern decision-making is no longer adequately captured by the logic of individual maximisation alone. Strategic agents today must learn, adapt, forecast others' behaviour, and operate under asymmetric or incomplete information. In such settings, tools like agent-based simulations, neural networks, and evolutionary tournaments (e.g., Axelrod's framework, Axelrod, 1984) have become increasingly valuable.

Brandenburger and Nalebuff (1996), through their concept of *co-opetition*, expanded the scope of game-theoretic reasoning beyond conflict and competition, framing strategy as an interaction of players who simultaneously cooperate and compete. Their work blends traditional models with real-world business insight, emphasising that competitive advantage often emerges not from dominance, but from shaping the rules of the game itself. Likewise, Myerson (1991) contributed a foundational mathematical formalism that allowed game theory to move beyond stylised examples and into complex institutional applications. His analysis of signalling, auctions, and bargaining provided the structural backbone for applying game theory to international relations, finance, and public policy.

This intellectual evolution also reframes how we view foundational metaphors like Adam Smith's "invisible hand". While once regarded as a guiding principle for spontaneous market order, in contemporary political economy this concept often serves more as an aspirational metaphor than a reliable mechanism. In practice, modern economies are shaped by regulation, lobbying, informal networks, and institutional inertia. The true "hand" guiding behaviour is often invisible not because it is emergent, but because it is obscured by competing interests, asymmetric power, or intentional design.

Thus, in a world of interconnected systems and strategic competition, game theory offers more than a predictive tool – it provides a language for interpreting behaviour, mapping power dynamics, and navigating uncertainty. Strategic thinking today is not merely about optimising within a set environment, but about shaping that environment itself. Whether in financial markets, wartime decision-making, corporate strategy, or international relations, actors must anticipate reactions, manage perceptions, and sometimes strategically distort information to achieve long-term advantage. Within this framework, classic models like the Prisoner's Dilemma (PD) take on renewed relevance – not just as teaching tools, but as heuristics for understanding institutional choices and systemic risk. Later in this text, we will explore how tournament-based simulations, such as those pioneered by Axelrod (1984), and models like Fama–French, can be employed to analyse real-world strategic behaviour – from military strategy and energy policy to corporate competition and postwar institution-building.

Building on these foundational developments, one of the reasons game theory has remained both analytically powerful and widely teachable is its use of vivid, simplified stories that encapsulate core strategic dilemmas. From pirates dividing treasure to prisoners negotiating silence, these stylised examples help illustrate otherwise abstract logic in relatable, memorable terms. For those seeking to engage their audience more vividly, it may be worth beginning with the tale of the division of treasure among pirates, where a younger pirate is often forced to accept a symbolic share or face being thrown overboard. Game theory is surrounded by such thought-provoking and illustrative scenarios. This type of analysis is classically framed through the well-known PD (Table 1.1). The scenario involves two bank robbers who, after a successful heist, decide to hide from further criminal investigation by spending time in prison. To do so, they stage a car theft and allow themselves to be caught in the act. Once apprehended, the prosecutor isolates them and offers each a deal: confess and walk free while the other takes the full blame, or remain silent and risk a shared sentence. If both confess, they each receive moderate punishment. If both stay silent, their cooperation leads to minimal sentencing. But if one betrays and the other stays loyal, the betrayer goes free while the other receives the harshest penalty. The resulting matrix of possible outcomes encapsulates the central problem of trust, risk, and strategy in a world of incomplete information and conflicting incentives.

The suspicious behaviour of the two suspects – who did not appear to be outright fools – prompted the prosecutor to investigate recent robbery cases. Given a resemblance between the suspects and descriptions from prior incidents, he hypothesised that these two were responsible for a recent bank robbery. To extract a confession, the prosecutor employed a classic strategy: he placed the suspects in separate rooms and attempted to convince each of them that the other could not be trusted and was likely to act in pure

Table 1.1 Prisoner's Dilemma (Example Scenario – Sentences in Years)

		Player 2 (Thief 2)	
		Confess	*Don't confess*
Player 1	*Confess*	6; 6	0; 10
(Thief 1)	*Don't confess*	10, 0	1; 1

Source: Based on the classical formulation of the Prisoner's Dilemma, as presented in Dixit and Nalebuff (2008).

self-interest. He promised freedom – or a minimal sentence – to the suspect who confessed. However, if one suspect remained silent while the other confessed, the silent party would receive the maximum sentence of ten years. If both confessed, they would each receive six years. If both remained silent, they would only be charged with the attempted (staged) car theft and sentenced to one year each. Although the exact lengths of sentences may vary in different versions of this matrix, the fundamental logic of the PD remains intact.

Thanks to John Nash's theoretical insights, we can identify a solution in which each player's best decision aligns with that of the other – the so-called Nash equilibrium. A simple method exists to find this equilibrium: cover one column of the payoff matrix and identify the best response in the remaining cells. Repeat the process across both dimensions (columns and rows). If the best responses of both players intersect in a single cell, Nash equilibrium is present. Yet a natural question arises: why would two relatively intelligent individuals – clever enough to design a plan to hide in prison – fail to coordinate their interrogation strategies? Could the explanation lie in psychological vulnerability or behavioural heuristics previously observed by the prosecutor? If so, we are dealing with a form of repeated game – at least in the prosecutor's mind. Without such a premise, the standard PD scenario can appear somewhat artificial in its assumptions about communication and rationality.

The general form of this payoff matrix is presented in Table 1.2. The symbols *R*, *T*, *S*, and *P* represent typical payoff values used in general two-player, two-strategy games such as the PD.

The broader perspective allows us to identify several key game types that meaningfully expand the traditional framework dominated by selfish, distrustful agents – such as those represented in the PD – who are unable to manage even a limited range of future contingencies (Figure 1.1). It is important to emphasise that the game types discussed here are, in most cases, symmetric, meaning that the payoffs for equivalent strategic choices are identical for both players. However, when such symmetry is absent – i.e., when players in equivalent positions receive unequal payoffs – the model must be reformulated. A prominent example of such asymmetry is found in the *Subordination Game*, which will be analysed in a later section.

The *PD* no longer adequately reflects the complexity of modern strategic environments. It has become increasingly difficult to model long-term planning for agents in a world where communication is no longer severely restricted. In today's digitally interconnected ecosystem, traditional barriers to communication and information are often removed. However, in certain geopolitical contexts – such as in China or Russia – where communication platforms may be censored or functionally restricted, the psychological or structural features of the PD can still be effectively replicated. In contrast, within cooperative or innovation-driven environments – such as open-business ecosystems, collaborative governance frameworks, or joint scientific ventures – mutual cooperation

Table 1.2 General Presentation of Payoff Matrix

		Player 2	
		Confess	*Don't confess*
Player 1	*Confess*	*R; R*	*S; T*
	Don't confess	*T; S*	*P; P*
Symbol		*Meaning*	*Description*
T		Temptation to defect	One player defects while the other cooperates. The defector gets the best individual outcome.
S		Sucker's payoff	One player cooperates while the other defects. The cooperator gets the worst outcome.
R		Reward for mutual defection	Both players defect (e.g., both confess). This outcome is moderately bad for both.
P		Reward for mutual cooperation	Both players cooperate (e.g., both remain silent). This is the best outcome for both.

Source: Own elaboration based on the classical formulation of the Prisoner's Dilemma, as presented in Dixit and Nalebuff (2008).

Note: In this version of the dilemma, "cooperation" refers to mutual silence (not confessing), and "defection" refers to confession. As such, the best collective outcome (P) occurs when both players remain silent and receive minimal sentences.

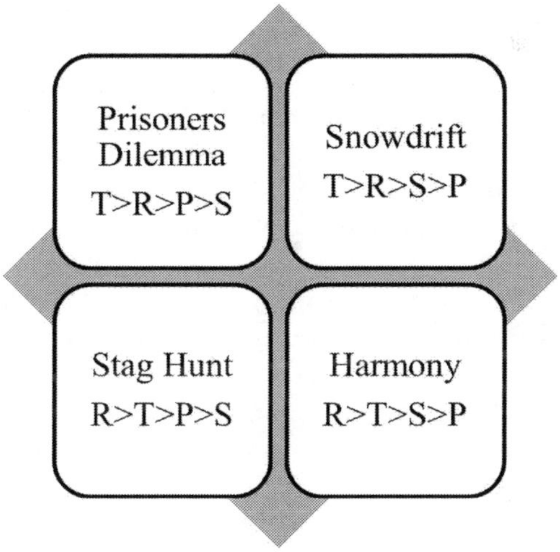

Figure 1.1 Classification of Main Symmetric Games Based on Payoff Structure.

Source: Own elaboration.

often yields the most optimal and sustainable results. In these cases, the *Harmony Game* better captures the strategic landscape than the PD, as cooperation becomes not only rational but also inherently rewarding for all involved.

At the opposite end of the strategic spectrum lies the *Chicken Game* (also referred to as the *Snowdrift Game*), which models high-stakes competition and brinkmanship. A well-known cultural reference is the expression "Trump Always Chickens Out" (Financial Times, 2025). Traditionally, the *Chicken Game* describes two drivers accelerating towards each other: the first to swerve is labelled the "chicken", while the one who continues on becomes, temporarily at least, the victor. However, if neither swerves, both risk mutual destruction. If both swerve, they suffer shared embarrassment. Though simple in concept, the *Chicken Game* captures real-world dilemmas in areas such as business strategy, international diplomacy, and market innovation. Take, for example, two firms contemplating entry into an emerging market with a revolutionary product. This move demands substantial investment in R&D and infrastructure. The first mover assumes high risks, while the second mover may benefit disproportionately from the former's efforts. In this case, the "chicken" is the firm that takes the initiative alone and is left exposed. If neither firm takes the risk, the opportunity may be lost – potentially to a disruptive third entrant. This dynamic unfolded in the photography industry, where Kodak, despite having invented a prototype digital camera, failed to act. Polaroid, a possible fast follower, also failed to adapt – and both lost market relevance. If both firms invest, the shared payoff is typically less than if one could exploit the other's investment. The *Chicken Game*, therefore, effectively illustrates the dilemma of risk leadership versus strategic delay in innovation contexts.

Another illustrative model is the *Stag Hunt Game*, which contains two Nash equilibria: one where both players cooperate to secure a high reward (e.g., hunting a stag together), and another where both defect and settle for a lower payoff (e.g., individually hunting hares). Both equilibria are stable, but the cooperative one yields the greatest mutual benefit. The Stag Hunt captures the importance of coordination, mutual expectations, and trust in achieving socially optimal outcomes. In contrast, the *Subordination Game* addresses asymmetric power relationships between players. A weaker player may choose to wait for a dominant actor to take initiative, thereby reducing risk and securing a share of the results. This model is particularly useful for understanding strategic behaviour in post-Soviet societies, where civil society actors often responded reactively to the decisions of oligarchic elites, as seen in Ukraine in the early 2000s.

Beyond classifying game types, one of the most influential developments in the strategic modelling of human and institutional behaviour has been the introduction of the *Axelrod Tournament*. Repeated games – far more representative of real-world dynamics than single-shot decisions – can now be effectively explored through algorithmic simulation.

In the Axelrod framework, players repeatedly choose whether to cooperate (C) or defect (D), guided by a variety of predefined or user-created strategies. The tournament allows not only for testing standard behaviours (such as *Tit-for-Tat [TFT]*, *Always Defect [AllD]*, or *Random*) but also for inserting new, custom-designed strategies into a shared competitive environment (Table 1.3). Over time, even classical strategies have evolved. Variants such as *Generous Tit-for-Tat (GTFT)* or more punitive "grim trigger" approaches have added nuance to the strategic toolkit. In recent years, AI techniques – particularly artificial neural networks (ANNs) – have also been introduced, enabling adaptive and learning-based strategies.

The *Axelrod Tournament* thus offers a flexible, accessible, and intellectually rigorous platform for exploring strategic behaviour across a wide range of dilemmas (Table 1.3). It enables users to test, refine, and even evolve their strategic thinking in a simulated environment that mirrors the uncertainties and repetitions of real-world interactions.

Table 1.3 Selected Behavioural Strategies in the Axelrod Tournament

Strategy	*Short Description*
Adaptive	An adaptive strategy that updates its internal state based on the previous round of play.
Backstabber	Forgives the first three defections, but on the fourth, defects permanently. Unconditionally defects in the last two rounds. "Even my patience has limits".
Collective.Strategy	Always cooperates in the first move and defects in the second. If the opponent follows the same pattern, it continues to cooperate until defection. Otherwise, it defects unconditionally.
Cycler CCCCCD, Cycler CCCDCD	Cyclical strategies combining cooperative and defecting actions in predefined sequences.
Evolvable ANN	A neural-network-based strategy using 17 features and a hidden layer of size 10, trained to optimise performance through evolution.
Gambler	A stochastic variant of LookerUp that selects actions probabilistically in certain cases.
Grumpy	Defects once a certain "grumpiness" threshold is crossed. Grumpiness increases with opponent defections and decreases with cooperation.
GTFT, Hard TFT, Adaptive TFT	Variations of the TFT strategy, including Generous, Hard, and Adaptive forms based on prior opponent behaviour.
Handshake	Begins with "Cooperate, Defect". If the opponent mirrors this pattern, it cooperates indefinitely; otherwise, it defects permanently.
LookerUp	Uses a lookup table to determine actions based on previous outcomes.
Memory One Player	Uses a four-element probability vector to decide moves based on the last round only.

(*Continued*)

Table 1.3 (Continued)

Strategy	*Short Description*
Memory Two Player	Employs a 16-element vector to represent conditional probabilities based on both players' last moves.
Resurrection	Starts with cooperation. Defects whether the player has played more than five rounds and the last five rounds were defections. Otherwise, it behaves like TFT.
Short Memory	Cooperates for the first 10 rounds. Then analyses the opponent's last 10 actions and responds based on the ratio of defections to cooperation.
Stalker	A score-based strategy influenced solely by accumulated game points rather than opponent behaviour.

Source: Own elaboration based on Axelrod-Python (n.d.).

1.1.2 *Strategic Simulation and Institutional Behaviour*

Game 1: Create Your Version of the World – Strategic Simulation Using the Axelrod Tournament

Let's begin with an inspiring challenge: how would you design your own virtual world? What problems would exist, who would the players be, and how would they interact? This educational and strategic game is ideal for students and creative audiences – from future economists to political scientists – seeking to explore global dynamics through the lens of game theory. While identifying problems and choosing appropriate strategies is intellectually demanding but accessible, implementing simulations (particularly the *Axelrod Tournament*) requires only minimal knowledge of Python.

Step 1: Identify Key Global Problems or Challenges

Begin by selecting a range of relevant, real-world, or speculative issues. These may be positive or negative in nature and should offer rich ground for modelling strategic behaviour.

Examples include:

- The Russia–Ukraine war
- CO_2 emissions/climate crisis
- Virtualisation of reality and AI
- Electric vehicles (charging infrastructure, lithium mining, urban pollution)
- Robotics (efficiency vs. unemployment, cost of retraining)
- Drug addiction
- Pandemics
- Remote education (screen fatigue vs. accessibility)
- Hikikomori (voluntary isolation)

Let your imagination guide you, optionally adding geopolitical constraints:

- A world composed solely of authoritarian regimes
- A planet governed by decentralised self-rule
- Isolated island-states (e.g., a fragmented Indonesian archipelago)

Step 2: Assign Game Structures to Each Problem

Next, define which type of game best captures the strategic dynamics for each challenge:

- *PD* – when communication is limited, and betrayal is tempting;
- *Chicken Game* – when players face high risk and brinkmanship (e.g., racing towards danger);
- *Subordination Game* – when a few leaders act first while others passively follow;
- *Stag Hunt* – when trust is required for optimal mutual gains;
- *Harmony Game* or *Custom Designs* – for cooperative systems or unique dilemmas.

Examples:

- If all actors wait for others to act first → *Subordination Game*
- If trust is fragile and consequences are asymmetric → *PD*
- If mutual hesitation may cause shared catastrophe → *Chicken Game*

Custom payoff matrices can also be constructed to suit your scenario.

Step 3: Define Strategic Actors

For each challenge, assign real-world or fictional players such as countries, regions, or multinational corporations. Each actor receives a strategy archetype, and the *Axelrod Tournament* is used to determine the winning strategy.

You now run multiple separate tournaments – one per issue.

Examples:

- CO_2 Emissions:
  - USA – Defector
  - China – *Gambler*
  - Norway – *Defector Hunter*
  - Winner – *Gambler*
- Electric Vehicles:
  - China – Calculator
  - EU – *Cooperator*
  - Winner – *Cooperator*
- Continue for each scenario…

Step 4: Run a Final Meta-Game

Once each challenge has produced a winning player-strategy combination, collect all winners into a final global challenge, such as:

- Climate catastrophe
- Asteroid threat
- Global AI uprising
- Collapse of international order

Choose the appropriate game type for this universal challenge and run the final summary tournament, reusing or evolving strategies from previous rounds.

Step 5: Describe the World That Emerges

Based on the results, construct a narrative about the new world that emerges:

- Who holds influence?
- What power structures dominate?
- Is the system cooperative, competitive, or fractured?
- Which strategies tend to survive across multiple issues?

Optionally, visualise the result as a map, flowchart, or policy framework.

Step 6: Organise Data in Tabular Form

For clarity, all scenarios can be compiled into a single table for comparison (Table 1.4).

Therefore, "Create Your Version of the World" is more than just a game – it's a strategic foresight exercise, a classroom simulation, and a testbed for collective intelligence. By combining imaginative scenario design, strategic modelling, and iterative simulation, players gain insights into the dynamics of cooperation, leadership, and survival in complex systems. As we can observe, the outcome of each proposed scenario emerges through the framework of the *Axelrod Tournament*. The corresponding Python package can be easily installed and applied. The model offers flexibility in shaping the simulations – users can manipulate game types, introduce varying levels of randomness in decision-making (*noise factor*), and adjust the number of rounds (*turns factor*).

The world we have constructed – through this series of interconnected strategic challenges – shows promising signs of resilience, particularly in its high degree of readiness for cooperation. But one critical question remains: is this level of cooperation truly sufficient? Imagine the emergence of a catastrophic, previously unknown global threat – a crisis demanding entirely unconventional forms of interaction, the rapid deployment of new technologies, and transformations

Table 1.4 Problems and Strategy Interactions (Simplified)

Problem	*Main Participants*	*Strategies*	*Game Type & Ranking of Winners*
CO_2 emissions	Russia, USA, Saudi Arabia, Germany, France, Brazil, Argentina, EU	Gambler, Cooperator, Defector, Defector Hunter, Tricky Cooperator, Backstabber, etc.	**Chicken Game:** Cooperator, Tricky Cooperator, Defector Hunter
Wars	Russia, France & Germany, Belarus, Kazakhstan, USA, UK	Memory One/ Two Player, Resurrection, Defector Hunter, Handshake	**Stag Hunt:** Resurrection; Win-Stay, Lose-Shift; Handshake
Virtuality/AI invasion	Iceland, Japan, Afghanistan, USA, Northern Europe	Gambler, Cooperator, Stalker, Prober, Go by Majority, Short Memory	**Stag Hunt:** Go by Majority, Short Memory, Gambler
Hunger	African nations, EU, China, CEE countries, Türkiye	Collective Strategy, Gambler, Short Memory, Memory One Player	**Prisoner's Dilemma:** Collective Strategy, Memory One Player, Short Memory
Tragedy of the commons	Japan, China, India, USA, EU members	Cooperator, Defector, Cooperator Hunter, Defector Hunter, Go by Majority	**Prisoner's Dilemma:** Defector Hunter, Cooperator, Cooperator Hunter
Global catastrophe (space)	Winners of previous clusters	Strategies from previous clusters	**Chicken Game:** Cooperator, Defector Hunter, Resurrection, Go by Majority

Source: Own elaboration.

Note: Simulations were run using the Axelrod Python package. Results are simplified for educational purposes.

that challenge tradition rather than reinforce it. In such a context, a generalised willingness to cooperate – without strategic discernment – may backfire. Unconditional openness to collaboration can lead to exploitation, stagnation, or systemic paralysis. In light of this, it is worth examining the strategies that come to dominate this final world. Even in interactions involving AI, innovation and forward-thinking do not prevail. Instead, conservative, consensus-oriented approaches – such as *Go By Majority* – take the lead. This suggests a system that favours what is collectively safe and familiar over what is novel and potentially transformative. Similarly, the public – viewed as a collective actor – is not empowered through Ostrom-style community-led governance. Instead, it becomes the object of monitoring and control, as embodied in strategies like *Defector Hunter*. It stands in stark contrast to the decentralised, self-organising models championed by Nobel Laureate Elinor Ostrom. In her seminal work, *Governing the Commons: The Evolution of Institutions for Collective Action* (1990), Ostrom demonstrated how local communities, when endowed with autonomy and clear governance structures, can effectively manage common resources without coercion or privatisation. She identified key principles – such as clearly defined boundaries, collective-choice arrangements, and community-based monitoring – that enable robust, self-regulating systems capable of sustaining cooperation and preventing tragedy of the commons scenarios.

The intermediate simulations make another sobering point clear: fundamental challenges such as hunger, thirst, and ignorance are not resolved, even in the presence of a shared external threat. They persist across scenarios, revealing the limitations of strategic alignment when systemic inequalities remain unaddressed. It is true that cooperation and the advancement of science enable the world to avoid some existential threats. However, this cooperation appears to be driven more by conformity or strategic adaptation than by authentic collectivity or solidarity. The resulting world is one where strict rules and rigid behavioural expectations dominate. At the same time, however, this world retains a collective memory and the capacity for rebirth. Strategies such as *Resurrection* suggest that even in collapse, some systems or communities can re-emerge – revived through resilience, cultural memory, and local innovation. Thus, the paradox becomes clear – humanity will find a solution, but may prove incapable of recognising, supporting, or adopting it. Technological and strategic answers to the global crisis may exist – but without the right social, cultural, and institutional context, they may not survive long enough to matter.

This brings us to a more interactive and educational application of the Axelrod framework: the construction of strategic teams under pressure. To introduce participants to the *Axelrod Tournament* framework and the broader principles of strategy selection, an engaging exercise involves simulating the formation of an optimal team tasked with solving a problem characterised by a specific level of societal risk and a set of predefined rules. Initially, participants often gravitate towards well-known cooperative strategies such as the *Cooperator* or the *LookerUp*, which reflect a desire for mutual support and calculated decisions based on past interactions. However, as the game progresses, players typically recognise the need for more dynamic, flexible, and context-responsive agents within the team.

This leads to the inclusion of strategies such as:

- *Tricky Cooperator* – to introduce novel ideas or resolve impasses creatively;
- *Alternator* – to test group assumptions and provide constructive opposition;

- *Backstabber* or *Prober* – to inject realism into strategy modelling in risky environments.

The key insight is that in high-risk strategic settings, relying solely on straightforward cooperation (e.g., selecting a *Cooperator* or an *Average Copier* as a team leader) can lead to suboptimal or losing outcomes. Strategic diversity becomes essential.

Participants can be challenged to select a team of four agents to address a specified problem (e.g., geopolitical crisis, technological disruption). Using basic Python code and the Axelrod Python package, they can simulate interactions among their chosen strategies and assess which team configuration achieves the highest cumulative score or success rate. This exercise encourages reflection on diversity of strategic roles within effective teams; the nonlinearity of outcomes in cooperative environments; and the need for adaptive, even contradictory behaviours in uncertain systems.

Game 2: Predict the Revolution – Ukraine's Institutional Turning Point

This scenario models strategic interactions in a society characterised by entrenched inequality – specifically, the relationship between dominant elite (oligarchs) and the broader population. The game is best conceptualised as a *Game of Subordination*, in which strategic shifts – such as revolution – are seen as transitions in the structure of payoffs and expectations. Here, revolution is metaphorically interpreted as a systemic shift in societal strategy – from compliant cooperation to sustained resistance or retaliation. Although simplified and abstract, this framework provides insights into how long-term patterns of exploitation and response may evolve. It does not attempt to model real-world political dynamics in full, but rather uses game theory to illustrate strategic tipping points. Since the *Axelrod Tournament* does not support asymmetric payoffs natively, this simulation requires a custom implementation using Axelrod-compatible strategies but with a user-defined payoff matrix.

BASIC PAYOFF STRUCTURE (PRE-REVOLUTION)

- If the oligarch defects and society cooperates → (10, –2)
- If the society defects and oligarch cooperates → (3, 5)
- If both defect → (0, 0)
- If both cooperate → (8, –2)

Here, society gains little even when cooperating, while the oligarch benefits disproportionately. This reflects structural asymmetry in power and resources. Over time, society may shift towards defection as retaliation or survival strategy.

STRATEGY ASSIGNMENTS

Oligarch strategies may include:

- *Defector* – consistently exploitative;
- *Hard Prober* or *Sneaky* – feign cooperation, then test for vulnerability;
- *Double Crosser* – cooperative until betrayed, then punishes;
- *Risky Q Learner* – adapts based on long-term rewards;
- *Original Gradual* – oscillates between coöperation and punishment.

Society strategies may include:

- *Cooperator* – always compliant;
- *TFT* – reciprocal, but initially forgiving;
- *Grudger* – cooperates until betrayed, then stops;
- *GTFT* – allows occasional mistakes;
- *Appeaser* – overly compliant, even under exploitation;
- *Forgetful Fool Me Once* – forgives once, and then retaliates.

POST-REVOLUTION PAYOFF STRUCTURE

Assuming a revolutionary shift, society's strategic leverage increases and the payoff matrix transforms into a more symmetric model:

- $(C, C) = (4, 4)$
- $(C, D) = (2, 6)$
- $(D, C) = (2, 1)$
- $(D, D) = (0, 0)$

This reflects a new balance in influence and cost/reward dynamics.

SIMULATION CONCEPT: CALCULATING THE REVOLUTIONARY TURN

The simulation begins with the society deploying a forgiving cooperative strategy (e.g., *GTFT*, *Cooperator*), while the oligarch adopts a strategic defection model (e.g., *Hard Prober*). The system tracks shifts in payoffs and strategy reactions.

A revolutionary tipping point is reached when (Figure 1.2):

- The cooperative strategy no longer yields positive expected value for society.
- Accumulated defection by the elite exceeds a defined threshold (e.g., betrayal in >50% of interactions).
- The society switches to a defensive or retaliatory mode, e.g., from *GTFT* to *Grudger* or *TFT*.

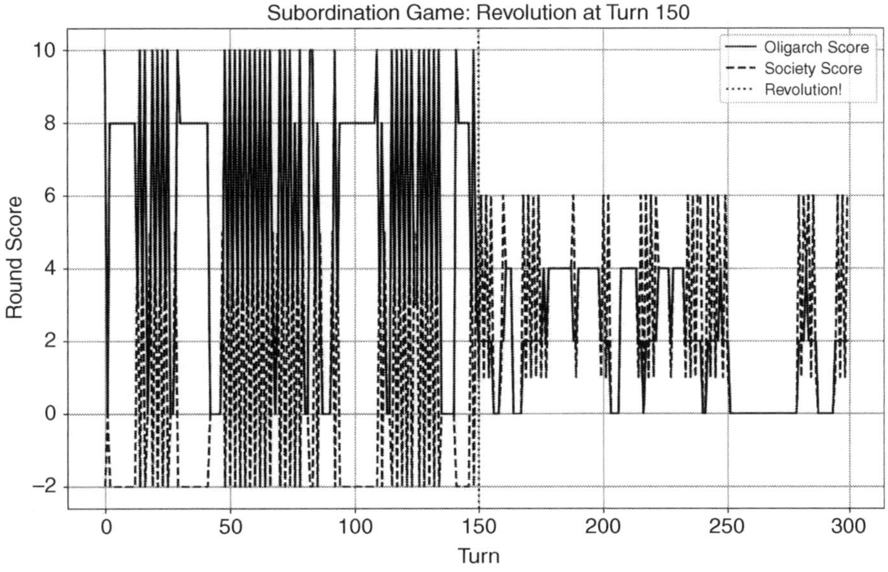

Figure 1.2 Simulated Revolution in Ukraine: Subordination Game Dynamics.

Source: Own elaboration.

Note: Results are generated using the Python packages Axelrod, random, matplotlib.pyplot, collections, and axelrod.random. The revolution is marked at Turn 150, indicating a strategic shift wherein society begins to push back. Following this point, the game's payoff structure becomes more favourable or equitable towards society.

This "turn" can be calculated in code by monitoring the cumulative payoff delta and behavioural shifts, identifying the first round when the cooperative strategy is no longer optimal (Figure 1.2).

In each round (turn), the following variables must be recorded: the payoff (score) for each player and the actions taken (Cooperate – *C*, or Defect – *D*). A "revolution trigger" is identified when one or more of the following criteria are met:

1 *Payoff imbalance* – the oligarchy's cumulative payoff becomes significantly higher than society's – e.g., more than twice as large.
2 *Repeated unreciprocated defection* – society has been defected upon more than *N* times without retaliating (where *N* is a predefined threshold).
3 *Strategic transformation* – society switches to a strategy such as *Grudger* or *AllD* – signalling a behavioural shift akin to revolution.

The first round in which such a strategic shift occurs is registered as the moment of revolution. While revolutions are commonly understood as major transformations in institutional structures, they can also be abstracted as strategic reconfigurations within repeated games. In the Ukrainian case, four major upheavals may be identified during the post-Soviet period: the Student Revolution on Granite, the Orange Revolution, the Revolution of Dignity, and the Tax Maidan. Excluding the first – largely associated with renouncing the Soviet legacy – these movements can be interpreted as iterative interactions between civil society and oligarchic elites, involving cycles of protest, elite concession or manipulation, and public disillusionment. In this context, the model provides a useful tool for periodisation and the prediction of political dynamics.

Game 3: Forecasting Institutional Tensions – The U.S. Spring 2025 Simulation

This modelling approach can also be applied to countries with more robust and proactive institutional systems. Even in such contexts, apparent political stability may mask underlying fragility. In this scenario, the elite strategy is represented by the Trump Administration (TA) as a Double Crosser – cooperative unless betrayed twice, after which it shifts to sustained defection. The society is initially modelled as a *Cooperator*, reflecting institutional trust and political naivety. Over time, TA begins defecting strategically: extracting gains and weakening institutional norms. In response, societal behaviour evolves. As trust erodes, the population may shift to more cautious or punitive strategies such as *Grudger*, *GTFT*, or *Forgetful Fool Me Once*. These transitions represent growing resistance, reduced tolerance for manipulation, and the beginning of systemic tensions.

Table 1.5 illustrates a selection of these cases, modelling different configurations of elite and societal behaviour, and identifying potential triggers for institutional strain or transformation. The framework is intentionally flexible, capable of accommodating a wide range of sociopolitical scenarios.

It is important to acknowledge that the "case" column in Table 1.5 allows for substantial variation. Researchers often apply different conceptual frameworks when analysing institutional reforms and prioritising key institutions. For some, the foundation lies in local governance, electoral systems, the judiciary, and law enforcement. Others may emphasise the institutional structure of business and market operations, while still others consider cultural orientation and societal values as central. In the authors' view, these differing emphases do not necessarily imply conflicting goals. On the contrary, they may converge towards a shared objective. The critical distinction lies not in the institutions themselves, but in the strategic behaviours they adopt – and in the broader context within which these strategies interact.

The outcomes summarised in Table 1.5 are based on simulated interactions using various strategic combinations. One illustrative case is the United States during the TA, where elite strategies of manipulation and delayed reform led to rising tensions. This is visualised in Figure 1.3, which shows the evolution of scores and resistance over time in a simulated 300-turn interaction between the TA (elite) and American society, representing

Table 1.5 Simulated Societal Responses to Elite Strategies in Subordination Game

Case	*Elite Strategy*	*Initial Society Strategy*	*Fake Reforms?*	*Trigger to Revolution*	*Revolution (Tensions) at Turn*	*Outcome Trend*
Trump admin – passive society	Double crosser	Cooperator	Growing tensions	Score imbalance exceeds threshold	~200	Rising tension leads to shift towards Grudger; scores stabilise
Trump admin – reactive society	Double crosser	TFT	Growing tensions	Repeated defection	~120	Earlier resistance; reduced exploitation
Ukraine – oligarch capture	Hard prober	Cooperator	Fake reforms	Gradual exposure of hidden exploitation	~250	Delayed resistance followed by sudden uprising
Ukraine – strong civil society	Hard prober	GTFT	–	Second betrayal	~150	Reforms are demanded earlier
Ukraine – media manipulation	Double crosser	Appeaser	Fake reforms	Information transparency breakthrough	~280	Unstable revolution with erratic patterns
Ukraine – real institutional reform	Golden (cooperative elite)	GTFT or Forgiving	–	Not applicable	–	Stable cooperation; no revolution required

Source: Own elaboration.

Notes:

- Results are generated using Python packages including Axelrod, random, matplotlib.pyplot, collections, and axelrod.random.
- All simulations use a *Subordination Game* framework; however, the game type can be modified depending on the context.
- "Turn" denotes the iteration in which a behavioural shift (revolution or tension) was observed.
- "Golden" strategy represents an elite actor committed to consistent cooperation and institutional strengthening.

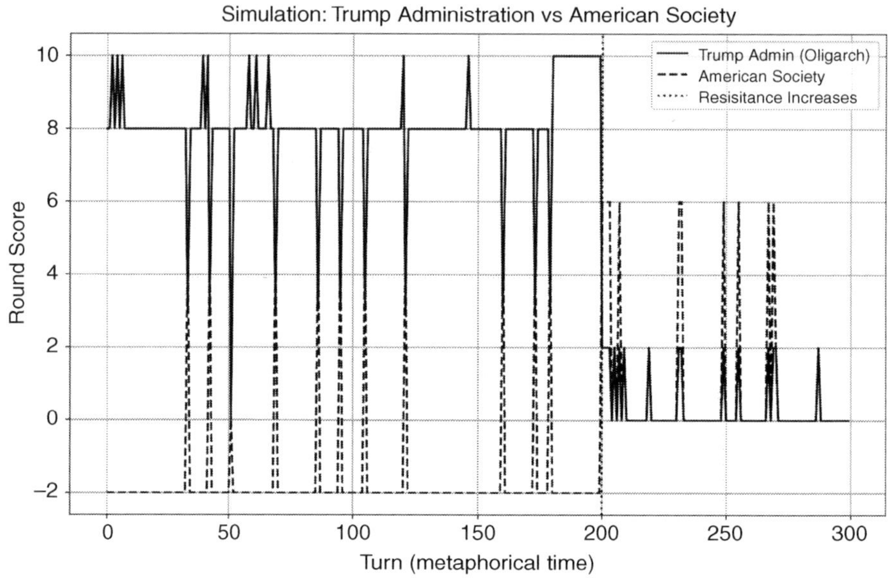

Figure 1.3 Strategic Simulation of Tensions: Trump Administration vs. American Society (Subordination Game).

Source: Own elaboration.

Notes: Results are generated using the Python packages Axelrod, matplotlib.pyplot, collections, and axelrod.random. From turn 150 onward, a "revolution" is marked – a behavioural shift where society pushes back and the game dynamics begin to favour more equitable outcomes.

approximately eight years of political time. Tensions intensify around turn 200, interpreted as increased resistance, electoral backlash, or institutional shifts. As illustrated in Figure 1.3, the simulation captures the moment when societal tensions escalate – represented metaphorically by the shift in behavioural strategies – marking a turning point in the elite–society interaction. This moment of transformation, whether interpreted as revolution or institutional recalibration, is critical for understanding long-term political dynamics.

Building upon this (with wide code manipulation), Figure 1.4 offers a detailed comparative view of cumulative payoffs in two distinct political environments: Ukraine (pre-war) and the United States (as projected in spring 2025). It highlights how elite and societal strategies evolve over time, how institutional structures modulate the pace and intensity of conflict, and when critical thresholds of dissatisfaction are reached. In Ukraine, a steep divergence in payoffs triggers a sharp revolution-like shift around Turn 190. In contrast, the U.S. exhibits a delayed and more buffered transition, with tension rising and then stabilising near Turn 230 – likely due to

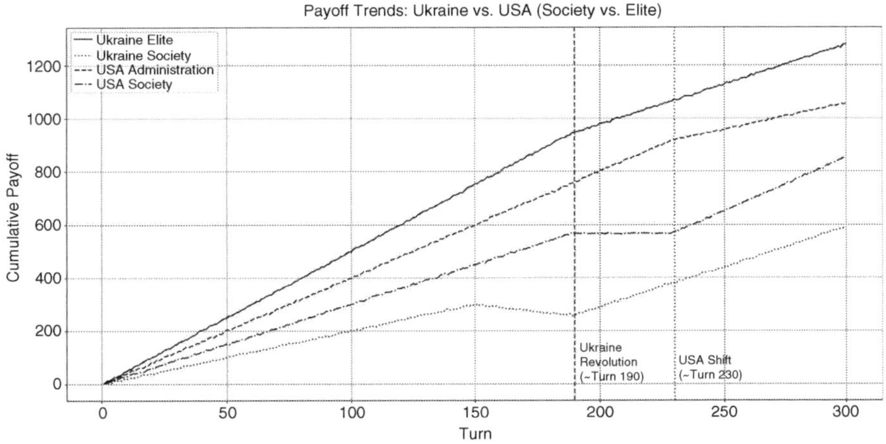

Figure 1.4 Comparative Payoff Dynamics: Ukraine vs. USA (Society and Elite Perspectives).

Source: Own elaboration.

Notes: This figure presents a comparative simulation of cumulative payoffs for elites and societies in Ukraine (pre-war) and the USA (spring 2025). The simulation is based on the Axelrod Python package and follows a Subordination Game framework with custom payoff structures. The Ukraine scenario shows rapid elite gain followed by a sharp drop in societal payoff, leading to a revolution around Turn 190. In contrast, the USA demonstrates a more gradual buildup of societal resistance, with a behavioural shift observed near Turn 230. Turn values serve as metaphors for political time, with each turn approximating one political cycle or strategic phase. The model illustrates how different institutional environments influence the timing and nature of tension and reform.

institutional safeguards such as judiciary oversight and academic autonomy. These contrasting payoff trajectories underscore the importance of trust, transparency, and institutional flexibility in preventing abrupt societal breakdowns.

Game 4: Strategic Redistribution Under Conflict – The War Outcome Game

While the *Axelrod Tournament* remains a robust framework for analysing repeated strategic interactions, other models – such as the *Vickrey–Clarke–Groves* (VCG) mechanism – offer powerful alternatives for simulating decision-making and distribution under conditions of strategic disclosure. Originally designed for the optimal allocation of public goods, the VCG mechanism has been adapted for diverse applied settings (Yoon, 2008). One of the best-known illustrations of the VCG model involves placing two streetlights on a street with five homes. Each resident reports how much they value lighting. Naturally, homeowners tend to exaggerate their preferences to secure the lights near their own property. However, overstatements come at a cost: increased tax liability. This trade-off between utility reporting and penalty creates a self-regulating incentive structure. Although war is not a public good – peace would more accurately fit that definition – a VCG-inspired war simulation can still provide valuable strategic insights.

THE VCG LOGIC APPLIED TO WAR

In the VCG model, players report their valuation of outcomes. Analogously, in the War Model, states report their *sensitivity to war*, which can be either transparent or strategically distorted. Some states might underreport sensitivity to appear more resilient; others might exaggerate to gain international support or attention. This introduces the concept of strategic misreporting. In the classic VCG model, the final decision is designed to maximise the total reported utility across all players. By contrast, the War Model uses aggregated reported influence to determine the shifting epicentre of the conflict. Rather than imposing financial penalties for misreporting – as the VCG mechanism does – the War Model inflicts unintended strategic consequences. These might include increased proximity to the conflict zone or elevated political risk. While the VCG framework enforces incentive compatibility through a clearly defined mathematical penalty rule, the War Model relies on indirect consequences. As a result, misreporting remains a rational strategy for states, especially in the absence of an enforcement mechanism. This creates fertile ground for deception, information asymmetry, and unanticipated power realignments.

INPUT PARAMETERS AND SCENARIOS

The war model incorporates multiple input factors: relative coordinates, sensitivity, concealment, political cost, sanction cost, influence loss, and military support. To explore this, we simulate three scenarios (Table 1.6):

1 *Scenario 1* – Expert-defined input values for key actors in the Russia–Ukraine war.
2 *Scenario 2* – AI-generated estimates of input factors, based on world media analysis from the past year.
3 *Scenario 3* – A hypothetical escalation scenario in which Ukraine gains indigenous missile production capability with foreign aid (e.g., from Germany).

Initial simulations (illustrated in Figures 1.5 and 1.6) show a drift of the conflict's influence centre towards countries such as Poland or Germany. This does not imply direct military engagement on their territories but rather highlights their strategic centrality in the evolving geopolitical structure – be presented through alliances, diplomacy, logistics, or defence posturing. In this VCG-inspired war simulation, Germany as the final influence centre means

Table 1.6 Scenario-Based Input Factors for Strategic War Impact Simulation

Scenario	*Input Source*	*Example Entries*
Expert estimation	Own selection of factors	Poland (0.4; 0.3; 0.6; 0.2), Germany (0.5; 0.4; 0.5; 0.1), USA (0.9; 0.7; 0.2; –0.5)
AI-based analysis	Press review (2024) → coordinates, sensitivity, concealment, political cost, sanction cost, influence loss, military support	Poland (0.6; 0.55; 0.8; 0.1; –0.3; –0.2; –0.2; +0.8)
Escalation scenario	Simulated data including Ukraine	Ukraine (50; 60; 0.9; 0.2; –0.1, –0.2; –0.1; +0.9); Russia (60; 60; 0.9; 0.1; 0.2; 0.1; 0.3; +0.6)

Source: Own elaboration.

Note: The selection of influential actors is inherently subjective. Input parameters can be easily updated in real time to reflect changes in political statements, military actions, or emergent state behaviour. The model is ideal for integrating AI-driven sentiment or media analysis, enabling dynamic re-calibration of simulations.

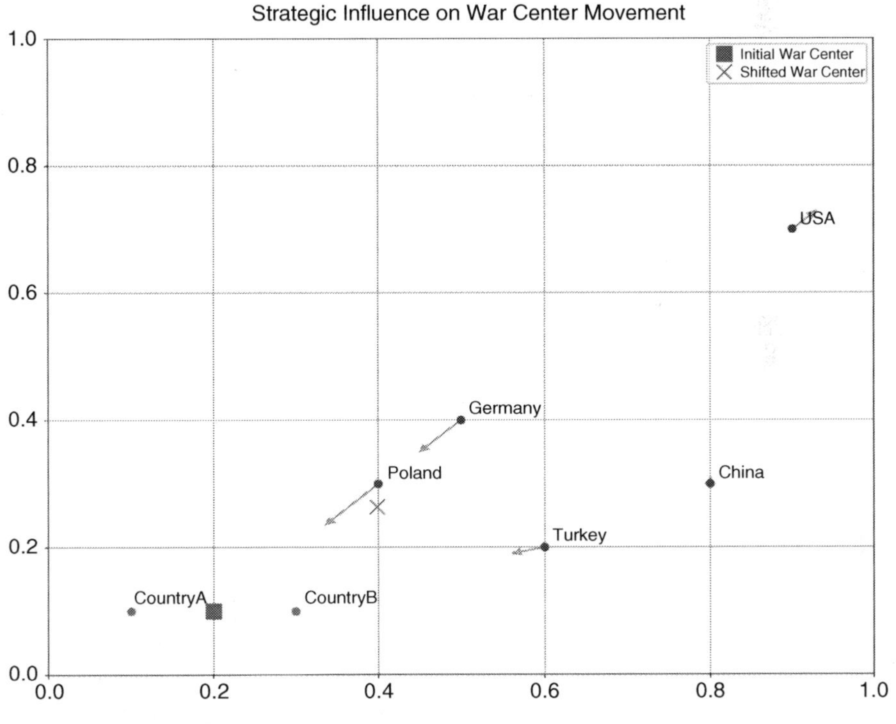

Figure 1.5 Scenario 1: Simulated Shift of War Influence Centre Towards Poland.

Source: Own elaboration.

Note: Based on expert-defined values for sensitivity, concealment, and positioning. Germany and Poland emerge as key pivot points under strategic misreporting assumptions.

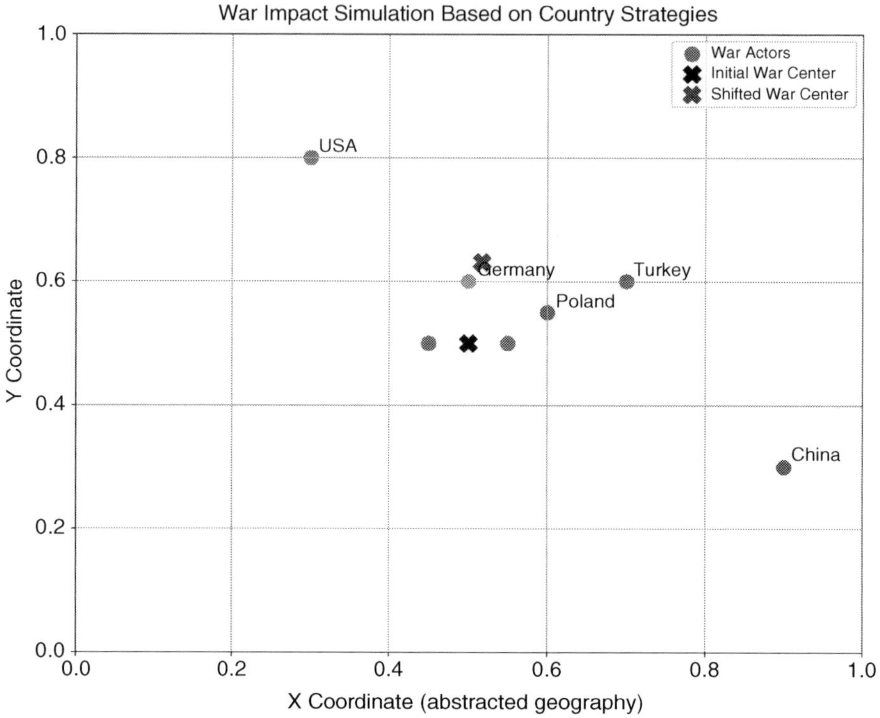

Figure 1.6 Scenario 2: Simulated Shift of War Influence Centre Towards Germany.

Source: Own elaboration.

Note: Calculations are based on AI-generated media sentiment analysis (2024). Germany appears as the primary actor influencing conflict outcome through strategic positioning and alliance dynamics.

it is the key actor shaping the eventual outcome, not necessarily the primary target or battlefield. The model thus provides a powerful tool to explore how strategic misreporting, alliances, and influence shape the trajectory of modern conflicts.

In technical terms, the simulation was conducted using Python's *matplotlib.pyplot, numpy,* and *dataclasses* packages. The goal of this model is to estimate the final location of the war centre. A central concept is the time-step function, governed by the formula:

$$\text{step\_time} = k\_\text{time\_scaling} \,/\, \text{total\_pressure} \tag{1}$$

Here, k_time_scaling is a constant representing the political-military inertia of the system (akin to friction), while total_pressure reflects the aggregated international influence exerted on the conflict's focal point. The higher the pressure, the more rapidly the war centre shifts geographically. In our case, we use a scaling constant of *k*_time_scaling = 5.0, intended to reflect the realistic tempo of developments observed during the Russia–Ukraine war. Given a total international pressure of 5.4, each simulation step represents approximately 0.93 months ($5.0 \div 5.4 \approx 0.9259$). After five simulated steps, this accumulates to about 4.63 months.

It is worth noting that adjusting the scaling constant has substantial implications:

- A value of $k = 1.0$ would accelerate the timeline unnaturally (one step ≈ 0.18 months);
- A value of $k = 20.0$ would imply sluggish evolution (one step ≈ 3.7 months), extending the conflict over many years.

Conceptually, one may imagine the war centre as a heavy object on a geopolitical plane, pushed and pulled by the international actors – each exerting force in the form of pressure. In this metaphor, total_pressure equates to the net force acting on the object, and *k*_time_scaling defines its resistance to movement.

Scenario 3, in which Ukraine initiates domestic long-range missile production with financial backing from Germany (Figure 1.7), appears to be the most plausible configuration. In May–June 2025, Germany formally committed to funding joint missile production in Ukraine with a reported budget of approximately €5 billion (Euronews, 2025). According to our simulation, such developments would enable the conflict to shift away from European territory in approximately 4.6 months. Given the nature of military-industrial projects – often withheld from public scrutiny – it is reasonable to assume that, at the time of writing, the first stages of this timeline may already be underway.

1.2 Institutions in Strategy Games: Modelling Societal Behaviour

If previous simulations and behavioural models appear too general or not sufficiently grounded in the structural features of a political system, a more in-depth academic perspective may be proposed – namely, an institutional interaction framework. This perspective focuses on how different social and political institutions behave strategically, especially in conditions of transformation. Such an approach builds upon foundational work in institutional theory, notably the frameworks developed by Ostrom (1990) and North (1990), who emphasised the adaptive and path-dependent nature of institutional change. March and Olsen (1989) further stressed the importance of institutional logics and symbolic roles, which often guide behaviour more effectively than individual rationality alone. In turn, Scharpf (1997) provides a valuable toolkit for simulating strategic interaction between real actors embedded in institutional constraints. These perspectives enrich simulation

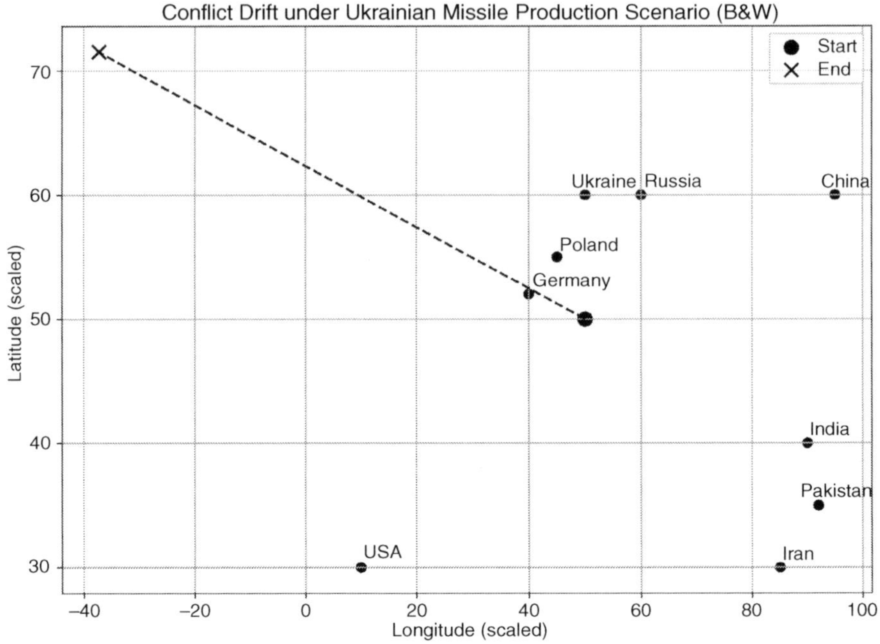

Figure 1.7 Scenario 3: Strategic Displacement of War Centre Beyond Europe (Missile Capability Shift).

Source: Own elaboration.

Notes: The graph illustrates the simulated displacement of the strategic conflict centre following Ukraine's acquisition of long-range missile capabilities. The trajectory indicates a shift away from European actors towards the broader Eurasian region. The final predicted conflict centre is located at coordinates (–37.31, 71.50), signalling reduced European exposure and elevated strategic pressure on actors such as China, Iran, and Pakistan.

models by anchoring agent behaviour in political norms, rule systems, and organisational routines, thereby enhancing both interpretability and predictive power.

A particularly illustrative case is that of modern Ukraine, currently undergoing profound change during wartime. Ukraine remains, in many respects, an oligarchic society. The separation of powers is fragile, and although the war has weakened the overt influence of oligarchs, their return to dominance is not only possible but also likely anticipated by many elites.

Let us briefly consider the strategic character of several core institutions.

Local self-governance in Ukraine is institutionally weak. Territorial communities lack legal personhood (unlike in European systems), have no power to initiate decisions between elections (e.g., through referenda), and are not formal founders of their governing bodies. Municipal taxes are centrally regulated, and the so-called community statute has little real application. These deficiencies make local governance highly unpredictable – hence, the *Gambler* strategy is appropriate to model its behaviour.

In the case of the electoral system, political parties are often controlled or financed by specific individuals or elite groups. They tend to function as vehicles for restoring previous power arrangements. This aligns closely with the *Resurrection* strategy, which embodies a return to earlier states after disruption.

Business actors experience continuous changes in regulatory norms, tax rules, and state priorities – even during the war. Despite consistent support from international allies, such volatility persists. This breeds both opportunism and frustration. The *Backstabber* strategy, which cooperates until a tipping point is reached before defecting permanently, reflects this institutional mood well.

Judicial institutions frequently engage in the appearance of anti-corruption enforcement without reaching guilty verdicts or substantive outcomes. Such performativity builds up institutional cynicism, moving slowly from cooperation to disengagement or retaliation – aptly captured by the *Grumpy* strategy. At the same time, some positive developments – such as judicial appointments via independent commissions – signal potential for reform, albeit limited.

Law enforcement, for its part, remains largely unreformed and reactive.

The volunteer movement – a key actor in Ukraine's resilience – is diverse and cannot be reduced to a single behavioural model. It includes both unwavering principled actors and those adapting flexibly to emerging conditions. Therefore, two strategies are applied here: *Grudger* (cooperative until betrayed) and *LookerUp* (adaptive, pattern-based response).

Lastly, external allies can be interpreted as *Punishers* – cooperative but ready to sanction defection – and the oligarchs themselves as *Retaliators*, who react strongly to perceived threats but can be cooperative under favourable conditions.

Table 1.7 presents the institutional mappings to their corresponding Axelrod strategies, followed by a ranking of their effectiveness based on tournament performance. Each institution is represented by a specific strategy from the Axelrod library, allowing for the modelling of interactions under conditions of limited cooperation, imitation, or conflict. The simulation runs for 365 turns using the classic *Chicken Game*, with a noise level of 0.1 to reflect real-world unpredictability and deviations from ideal behaviour. This setup enables us to explore how different institutional strategies perform over time and under pressure – mirroring real tensions within a transforming society.

The simulation results suggest a looming surge of resistance – possibly escalating to a full collapse of the existing institutional framework. It is crucial to emphasise that this analysis does not focus solely on the wartime period but encompasses a broader historical trajectory. In Ukraine, this cyclical breakdown and reassertion of institutional control has occurred multiple times. Such was the case during the Orange Revolution (2004–2005) and the Revolution of Dignity (2013–2014). Despite initial success, these uprisings failed to yield long-term institutional transformation. The victorious

Table 1.7 Institutional Behaviour Simulation: Strategic Mapping and Tournament Outcomes in the Ukrainian Context

Strategic Mapping of Ukrainian Institutions		*Ranking of Strategies by Tournament Success*
Institution	Strategy	Grumpy
Judiciary	Short Memory	LookerUp
Electoral system	Resurrection	Gambler
Local self-governance	Gambler	Short Memory
Business environment	Backstabber	Resurrection
Law enforcement	Grumpy	Punisher
War allies	Punisher	Backstabber
Oligarchy	Retaliate	Retaliate
Volunteers/post-military civilians	Grudger, LookerUp	Grudger

Source: Own elaboration by using the Axelrod package for Python.

Note: The tournament was conducted with the Chicken Game, run for 365 turns with noise = 0.1, simulating a year-long interaction cycle with moderate uncertainty.

strategies in these moments lacked constructive follow-through – gradually, over the span of months, oligarchic influence was re-established. These cycles of protest were followed by elite re-consolidation point to deep systemic inertia. By contrast, the Student Hunger Strike of the early 1990s – the so-called "Revolution on Granite" – was of a different character. At that time, most of today's political institutions did not yet exist. The players were new, informal, and often ad hoc. Consequently, a different strategic mapping would be required to model that period accurately. Still, across these distinct historical episodes, the underlying strategic game remains largely the same – a repeated *Chicken Game*, emblematic of Ukraine's broader political culture over the past four centuries. This structural pattern – oscillating between confrontation and stalemate – suggests the limitations of analysing institutional behaviour in isolation.

Therefore, this observation leads to a pivotal methodological shift. When institutions fail to deliver sustained strategic change, the analytical lens must descend: from the level of institutions to the level of individuals. As Granovetter (1985) argued in his theory of embeddedness, meaningful economic behaviour cannot be fully understood without reference to interpersonal networks and micro-level contexts. Similarly, Coleman's (1990) schema of social explanation advocates for tracing macro-level outcomes back to micro-level actions and their structural constraints. This bottom-up approach is further supported by agent-based models (Epstein, 2006), which simulate how institutional dynamics emerge from individual-level decisions, learning, and adaptation. In this sense, moving the analysis to the level of the individual is not a reduction but a reconstruction of institutional understanding through behaviourally grounded mechanisms (Hedström & Swedberg, 1998; Ostrom, 2005).

The next stage of modelling, accordingly, should explore how personal agency – embedded within informal networks, moral heuristics, or situational decision-making – can alter strategic dynamics in both local and national contexts. To further enhance the granularity of institutional and societal modelling, it becomes useful to integrate findings from sociological and behavioural segmentation studies. One such example comes from a 2007 study by GfK Ukraine, which identified several distinct subgroups within Ukrainian society, each characterised by different value systems, political attitudes, and economic behaviour (see Lviv Entrepreneurs Committee, 2007). To bridge this qualitative categorisation with quantitative game-theoretical modelling, we propose aligning these societal archetypes with selected *Axelrod Tournament* strategies. The distribution was as follows: Conscious Galicians (26%), Philistines (22%), Thrifty individualists (20%), Enterprising individuals (19%), and Postmodernists (13%). While this mapping is necessarily interpretative, it provides a plausible heuristic for simulating social behaviours in iterated games. Table 1.8 presents these subgroup-strategy correspondences. It should be acknowledged upfront that identifying perfect one-to-one equivalents is virtually impossible. Ideally, such a task would require the creation of custom-coded strategies tailored to each sociocultural profile. For the sake of illustration, however, a simplified approximation was employed.

To explore this mapping within a game-theoretical framework, we simulated a *Chicken Game* using the *Axelrod Tournament* environment and assigned these strategies accordingly. Unexpectedly, the *Stalker* strategy emerged as the winner under low-randomness conditions (1% noise), as shown in Table 1.9. The results suggest that in high-risk environments, entrepreneurial capabilities emerge as the primary drivers of societal advancement.

Table 1.8 Mapping Sociocultural Archetypes to Axelrod Strategies

Original Subgroup (GfK Ukraine)	*Proposed Axelrod Strategy*	*Strategy Description*
Conscious galician	Forgetful grudger	Starts with cooperation; defects after being betrayed but eventually forgives after a fixed memory length.
Philistine	Win-Stay, Lose-Shift	Also known as Pavlov; repeats a winning move, switches after a loss.
Thrifty individualist	Memory One Player	Makes decisions based only on the last round's outcomes using a 4-vector strategy matrix.
Enterprising	Stalker	Strategy influenced solely by score performance; defects whether average payoff exceeds a defined threshold.
Postmodern	AntiCycler	A strategy that avoids repeating sequences of behaviour; non-repetitive and less predictable.

Source: Own elaboration based on data from Lviv Entrepreneurs Committee (2007); Axelrod-Python. (n.d.); Chumachenko and Zadorozhna (2024).

Table 1.9 Comparative Performance of Sociocultural Subgroup Strategies Across Game Types

Game Description	*Ranking of Strategies*
Players, Game: Chicken, Turns = 300, Noise = 0.01	*Stalker*, AntiCycler, Win-Stay Lose-Shift, Generic Memory One Player, Forgetful Grudger
Players, Game: Prisoner's Dilemma, Turns = 300, Noise = 0.1	*AntiCycler*, Win-Stay Lose-Shift, Generic Memory One Player, Forgetful Grudger, Stalker
Players, Game: Prisoner's Dilemma, Turns = 300, Noise = 0.5	*Forgetful Grudger*, Win-Stay Lose-Shift, Generic Memory One Player, Stalker, AntiCycler
Players, Game: Stag Hunt, Turns = 300, Noise = 0.1	*Win-Stay Lose-Shift*, Forgetful Grudger, Generic Memory One Player, Stalker, AntiCycler
Players, Game: Stag Hunt, Turns = 300, Noise = 0.5	*Generic Memory One Player*, Forgetful Grudger, Win-Stay Lose-Shift, Stalker, AntiCycler

Source: Own elaboration by using the Axelrod package in Python.

Notes: Strategy performance was evaluated across different classic two-player symmetric games – *Chicken, Prisoner's Dilemma*, and *Stag Hunt* – under varying noise levels (representing randomness or miscommunication in interactions). Each simulation involved 300 turns. Ranking is ordered from most to least successful strategy in each game environment.

This aligns closely with real-world observations – particularly, the rapid growth of Ukraine's domestic drone industry during the initial three years of the large-scale Russian invasion. Such parallels lend empirical plausibility to the model. In a broader conceptual leap, these Lviv-specific sociocultural strategies were extrapolated imaginatively to the entire territory of Ukraine. Based on our analysis of Ukrainian society in 2025, we posit that the collective wartime experience – originally concentrated in Western Ukraine due to historical resistance to the Soviet regime (1942–1956) – has now dispersed nationally, shaping strategic behaviour across all regions. In this sense, a form of behavioural convergence is taking place, driven by shared exposure to conflict with a totalitarian adversary.

When simulating a fragmented or polarised society using the PD framework, Ukrainian adaptability and receptivity to innovation still hold. The strategy *AntiCycler* (Table 1.9), symbolic of nonlinear, anti-conformist behaviour, has deep cultural roots in Ukrainian history – reflected in past instances of resistance and reinvention. However, as the level of randomness in decision-making increases – driven by factors such as oligarchic manipulation, public disillusionment with imposed peace settlements, or war fatigue – the model indicates potential destabilisation. In such scenarios, strategies representing passivity or short-term pragmatism (e.g., *Philistine* = *Win-Stay Lose-Shift*) begin to dominate. The societal outlook under these conditions shifts towards short-lived gains and eroded cohesion.

The *Stag Hunt* simulation paints a particularly sobering picture (Table 1.9). This game poses a choice between cooperative efforts yielding high rewards and risk-averse individualism producing safer but suboptimal outcomes. Both are Nash equilibria, yet only the cooperative one maximises social welfare. When this dynamic plays out in geopolitical arenas – whether through appeasement of aggressors, hyper-nationalist isolationism (somewhat reminiscent "Make America Great Again"), or fragmented domestic alliances – the game structure replicates within societies. It manifests as inter-elite, interregional, or intergroup rivalries that stifle progress.

What we observe here is not only a series of isolated strategies but the emergence of societal behaviour patterns shaped by strategic interaction. The *Hunt Game* becomes a cautionary tale: a society that seeks "peace at any cost" without strategic coherence may find itself in a stagnant equilibrium – formally stable, but practically unproductive. This illustrates the potential of Axelrod-based strategy modelling as a powerful heuristic framework. While it requires some simplification – particularly in mapping sociocultural identities to predefined algorithmic behaviours – it offers valuable insight. Just as electoral shifts and financial markets often hinge on perception rather than underlying fundamentals, so too can our modelling benefit from a stylised, rule-based approach to strategy simulation. Ultimately, any society – or any political, military, or economic conflict – can be analysed through this lens. The real strength lies in the ability to simulate not just isolated outcomes, but systemic dynamics that evolve across time and under pressure.

1.3 Beyond Valuation: Strategic Reinterpretation of the Fama–French Framework

As strategic modelling expands to incorporate increasingly complex systems – from global conflicts to institutional resilience – it becomes essential to link macro-level simulation with microeconomic behaviour. Financial markets, and specifically stock price dynamics, offer a revealing window into how firms navigate risk, competition, and long-term positioning. In this context, asset pricing models do more than just predict returns: they offer a structural perspective on business strategies, market expectations, and firm-level decision-making under uncertainty (Bali, Cakici, & Whitelaw, 2011; Gu, Kelly, & Xiu, 2020).

Among the most influential models for interpreting financial performance is the Fama–French framework. Originally designed to improve asset return prediction by incorporating size and value effects (Fama & French, 1993), it has since evolved into a five-factor model reflecting deeper aspects of corporate behaviour, such as investment patterns and profitability (Fama & French, 2014). Although its primary role remains empirical in financial economics, this framework can be creatively reinterpreted to support institutional strategy classification – especially when paired with behavioural simulations such as Axelrod tournaments (Bender et al., 2013; Lo, 2005). This part outlines this dual application, bridging quantitative finance and strategic analysis.

The five-factor model time series regression traditionally could be presented (Fama & French, 2014):

$$Rit - RFt = ai + bi\,(RMt - RFt) + siSMBt + hiHMLt + riRMWt + ciCMAt + eit \quad (2)$$

where:

- *Rit* is the return of portfolio *i* at time *t*;
- *RFt* is the risk-free return;
- *RMt* is the return of the market portfolio;
- *SMBt*, *HMLt*, *RMWt*, and *CMAt* are the factor returns representing size, value, profitability, and investment styles, respectively;
- *ai, bi, si, hi, ri, ci* are regression coefficients;
- εit is the residual error term.

If the five factors fully capture variations in expected returns, then the intercept αi should theoretically be zero across all portfolios *i*. In strategic terms, applying the Fama–French framework means identifying key features of a business such as conservatism vs. aggressiveness, market capitalisation, risk profile, dividend policy, and other firm-level attributes. These components offer insights into a company's long-term behaviour and strategic positioning within a competitive, often regulated, stock market environment (Barber & Odean, 2001; Lakonishok, Shleifer, & Vishny, 1994).

1.3.1 Limitations and Strategic Gaps in Classical Financial Models

Before proceeding to modelling strategy, it is helpful to focus on one of the most informative factors within the Fama–French five-factor model: HML (High Minus Low). This factor represents the return spread between value stocks – companies with high book-to-market ratios – and growth stocks – firms with low book-to-market ratios. Value stocks (high HML) are typically perceived as undervalued by the market and are often associated with more stable, mature firms. These companies tend to offer above-average returns over the long run, a pattern supported by empirical studies (e.g., Fama & French, 1993; Lakonishok, Shleifer, & Vishny, 1994). Growth stocks (low or negative HML), on the other hand, are often characterised by high expectations of future earnings, and reflected in their high price-to-earnings (P/E) ratios. These firms generally reinvest earnings rather than issuing dividends, relying on capital gains for investor returns. The dividend factor – closely tied to value orientation – has also been shown to play a crucial role in investor behaviour and long-term performance. Studies such as those by Baker and Wurgler (2004) demonstrate that dividend-paying stocks are more attractive to investors seeking income stability, and that dividend policy can signal management's confidence in future earnings. Thus, HML is not only statistically significant in pricing models but also strategically revealing. It allows analysts to infer behavioural tendencies of firms – such as conservatism, maturity, or speculative growth orientation – which are foundational for mapping corporate actors to strategic archetypes in simulations such as Axelrod's tournaments.

Despite its robustness in financial econometrics, the Fama–French framework operates on statistical abstractions – aggregating knowledge of firms' external characteristics such as size, value orientation, profitability, and investment intensity. While this approach is powerful for understanding systematic return variation, it lacks granularity when it comes to revealing strategic behaviour or decision-making under uncertainty. As noted by Lo (2005), financial models built on rational equilibrium assumptions often underperform in environments characterised by adaptive complexity, where actors learn and evolve over time. This shortcoming becomes particularly evident in innovation-intensive sectors, such as electric vehicles (Table 1.10), where company trajectories are shaped not only by financial fundamentals but also by technological bets, regulatory risk, leadership volatility, and nonlinear market responses (Bender et al., 2013).

In such contexts, two firms with similar Fama–French profiles might pursue radically different strategies: one might invest in autonomous technology and accept short-term losses, while another optimises cost efficiency and market share through incremental innovation. The statistical model treats them similarly – but their strategic postures differ markedly. This is why we propose supplementing Fama–French insights with behavioural strategy analogies, based on the *Axelrod Tournament* framework, to better reflect corporate decision-making logic in competitive simulations.

Table 1.10 illustrates the application of the Fama–French five-factor model to a selected group of electric vehicle producers. The Adjusted R^2 values vary significantly across firms, reflecting differing degrees of model fit. For example, General Motors (GM) shows relatively high explanatory power (R^2 = 0.48), suggesting that traditional financial factors (like value and market risk) offer a reasonable account of its stock performance. In contrast, companies like Hyundai (005380.KS) or NIO display much lower R^2 values (0.208 and 0.19, respectively), indicating that a large portion of return behaviour remains unexplained by the standard model – likely due to country-specific volatility or innovation-driven dynamics.

The HML coefficients offer insight into each firm's valuation status. Tesla and NIO exhibit negative HML values, signalling a "growth stock" profile with high market valuations and limited dividend signalling – typical of companies betting heavily on innovation. By contrast, GM and Volkswagen (VOW.DE) show positive HML values, suggesting traditional "value stock" characteristics, possibly indicating a conservative or risk-adjusted growth trajectory. Meanwhile, the Mkt-RF coefficients highlight the firms' sensitivity to general market conditions. Tesla (2.11) and Ford (1.59) exhibit high exposure to systematic market risk, implying strong reactions to macroeconomic shocks.

Therefore, the results presented in Table 1.10 illustrate the limitations of the Fama–French model in strategic profiling. While the model captures key statistical relationships – such as sensitivity to market risk or valuation style – it does not fully account for firm behaviour in the context of technological disruption, innovation cycles, or institutional complexity.

1.3.2 Mapping Financial Archetypes to Strategic Game Theory Behaviours

Fama–French regression results – alongside knowledge of firms' institutional environments – help us draw analogies with *Axelrod Tournament* strategies. Thus, we propose the following analogies between Fama–French profiles and *Axelrod Tournament* strategies:

- Tesla (TSLA) – *Tricky Cooperator;*
- Hyundai (005380.KS) – *Cooperator;*
- General Motors (GM) – *Stalker;*
- Volkswagen (VOW.DE) –*TFT;*
- NIO – *Memory One Player;*
- Ford (F) – *Resurrection.*

An instructive example is Ford (F), a company with a long industrial legacy that, despite occasional setbacks such as recalls related to transmission issues, has demonstrated no intention of reversing its strategic direction towards electric mobility. Its recurring pattern of decline and recovery lends itself well to the *Resurrection* strategy in the *Axelrod Tournament* framework. Hyundai (005380.KS), rooted in a corporate culture marked by cooperation and shaped by the strategic imperative of entering foreign markets, closely resembles the *Cooperator* strategy. This role reflects both its adaptability and its preference for inclusive, consensus-driven expansion. General Motors (GM),

Table 1.10 Fama–French Model Applied to a Group of E-Vehicle Producers (Selected Factors)

Ticker	*Adjusted* R^2	*HML (Significance)*	Mkt-RF *(Significance)*
GM	0.48	0.66 (0.004)	1.27 (0.000)
005380.KS	0.208	−0.88 (0.07)	0.98 (0.001)
VOW.DE	0.23	0.67 (0.23)	1.17 (0.001)
NIO*	0.19	−2.43 (0.04)	1.5 (0.03)
F	0.36	0.38 (0.46)	1.59 (0.000)
TSLA	0.42	−1.48 (0.07)	2.11 (0.000)

Source: Own elaboration.

Notes: Models estimated using Python packages: *numpy, pandas, pandas_datareader,* and *yfinance*. Period: max available.

*For NIO, SMB = 3.75 (0.008).

in contrast, has committed to an aggressive transformation – investing heavily in electric vehicles, battery technologies, and autonomous driving – while simultaneously resisting populist political pressures to reshuffle production networks. These behaviours suggest a calculated, performance-driven approach best represented by the *Stalker* strategy, where decisions are influenced by accumulated gains rather than fixed patterns of response. GM also fits the profile of a value stock: undervalued on the surface, yet carrying significant underlying risk and innovation potential. Tesla (TSLA) represents a more complex case. Characterised by extreme volatility and unpredictable decision-making, particularly at the executive level, it resists stable strategic classification under the Fama–French model. It's erratic but often highly innovative actions align best with the *Tricky Cooperator* strategy – a hybrid approach that mixes collaboration with tactical opportunism. Volkswagen (VW), on the other hand, tends to respond belatedly to strategic inflection points, displaying a degree of inertia in adapting to market signals. Combined with inconsistent responsiveness to valuation factors, this behavioural profile resembles the *TFT* strategy, which emphasises conditional cooperation – responding only after being provoked or challenged. Finally, NIO stands apart due to the opaque nature of its operational environment. With indirect support from the Chinese government and a reliance on internal data systems that remain largely inaccessible to external observers (auditors), its strategic behaviour appears to be driven primarily by short-term feedback loops. This aligns with the *Memory One Player* strategy, in which actions depend almost entirely on the outcomes of recent interactions, rather than long-term planning or transparent rules.

It should be noted at the outset that the choice of strategies assigned to each firm is not the only possible mapping. Nevertheless, we argue that the resulting outcomes in the *Axelrod Tournament* should remain reasonably consistent, capturing the strategic nature of each company under different game-theoretic conditions (Table 1.11).

In a high-risk environment – characterised by ongoing tariff wars, disruptions in supply chains, and geopolitical instability – GM, modelled as the *Stalker* strategy, emerges as the consistent leader in both short-term (10 turns) and long-term (300 turns) interactions (Table 1.11). This dominance reflects GM's calculated, performance-driven strategic posture. In such environments, the randomness (*noise*) in decision-making is minimised, aligning with real-world patterns where high stakes reduce tolerance for erratic behaviour. In a more selfish and fragmented world, modelled by the PD, the outcomes shift dramatically. Here, Hyundai, represented by the *Cooperator*, consistently ranks first. The game assumes limited trust and high incentives for betrayal – highlighting how adaptive and compliant strategies gain an edge. The increasing uncertainty (*noise*) in decisions mirrors real-life instability in policy environments and supply constraints, placing risk-averse actors in favourable positions. The *Stag Hunt Game*, which features multiple possible equilibria, yields a nuanced strategic landscape. In the short

Table 1.11 Comparative Outcomes of Strategic Interactions Among E-Vehicle Producers in Repeated Game Simulations

Chicken Game: Strategic Interactions Among E-Vehicle Producers

Players: Tricky Cooperator (Tesla), Cooperator (Hyundai), Stalker (GM), GTFT (Volkswagen), Memory One Player (NIO), Resurrection (Ford)
Settings: game = Chicken, noise = 0.01

Turns	*Ranking of Strategies*
10	Stalker, Cooperator, Resurrection, Memory One Player, GTFT, Tricky Cooperator
300	Stalker, GTFT, Memory One Player, Tricky Cooperator, Cooperator, Resurrection

Prisoner's Dilemma: Strategic Behaviour Under Competitive Pressure

Players: Tricky Cooperator, Cooperator, Stalker, GTFT, Memory One Player, Resurrection Settings: game = Prisoner's Dilemma, noise = 0.1

Turns	*Ranking of Strategies*
10	Cooperator, Tricky Cooperator, GTFT, Resurrection, Memory One Player, Stalker
300	Cooperator, GTFT, Tricky Cooperator, Resurrection, Memory One Player, Stalker

Stag Hunt Game: Strategic Coordination with Shared Payoff Potential

Players: Tricky Cooperator, Cooperator, Stalker, GTFT, Memory One Player, Resurrection Settings: game = Stag Hunt, noise = 0.1

Turns	*Ranking of Strategies*
10	GTFT, Stalker, Resurrection, Tricky Cooperator, Memory One Player, Cooperator
300	Resurrection, Cooperator, Stalker, GTFT, Tricky Cooperator, Memory One Player

Source: Own elaboration.

Notes: Simulations executed using the Python Axelrod package.

term, Volkswagen's approach (*GTFT*) leads, benefiting from stable European market conditions and tactical flexibility abroad. However, over a longer horizon, Ford – modelled with the *Resurrection* strategy – surpasses competitors. Ford's resilience, government backing, and ability to rebound after downturns make it well-suited for an environment that rewards long-term coordination.

1.3.3 Neural Networks as Predictive Tools for Strategic Forecasting

The Fama–French model is traditionally divided into two streams: one for developed markets and another for emerging economies. While moderately diversified environments can often be modelled effectively using linear assumptions, applying the same framework globally – across heterogeneous markets and regulatory regimes – reveals significant shortcomings (Gu, Kelly, & Xiu, 2020). However, what appears as a limitation in linear models reveals new potential when approached through nonlinear methods and neural networks. Increasing the number of hidden layers in deep learning architectures enhances a model's ability to capture complex, nonlinear relationships – essential in modelling multi-regional strategies. Of course, this also introduces challenges such as overfitting, increased computational cost, and diminishing returns on complexity. Ultimately, identifying the optimal architecture (e.g., number of hidden layers, regularisation techniques, learning rate) is problem-specific and often determined empirically. The use of a nonlinear approach with hidden layers allows for a significant increase in the model's coefficient of determination (R^2), thereby enhancing the reliability of both price prediction and survival strategy testing under different market conditions. This is particularly relevant in the case of diversified or volatile sectors, such as electric vehicle production or banking in emerging markets. This approach has been increasingly validated in the literature. Studies show that neural networks, including LSTM models and deep learning architectures, can outperform traditional models in predicting financial returns and identifying patterns in volatile or high-dimensional environments (Henrique et al., 2019; Fischer & Krauss, 2018; Patel et al., 2015; Ticknor, 2013; Wang et al., 2012; Zhang, 2003).

As shown in Table 1.12, different neural network architectures (NNAs) yield varying levels of accuracy across electric vehicle producers, reflecting

Table 1.12 Neural-Network-Based Performance Across E-Vehicle Companies

Ticker	*Neural Network Architecture*	*Error*	*Steps*	*Accuracy*
GM	1 hidden layer, 2 neurons	0.323	14	0.87
GM	c(4, 2)	0.320	26	0.87
005380.KS	1 hidden layer, 2 neurons	0.250	12	0.73
005380.KS	c(4, 2)	0.260	19	0.724
005380.KS	c(6, 2)	0.259	9	0.718
VOW.DE	c(6, 2)	0.386	21	0.924
VOW.DE	1 hidden layer, 2 neurons	0.386	15	0.923
NIO	1 hidden layer, 2 neurons	2.274	19	0.916
NIO	c(6, 2)	2.272	7	0.920
F	c(6, 2)	0.395	19	0.945
F	1 hidden layer, 2 neurons	0.394	16	0.946
TSLA	1 hidden layer, 2 neurons	0.737	15	0.985
TSLA	c(6, 2)	0.740	10	0.963

Source: Own elaboration.

Notes: Results obtained using R libraries: *stats*, *dplyr*, *ggplot2*, *ggfortify*, and *neuralnet*. The notation c(n, m) refers to a neural network with two hidden layers comprising *n* and *m* neurons, respectively.

the complexity and volatility of each firm's data profile. For instance, Ford (F) and Volkswagen (VOW.DE) demonstrate high predictive accuracy (above 90%) even with relatively simple architectures, suggesting more stable or pattern-consistent market behaviour. In contrast, NIO exhibits a high error despite strong accuracy values, indicating significant fluctuations or outlier sensitivity in the training set – typical for emerging market firms operating under opaque governance structures. Tesla (TSLA) also reaches high accuracy (0.985) with minimal network depth, but a slight drop when the architecture is expanded to two hidden layers suggests possible overfitting or redundancy in model complexity. Meanwhile, Hyundai (005380.KS) displays lower accuracy (around 0.72–0.73) across all configurations, potentially due to complex externalities tied to its mixed strategic posture (e.g., domestic conservatism vs. global expansion), which are harder to capture without context-aware features. GM maintains consistent accuracy (~0.87) across both simple and deeper networks, showing a robust yet moderately complex signal. This stability aligns with GM's strategy of calculated innovation under pressure, as reflected in prior tournament simulations.

Thus, firms operating in more transparent or regulated environments (e.g., Ford, GM, and Volkswagen) tend to exhibit stronger predictive alignment. In contrast, companies shaped by geopolitical uncertainty or aggressive innovation (such as NIO and Tesla) require more nuanced, adaptive modelling. This underscores the value of NNAs not only in boosting numerical performance but also in mapping strategic complexity and diverse risk profiles across market systems. Even when linear models offer only moderate explanatory power (e.g., R^2 values between 0.2 and 0.4), neural architectures can substantially improve predictive accuracy – making them better suited for price forecasting and stress-testing strategic responses in volatile environments. Beyond prediction, these models also enable the simulation of firm behaviour under crisis conditions. For example, they allow analysts to test how a company's stock price might react to different Axelrod strategy profiles, offering insights into the long-term viability of specific business models.

Therefore, the findings highlight the capacity of neural networks to uncover non-obvious patterns in complex datasets – particularly where traditional models fall short. The high accuracy achieved, even with relatively simple NNAs, suggests that well-calibrated nonlinear approaches can reveal meaningful firm-level dynamics. The observed variation in performance further indicates that predictability depends on a firm's strategic transparency, innovation behaviour, and market context. This becomes especially important when examining sectors like banking, where investor sentiment, political risks, and cross-border exposure complicate standard valuation models. The next part of the study demonstrates this by applying a neural network framework to OTP Bank (Hungary) – an institution that combines high-risk positioning with a resilient strategic posture – to test its performance under simulated crisis conditions. For the purpose of analysis, a 15-year dataset of OTP's closing stock price was evaluated. Given the nature of emerging markets, an adjusted R^2 of 0.328 was deemed satisfactory. Additionally, the F-statistic confirms the model's statistical relevance.

Key findings from the Fama–French model:

- $Mkt - RF = 0.678 \rightarrow$ lower volatility than the market average.
- $HML = 1.39(p = 0.000) \rightarrow$ indicates strong value stock characteristics.
- $CMA = -1.4764(p = 0.002) \rightarrow$ reflects highly aggressive investment behaviour.

Despite being a bank – a sector typically associated with conservative profiles – OTP shows signs of risk-prone positioning, likely shaped by geopolitical nuances. For instance, the bank has maintained operations in both Russia and Ukraine during the 2022–2025 conflict, indicating possible back-channel agreements or diplomatic insulation from sanctions. This positions OTP as a value stock with aggressive behaviour – and yet less market risk. The combination is counterintuitive, underscoring the non-economic and strategic political factors influencing OTP's business model. Given that only 32% of the return variance is explained by the linear model, neural networks are necessary to capture the hidden layers of influence – ranging from cross-border permissions to EU dynamics and local legislative shifts. This reinforces the importance of multilayer architectures with more neurons than input factors to address the informational complexity of emerging markets.

To further enhance the reliability of our forecasting model, we implement a deep NNA with three hidden layers consisting of 8, 5, and 3 neurons, respectively – denoted as c(8, 5, 3). This architecture achieves an impressive prediction accuracy of 98.3%. The model is trained using the classical backpropagation algorithm with a learning rate of 0.01. The dataset is divided into two parts: the first 100 rows for training and the last 75 rows for testing, ensuring out-of-sample validation.

To test the strategic robustness of the OTP Bank under real-world stress conditions, we simulate its stock behaviour during a known crisis period. For this purpose, we select March to November 2001 as a representative phase of heightened market volatility, applying the corresponding segment of the Fama–French factor matrix to reflect general market behaviour during that time. The resulting performance of OTP's strategy – modelled through the neural network – is illustrated in Figure 1.8. As the simulation shows, the chosen strategy proved effective in preserving the attractiveness and resilience of the bank's shares, even under crisis dynamics. This supports the view that OTP's approach, while aggressive, maintained investor confidence during a downturn, offering valuable insight into strategic behaviour under pressure.

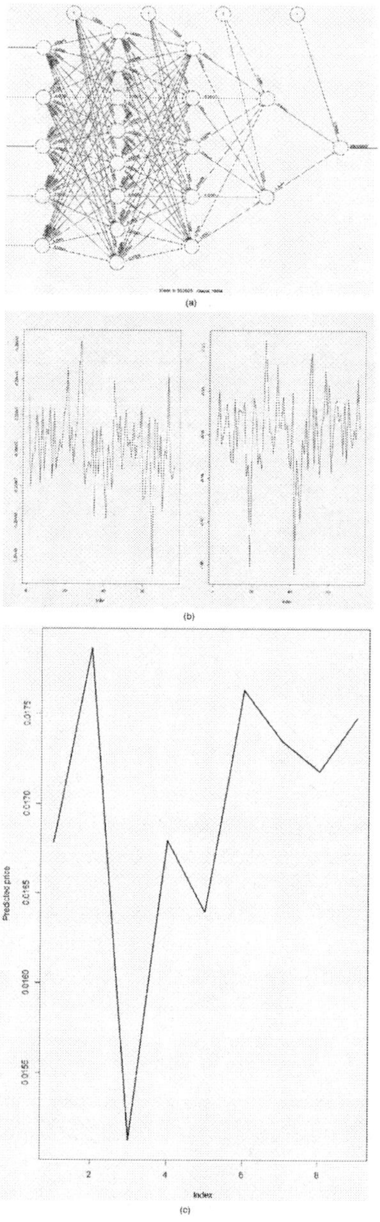

Figure 1.8 Strategy Testing and Price Prediction for OTP Using Neural Network Architecture.

Source: Own elaboration.

Notes: Results were obtained using the R libraries: *stats, dplyr, ggplot2, ggfortify*, and *neuralnet*. The far-left panel visualises the weight coefficients and biases of the neural network model. The two central graphs display the alignment between predicted and actual values during the testing phase. The far-right graph illustrates the projected dynamics of OTP Bank's share price during a selected crisis period, reflecting the strategic behaviour simulated by the model.

1.4 Econophysics and Strategic Capital Modelling: A New Paradigm

Econophysics, a research field at the intersection of statistical physics and financial economics, emerged in the 1990s and is considered to have two primary origins: one in Boston, USA, under the leadership of Eugene Stanley, and the other in Budapest, Hungary, with Imre Kondor. Both scholars permitted their students to apply methods of statistical mechanics to financial data in their graduate theses – an unprecedented shift at the time. As Stanley and colleagues noted in their seminal 1999 paper,

> economic time series, as e.g., stock market indices or currency exchange rates depend on the evolution of a large number of strongly interacting systems, and belong to the class of complex evolving systems. Thus, the statistical properties of financial markets have attracted the interests of many physicists
>
> (Stanley et al., 1999, p. 156)

The movement was not simply methodological, but paradigmatic. As Jovanovic and Schinckus (2013) argue, econophysics represents a distinct epistemological rethinking of modern financial theory. Rather than relying exclusively on rational expectations or equilibrium models, it embraces stochasticity, emergent patterns, and power-law distributions – phenomena well known in physics but often underutilised in traditional economics.

According to Nicolescu (2010), the first step towards constructing a transdisciplinary methodology involves identifying formal analogies between scientific domains. Such analogies may manifest as similar statistical properties (e.g., fat tails or volatility clustering in both turbulence and asset returns), or as shared mathematical structures (e.g., differential equations, entropy models, or phase transitions). This conceptual overlap legitimises the application of physical models to financial markets, especially where conventional economic tools have failed to predict systemic crises or cascading failures. Additional support for the application of physics-based models in economics comes from Estola (2017), who proposed a dynamic extension of neoclassical microeconomics inspired by Newtonian mechanics. Estola's work treats agents as dynamic objects subject to forces, inertia, and constraints, mirroring the laws of motion in classical physics.

Given this framework, it becomes natural to ask whether the collective behaviour of millions of investors resembles the dynamics of physical particles. In both domains, agents (or particles) operate under constraints, exhibit localised and system-wide interactions, and are subject to external shocks – be they economic news or energy fluctuations. In this analogy, asset prices arise from the aggregation of countless micro-interactions – akin to the collisions and energy exchanges in a physical system. Importantly, this analogy is most applicable to developed markets with high liquidity, large numbers of participants, and observable feedback loops. Smaller or opaque markets, by contrast, may lack the statistical robustness needed for meaningful modelling.

As computational power has increased, it is now feasible to simulate these interactions at scale. Agent-based models, neural networks, and Monte Carlo simulations allow researchers to mimic the behaviour of financial particles (investors) and track the emergent properties of the market system – much as physicists model molecular behaviour in closed systems. What matters now is not ideological allegiance to one discipline or another, but rather the pragmatic value of borrowing tools, data, and metaphors across domains. As in the longstanding debate over string theory in physics, disagreement should not preclude exploration – particularly when real-world systems defy reductionist models.

A notable tension persists between traditional economists and researchers with backgrounds in physics. As Jovanovic and Schinckus (2013) observe, this intellectual divide stems largely from foundational assumptions. Economists traditionally rely on Gaussian distributions to model asset returns, emphasising expected return as the investor's goal and standard deviation as the proxy for risk. This approach implicitly assumes a world governed by equilibrium and moderate variability. In contrast, econophysicists tend to apply Lévy stable distributions or power-law frameworks, which account for the heavy tails observed in real-world financial data – offering a more realistic probability of rare but severe events, such as market crashes or sudden price surges.

1.4.1 *Econophysical Forces in Action: Capital Flow and Strategic Friction*

Rather than engaging in this methodological debate, our approach bypasses the issue by focusing on the core mechanics of interaction among economic forces – irrespective of disciplinary boundaries. Our objective is to embed econophysical thinking into strategic modelling, especially where uncertainty, adaptive dynamics, and complex interdependencies are involved. Imagine, for example, the process of launching a business venture. An entrepreneur – armed with education, ideas, and partial market knowledge – requires capital to bring the project to life. Over time, four principal funding sources become relevant: (1) bank credit, (2) equity financing through capital markets (particularly under incentive schemes for SMEs), (3) public financing via national or municipal budgets, and (4) informal financing or shadow capital (Figure 1.9). The interaction of these capital flows, much like interacting physical forces, results in the emergence (or erosion) of economic value. However, these interactions are not always productive. They can be dampened by frictions and manipulations – what we call *vibrational forces* of the system. These include lags or volatility in receivables and payables, illiquid inventories, excess reserves, or fluctuating credit conditions. In other words, not all

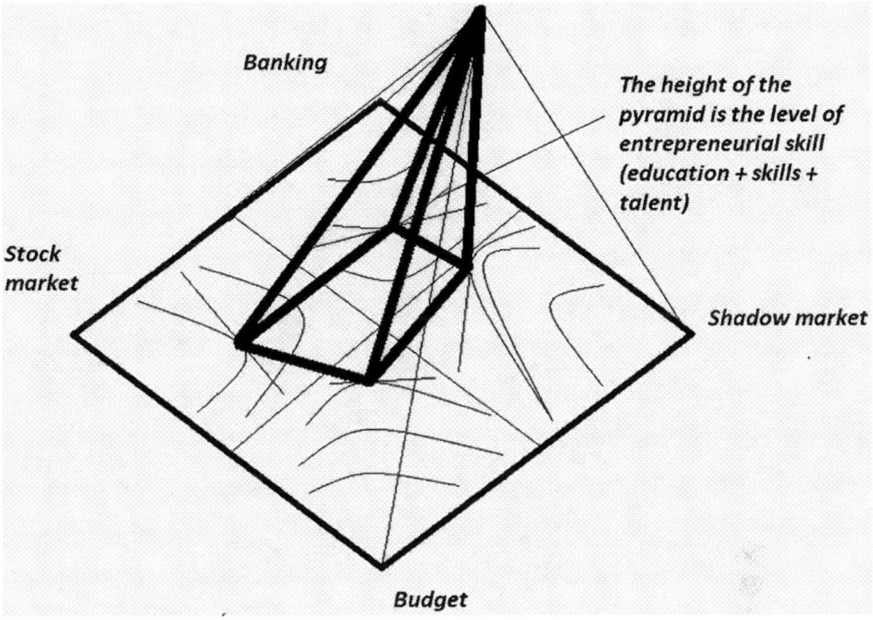

Figure 1.9 Strategic Capital Pyramid: Primary Sources of Economic Force.
Source: Own elaboration.

forces act in synchrony or with equal efficiency. Figure 1.10 illustrates this concept, drawing attention to the vibrational and inertial drag exerted by financial frictions on value creation. It extends the concept by depicting how capital flows between key institutions (e.g., stock markets and banks) are affected by vibrational forces – such as receivables, payables, and inventory dynamics – that introduce systemic drag and instability. These distortions can undermine value creation, similar to friction in physical systems. As illustrated in Figure 1.9, the strategic potential of a business venture is shaped not only by available capital channels but also by the entrepreneur's capacity to access and leverage these resources. However, Figure 1.10 reveals that this system is far from frictionless – vibrational forces can impede capital flow, introducing instability or inefficiency into the system.

Meanwhile, Estola (2017) offers a formal Newtonian microeconomic framework that can represent such interactions. Building on that concept, our team proposed a model in which economic value behaves analogously to a mass subjected to multiple forces. The simplified dynamic equation – rooted in classical mechanics but applied to finance – can be written as follows (see also Hurnyak, Struk & Kordonska, 2021):

$$m_{EV}\overrightarrow{\dot{EV}} = -\, m_{AP}\overrightarrow{AP} + m_{AR}\overrightarrow{AR} + m_{I}\vec{I} + m_{\text{Debt}}\overrightarrow{\text{Debt}} + m_{\text{Equity}}\overrightarrow{\text{Equity}}, \quad (3)$$

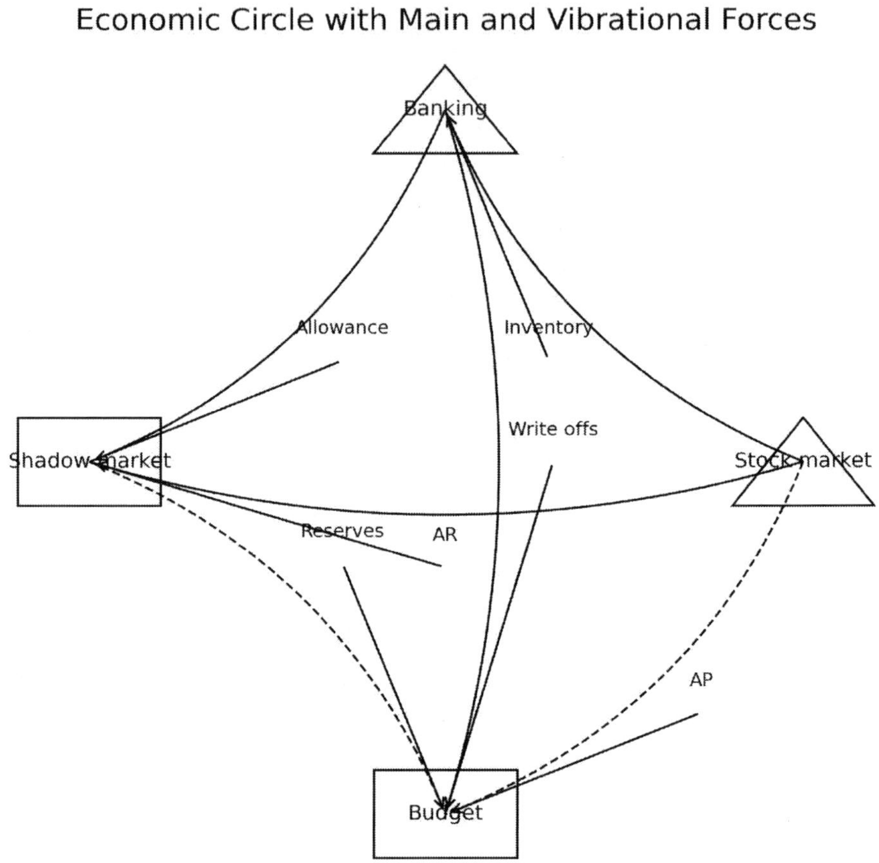

Figure 1.10 Interplay of Primary and Vibrational Economic Forces.

Source: Own elaboration.

where:

- m_{EV}; m_{AP}; m_{AR}; m_I; m_{Debt}; and m_{Equity} represent the inertial resistance associated with accounts payable, receivable, inventory, debt, and equity, respectively;
- the vectors denote the direction and intensity of each economic force.

This model captures how different funding or frictional components exert push or drag on value creation. The forces can be conceptualised linearly or, in more advanced treatments, with feedback loops, delay differentials, or nonlinear interaction terms. In the linear case, the equation offers tractable insights into liquidity bottlenecks, financial leverage effects, or operational slack. In nonlinear extensions, the system can exhibit oscillations, bifurcations, or chaotic behaviour – mirroring what we observe in stressed financial environments. Ultimately, this framework supports a dynamic, interdisciplinary understanding of value generation, where econophysical principles – mass, inertia, force – are not metaphors but structural analogues. They provide tools to analyse how strategic decisions ripple through complex financial ecosystems. For example, in certain institutional environments, it may be possible to accumulate investment resources not through conventional funding channels, but by delaying payments to suppliers, deferring employee wages, or postponing tax obligations. These forms of internal financial manipulation reflect what we refer to as vibrational forces – factors that distort the flow of capital and contribute to systemic risk. When strategic profiling is based solely on market dynamics – such as those captured in the Fama–French model, which reflects external valuation – such internal turbulence often remains hidden. Therefore, it becomes logical to incorporate both basic and vibrational forces into the analysis, especially when drawing on internal firm-level accounting data. Figure 1.10 visualises this dual structure under two scenarios. The upper part of the diagram represents a normal state in which primary capital flows (banking, equity, budgets) dominate. In contrast, the lower part illustrates crisis conditions, where these main forces are suppressed and vibrational forces (such as accounts payable, inventory drag, or unstable receivables) become the dominant drivers of economic outcomes. In such situations, external strategic signals become less reliable, and internal balance sheet behaviour gains greater predictive power.

1.4.2 Quantifying Economic Vibrations: A Regression-Based Perspective

To operationalise this approach in a replicable and transparent manner, we simplify the system into a linear regression model, using economic value added (EVA) as the dependent variable. For input data, we rely on industry-level financials provided by Professor Aswath Damodaran, ensuring both transparency and reproducibility for researchers familiar with standard econometric techniques (see Damodaran, n.d.).

Table 1.13 presents the results of the econophysical regression model examining the determinants of EVA across three macro-regions: Europe, Emerging Markets, and the United States. As the adjusted R^2 values suggest, the model explains EVA variation most effectively in the U.S. ($R^2 = 0.98$), with lower but still statistically significant explanatory power in Europe ($R^2 = 0.56$) and emerging markets ($R^2 = 0.50$). The standardised regression coefficients reveal notable regional differences. For example, the book value of equity (BV_E) has a strong positive effect on EVA in Europe but turns significantly negative in the U.S., indicating divergent capital market dynamics and possibly differences in investor expectations or capital structures. Interestingly, account receivables to sales (AR/S) have a strong negative effect only in the U.S. context, perhaps suggesting more rigid expectations regarding

Table 1.13 Impact of Structural and Vibrational Forces on Economic Value Added Across Regions: Results of the Econophysical Regression Model

Indicator of Force	*Europe*	*Emerging Markets*	*USA*
Adj R^2	0.56	0.5	0.98
F (Sign.)	23.7 (0.000)	18.8 (0.000)	1297.7 (0.000)
BV_E (Sign.)	0.73* (0.000)	−0.08 (0.3)	−0.16* (0.000)
ADV_T_R (Sign.)	−0.22* (0.002)	−0.125** (0.1)	−0.01 (0.411)
AR/S (Sign.)	−0.08 (0.242)	0.05 (0.59)	−0.96* (0.000)
I/S (Sign.)	−0.03(0.66)	−0.39* (0.000)	0.01 (0.435)
AP/S (Sign.)	−0.05(0.46)	−0.54*(0.000)	0.038** (0.08)

Notes: Standardised coefficients are presented. All models met multicollinearity criteria (acceptable VIF or Tolerance values).

The dependent variable is Economic Value Added (EVA), calculated as:

$$EVA = NOPAT - (\text{Invested Capital} \times WACC).$$

Data reflect January 2025 values (covering the previous fiscal year).

Sample size: 90 firms.

Independent variables include: BV_E – Book Value of Equity; ADV_T_R – Inverse Tax Rate (1/tax rate); AR/S – Accounts Receivable to Sales Ratio; I/S – Inventory to Sales Ratio; AP/S – Accounts Payable to Sales Ratio.

Statistical analysis was performed using SPSS.

* indicates significance at the 10% level ($p < 0.10$);

** indicates significance at the 1% level ($p < 0.01$).

liquidity and cash conversion efficiency. In contrast, inventory to sales (I/S) and accounts payable to sales (AP/S) ratios exert significant negative impacts in emerging markets, where operational inefficiencies and low automation may amplify the cost of holding or delaying financial obligations. The inverse tax rate (ADV_T_R) – interpreted here as a proxy for fiscal efficiency or burden – is negatively associated with EVA in Europe and emerging markets but proves insignificant in the U.S. These findings suggest that, during the analysed period (data as of January 2025), so-called vibrational forces – such as the management of receivables, inventory, and payables – played a more substantial role in shaping EVA in the U.S. than in other regions. This reinforces the relevance of micro-level frictions in strategic financial modelling, particularly when using econophysical analogies.

1.4.3 Building Strategic Futures: Neural Network Scenarios for EVA Forecasting

Figure 1.11 presents the structure of a neural network trained to model the EVA coefficient based on 90 industry-specific observations. This multilayer perceptron architecture, implemented in *R* using the neuralnet package, uses a configuration of three hidden layers with 8, 5, and 2 neurons respectively – denoted as c(8, 5, 2). Each input variable corresponds to one of

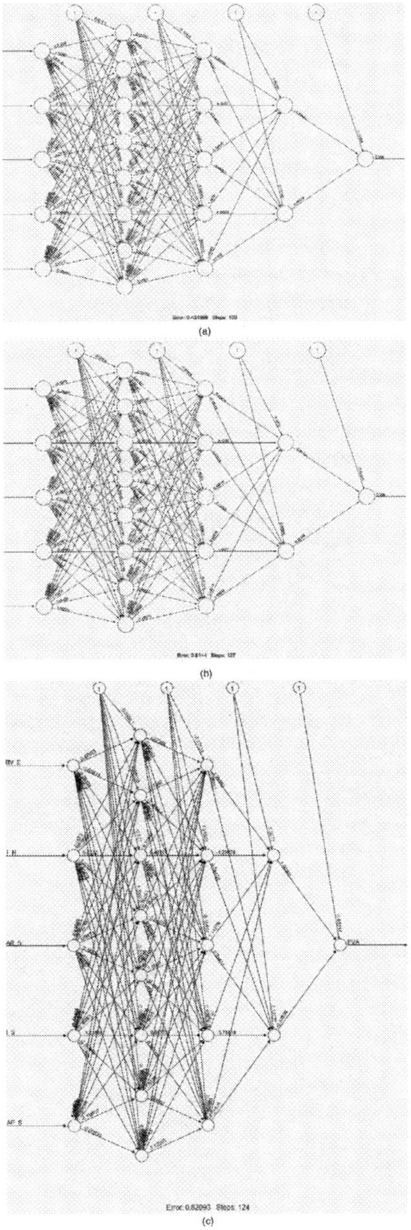

Figure 1.11 Simulated Economic Value Added (EVA) Changes Across Industries Under Variable Stress Scenarios.

Note: Results were achieved based on R libraries: *stats*, *dplyr*, *ggplot2*, *ggfortify*, and *neuralnet*. Model accuracy: Europe = 0.935; Emerging markets = 0.939; USA = 0.983. Neural network architecture: c(8, 5, 2). Dataset: 90 industries.

Source: Own elaboration.

the economic forces discussed earlier: both *basic forces* (such as equity capital and tax efficiency) and *vibrational forces* (like accounts payable, receivable, and inventory ratios).

The model achieves exceptionally high levels of accuracy, with coefficients of determination (R^2) for Europe – 0.935; Emerging markets – 0.939; and USA – 0.983, which significantly surpass the results of earlier linear regression models (Table 1.13). Training was performed using classical backpropagation, and convergence was achieved within acceptable error bounds (e.g., error = 0.834 for the European dataset after 123 steps).

The neural network allows for advanced scenario testing. Because of its high explanatory power, the model can simulate how EVA would respond to strategic changes such as a 20% increase in share capital (proxy: BV_E) – modifying the effective tax rate (ADV_T_R = 1/tax rate), changes in payment policies (AR/S, AP/S), and inventory optimisation (I/S). These manipulations are critical in planning resilient business strategies under uncertainty, especially when evaluating the elasticity of EVA in response to internal managerial actions or external financial conditions. As shown in subsequent tables and figures (e.g., Table 1.14 and Figure 1.12), changes in these forces lead to divergent EVA responses across industries.

These results underscore the strategic relevance of nonlinear modelling for capturing sector-specific dynamics. As seen in Table 1.14 and illustrated in Figure 1.12, the EVA response to changes in core input variables (such as share capital, tax conditions, and working capital elements) is not uniform across industries. For example, sectors such as Computer Services or Telecom exhibit relatively minor changes under most manipulations, suggesting a level of operational or financial inertia. In contrast, sectors like Healthcare or Advertising show pronounced sensitivity, particularly to receivables and tax regime alterations, indicating that their EVA generation is tightly coupled with external

Table 1.14 Simulated Impact of Financial Policy Adjustments on EVA Across Industries (Neural Network Model)

Industry	*No Changes*	*BV_E/S * 1.2, I/S *0.5*	*T_R *0.9, AR/S *0.5, AP/S *2*
Education	0.2241953	0.2244735	0.2237693
Computer services	0.2211056	0.2214982	0.2211511
Advertising	0.2235288	0.2235422	0.2227886
Entertainment	0.2238877	0.2241965	0.2273987
Healthcare support services	0.2203716	0.2212497	0.2218010
Information services	0.2246049	0.2246117	0.2240494
Telecom. services	0.2236759	0.2242802	0.2237536

Source: Own elaboration.

Notes: The table presents EVA outcomes under different manipulations of input financial indicators across seven industries. Input changes reflect strategic decisions such as tax optimisation (T_R), working capital adjustments (AR/S, AP/S), and capital structure shifts (BV_E). All values are normalised; model trained using 90 observations (industries).

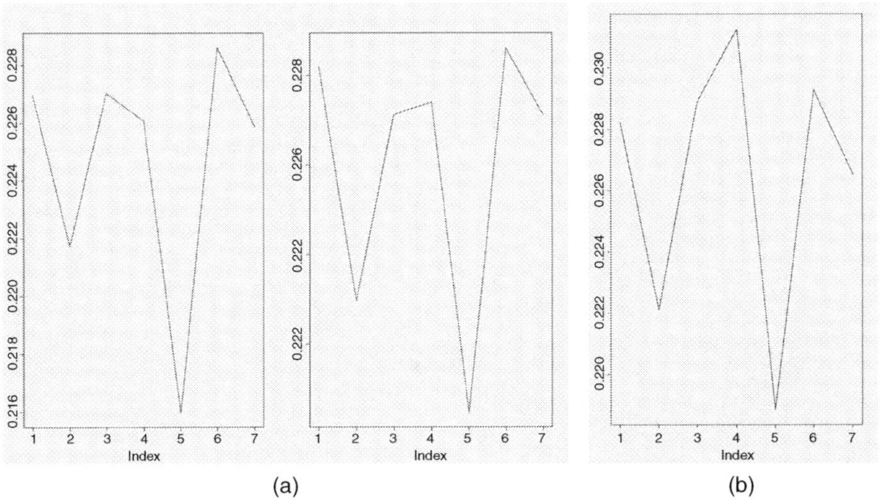

Figure 1.12 Visual Representation of EVA Sensitivity to Strategic Financial Adjustments.

Source: Own elaboration.

Notes: The plots illustrate normalised changes in EVA under different input configurations across industries. Data corresponds to scenarios detailed in Table 1.14. Results highlight variance in sectoral sensitivity to input perturbations.

fiscal levers or internal liquidity cycles. The graphs in Figure 1.12 visualise these nonlinearities more clearly, revealing abrupt jumps or non-monotonic patterns in EVA outcomes – behaviour that traditional linear regressions may fail to capture. Such responsiveness may also point to exploitable strategic leverage: where small shifts in financial structure or capital efficiency produce disproportionate changes in economic value. In practice, this modelling framework can support proactive strategy design. A firm could simulate hypothetical shifts (e.g., doubling accounts payable or halving tax obligations) and observe how these ripple through EVA in its specific sectoral context. This empowers decision-makers to optimise resource allocation and timing under varied macroeconomic or policy scenarios, moving beyond static benchmarking towards adaptive, scenario-responsive modelling.

The presented modelling framework offers practical benefits for decision-makers seeking to navigate financial complexity with greater precision. Neural networks trained on firm-level or industry-specific data allow managers to simulate the impact of various strategic options on EVA, including adjustments to capital structure, tax regimes, or working capital management. These simulations enable pre-testing of strategies under different macroeconomic or institutional scenarios, reducing reliance on intuition or oversimplified heuristics. From a managerial standpoint, the key advantage lies in the ability to model nonlinear cause-and-effect relationships. Unlike traditional regression models, neural networks can account for threshold effects, feedback loops, and sector-specific sensitivities. For instance, companies in healthcare or technology may show disproportionate EVA sensitivity to minor shifts in receivables or inventory levels – insights that are critical for strategic planning. Moreover, the model's flexibility allows for scenario-based stress testing, helping firms prepare for crisis situations or policy shocks. Managers can explore what-if cases: what happens to EVA if interest rates rise? How does the supplier delay ripple through value creation? This supports proactive rather than reactive financial management.

Looking ahead, this modelling architecture can be expanded in several directions:

- Integration of ESG data, enabling firms to evaluate how environmental, social, and governance performance interacts with financial value;
- Embedding game-theoretical interactions, such as Axelrod-style simulations, to assess how competitive behaviour influences long-term survival and profitability;
- Application to crisis modelling, especially in emerging markets where volatility and institutional uncertainty amplify the role of vibrational forces;
- Agent-based extensions, allowing for bottom-up simulations of investor behaviour, liquidity shocks, or supply chain disruptions across interconnected industries.

Consequently, econophysical and neural approaches do not replace traditional strategic thinking – they enrich it. They offer a quantitative lens through which complexity can be operationalised, uncertainty managed, and long-term value better understood.

1.5 Implications and Strategic Reflections

This chapter introduced a comprehensive, multidisciplinary rethinking of strategy within the context of today's volatile, uncertain, complex, and ambiguous economic landscape. Drawing on tools from game theory, financial econometrics, nonlinear modelling, and econophysics, we proposed a layered approach to strategic analysis – one that is adaptive, empirically grounded, and capable of addressing both external dynamics and internal firm behaviour.

Traditional approaches to strategy, focused on equilibrium assumptions and rational actors, are increasingly insufficient in explaining market behaviour, especially in sectors marked by innovation cycles, institutional fragmentation, or systemic uncertainty. In response, this chapter introduced an expanded strategic toolkit that integrates:

- Axelrod tournaments, for simulating interactive behaviour and testing cooperation under evolving rules;
- VCG mechanism offering powerful alternatives for simulating decision-making and distribution under conditions of strategic disclosure;

- Fama–French financial modelling, reinterpreted to detect deeper business strategy profiles based on market risk, value orientation, and profitability;
- Neural networks, which model nonlinear interactions and support scenario testing of financial strategies;
- Econophysical modelling, using the concepts of fundamental vs. vibrational forces to identify the role of internal frictions on value creation.

Underlying this toolkit is the principle of econothinking – a mindset that approaches strategic decisions with an awareness of how economic dynamics, geopolitical forces, and institutional structures intertwine. Econothinking emphasises systemic connections rather than isolated analyses, enabling strategists to anticipate how local actions ripple outward to influence broader economic and political patterns. By combining these perspectives, we moved from a view of strategy as static optimisation to one rooted in adaptive modelling and systemic thinking. The core insight is that strategic resilience cannot be separated from a firm's behavioural dynamics, institutional environment, and capacity to respond to both predictable and chaotic change. This reimagined approach allows for more than just tactical adaptation – it enables firms to simulate and stress-test their decisions in advance, assessing not only financial return but also long-term viability and structural integrity. It also shifts the concept of strategic success away from short-term gain towards sustainable value creation.

Thus, Chapter 1 lays the methodological and conceptual foundation for an advanced, data-driven, behaviourally sensitive model of strategy. It connects micro-level indicators with macro-level patterns, offering a way forward for institutions, managers, and policymakers operating in increasingly entangled environments.

References

Axelrod, R. (1984). *The evolution of cooperation*. New York: Basic Books.

Axelrod-Python. (n.d.). *Strategy index*. Axelrod Project Documentation. Retrieved June 21, 2025, from https://axelrod.readthedocs.io/en/dev/reference/strategy_index.html

Baker, M., & Wurgler, J. (2004). A catering theory of dividends. *The Journal of Finance*, *59*(3), 1125–1165. https://doi.org/10.1111/j.1540-6261.2004.00658.x

Bali, T. G., Cakici, N., & Whitelaw, R. F. (2011). Maxing out: Stocks as lotteries and the cross-section of expected returns. *Journal of Financial Economics*, *99*(2), 427–446. https://doi.org/10.1016/j.jfineco.2010.08.014

Barber, B. M., & Odean, T. (2001). Boys will be boys: Gender, overconfidence, and common stock investment. *Quarterly Journal of Economics*, *116*(1), 261–292. https://doi.org/10.1162/003355301556400

Bender, J., Briand, R., Melas, D., & Subramanian, R. (2013). *Foundations of factor investing*. MSCI Research. https://www.msci.com/documents/1296102/1336482/Foundations_of_Factor_Investing.pdf

Binmore, K. (2007). *Playing for real: A text on game theory*. Oxford: Oxford University Press.

Brandenburger, A., & Nalebuff, B. (1996). *Co-opetition*. Doubleday.

Camerer, C. F. (2003). *Behavioral game theory: Experiments in strategic interaction*. Princeton, NJ: Princeton University Press.

Chumachenko, M., & Zadorozhna, Y. (2024). Strategic behavioral modeling of social archetypes: Interpreting Axelrod tournament strategies in the Ukrainian context. *Journal of Institutional Studies and Political Economy*, *5*(2), 115–134. https://www.ceeol.com/search/article-detail?id=1264928

Coleman, J. S. (1990). *Foundations of social theory*. Cambridge, MA: Harvard University Press.

Committee of Entrepreneurs of Lviv Oblast. (2007, October 8). Lviv entrepreneurs researched the values of the residents of their city. *KPL*. https://kpl.org.ua/news/2007/10/08/447

Damodaran, A. (n.d.). *Data archive*. New York University Stern School of Business. Retrieved June 22, 2025, from https://pages.stern.nyu.edu/~adamodar/

Dixit, A., & Nalebuff, B. (2008). *The art of strategy: A game theorist's guide to success in business and life*. New York: W. W. Norton & Company.

Epstein, J. M. (2006). *Generative social science: Studies in agent-based computational modeling*. Princeton, NJ: Princeton University Press.

Estola, M. (2017). *Newtonian microeconomics: A dynamic extension to neoclassical micro theory*. London: Palgrave Macmillan.

Euronews. (2025, May 28). Germany to jointly produce long-range weapons with Ukraine, Friedrich Merz says. https://www.euronews.com/my-europe/2025/05/28/germany-to-jointly-produce-long-range-weapons-with-ukraine-friedrich-merz-says

Fama, E. F., & French, K. R. (1993). Common risk factors in the returns on stocks and bonds. *Journal of Financial Economics*, *33*(1), 3–56. https://doi.org/10.1016/0304-405X(93)90023-5

Fama, E. F., & French, K. R. (2014). A five-factor asset pricing model. *Fama-Miller Working Paper*. https://doi.org/10.2139/ssrn.2287202

Financial Times. (2025, May 12). Trump always chickens out. *Financial Times*. https://www.ft.com/content/714c1096-eb17-40b0-a570-8a051406bc75

Fischer, T., & Krauss, C. (2018). Deep learning with long short-term memory networks for financial market predictions. *European Journal of Operational Research*, *270*(2), 654–669. https://doi.org/10.1016/j.ejor.2017.11.054

Fudenberg, D., & Tirole, J. (1991). *Game theory*. Cambridge, MA: MIT Press.

Gintis, H. (2009). *The bounds of reason: Game theory and the unification of the behavioral sciences*. Princeton, NY: Princeton University Press.

Granovetter, M. (1985). Economic action and social structure: The problem of embeddedness. *American Journal of Sociology*, *91*(3), 481–510. https://doi.org/10.1086/228311

Gu, S., Kelly, B., & Xiu, D. (2020). Empirical asset pricing via machine learning. *The Review of Financial Studies*, *33*(5), 2223–2273. https://doi.org/10.1093/rfs/hhaa009

Hedström, P., & Swedberg, R. (1998). *Social mechanisms: An analytical approach to social theory*. Cambridge: Cambridge University Press.

Henrique, B. M., Sobreiro, V. A., & Kimura, H. (2019). Literature review: Machine learning techniques applied to financial market prediction. *Expert Systems with Applications*, *124*, 226–251. https://doi.org/10.1016/j.eswa.2019.01.012

Hurnyak, I., Struk, N., & Kordonska, A. (2021). Value added from the perspective of econophysics. *Comparative Economic Research. Central and Eastern Europe*, *24*(4), 137–152. https://doi.org/10.18778/1508-2008.24.35

Jovanovic, F., & Schinckus, C. (2013). The history of econophysics as a new approach in modern financial theory. *History of Political Economy*, *45*(Supplement), 443–474. https://dx. doi.org/10.1215/00182702-2334758

Lakonishok, J., Shleifer, A., & Vishny, R. W. (1994). Contrarian investment, extrapolation, and risk. *The Journal of Finance*, *49*(5), 1541–1578. https://doi.org/10.1111/j.1540-6261.1994.tb04772.x

Lo, A. W. (2005). Reconciling efficient markets with behavioral finance: The adaptive markets hypothesis. *Journal of Investment Consulting*, *7*(2), 21–44. https://papers.ssrn.com/sol3/papers.cfm?abstract_id=1702447

March, J. G., & Olsen, J. P. (1989). *Rediscovering institutions: The organizational basis of politics*. New York: Free Press.

Myerson, R. B. (1991). *Game theory: Analysis of conflict*. Cambridge, MA: Harvard University Press.

Nash, J. (1950). Equilibrium points in n-person games. *Proceedings of the National Academy of Sciences*, *36*(1), 48–49. https://doi.org/10.1073/pnas.36.1.48

Nicolescu, B. (2010). Methodology of transdisciplinarity — Levels of reality, logic of the included middle and complexity. *Transdisciplinary Journal of Engineering & Science*, *1*, 17–18. https://doi.org/10.22545/2010/0009

North, D. C. (1990). *Institutions, institutional change and economic performance*. Cambridge: Cambridge University Press.

Ostrom, E. (1990). *Governing the commons: The evolution of institutions for collective action*. Cambridge: Cambridge University Press.

Ostrom, E. (2005). *Understanding institutional diversity*. Princeton, NJ: Princeton University Press.

Patel, J., Shah, S., Thakkar, P., & Kotecha, K. (2015). Predicting stock and stock price index movement using trend deterministic data preparation and machine learning techniques. *Expert Systems with Applications, 42*(1), 259–268. https://doi.org/10.1016/j.eswa.2014.07.040

Scharpf, F. W. (1997). *Games real actors play: Actor-centered institutionalism in policy research*. Boulder, CO: Westview Press.

Selten, R. (1975). Reexamination of the perfectness concept for equilibrium points in extensive games. *International Journal of Game Theory, 4*(1), 25–55. https://doi.org/10.1007/BF01766400

Stanley, H. E., Amaral, L. A. N., Canning, D., Gopikrishnan, P., Lee, Y., & Liu, Y. (1999). Econophysics: Can physicists contribute to the science of economics? *Physica A: Statistical Mechanics and Its Applications*, *269*(1), 156–169. https://doi.org/10.1016/S0378-4371(99)00185-5

Ticknor, J. L. (2013). A Bayesian regularized artificial neural network for stock market forecasting. *Expert Systems with Applications, 40*(14), 5501–5506. https://doi.org/10.1016/j.eswa.2013.04.013

von Neumann, J., & Morgenstern, O. (1944). *Theory of games and economic behavior*. Princeton, NJ: Princeton University Press.

Wang, J., Wang, J., Zhang, Z., & Guo, S. (2012). Forecasting stock indices with back propagation neural network. *Expert Systems with Applications, 38*(11), 14346–14355. https://doi.org/10.1016/j.eswa.2011.11.032

Yoon, K. (2008). The participatory Vickrey–Clarke–Groves mechanism. *Journal of Mathematical Economics*, *44*(3–4), 324–336. https://doi.org/10.1016/j.jmateco.2007.05.009

Zhang, G. P. (2003). Time series forecasting using a hybrid ARIMA and neural network model. *Neurocomputing*, *50*, 159–175. https://doi.org/10.1016/S0925-2312(01)00702-0

2 Human Behaviour and Market Dynamics in the Age of Competition

2.1 Progress, Digital Transformation, and Strategic Adaptability

The notion of progress has been interpreted in many ways over time. The Oxford English Dictionary defines it as "advancement to a further or higher stage, or to further or higher stages successively; growth; development, usually to a better state or condition; improvement (...) applied especially to manifestations of social and economic change or reform" (Simpson & Weiner, 1989). However, this definition only scratches the surface. Xingfu and Siming (2020), drawing on Marxist critiques of the paradoxes inherent in capitalist progress and Habermas's reconstruction of social evolution, emphasise that progress should not be understood as an automatic or intrinsic trend in history. Rather, it is a historical-practical project undertaken by humanity. This deeper questioning of progress has been explored by the Conversations on Rethinking Human Development project team. In a report from the International Science Council (2020, pp. 75–76), they pose essential questions: do we define progress as mastery over the universe and technology, or as our capacity to build relationships and solidarity with one another? Equally crucial is the question of what it means to be human. Is our essence captured by the notion of Homo economicus – a human being primarily driven by economic motives – or is this merely a framework shaped by a system where individual competition and profit dominate all other considerations? Moreover, how do our collective responsibilities evolve in the face of challenges such as material provisioning, economic life, technological advances, and artificial intelligence? (International Science Council, 2020, p. 76).

Ruzzeddu (2022) offers another dimension, describing modernisation as a process in which traditional ascribed characteristics – such as gender, religion, and ethnicity – gradually lose their rigid role in defining personal identity. Instead, personal achievements increasingly shape how individuals are perceived and how they perceive themselves. Alongside this societal shift, the US-based Partnership for 21st century Learning proposes the "Framework for 21st Century Learning", identifying four critical categories of skills: critical thinking, communication, collaboration, and creativity (Joynes et al., 2019).

DOI: 10.4324/9781003660194-2

The so-called "4Cs" model reflects the belief that 21st-century challenges demand a broad skill set, encompassing not just core academic knowledge but also social and cross-cultural competencies, multilingual proficiency, and a nuanced understanding of economic and political forces (Joynes et al., 2019, p. 12). At an even deeper level, the framework emphasises lifelong learning, problem-solving, self-management, and teamwork – key elements in navigating an era of rapid change (Chalkiadaki, cited in Joynes et al., 2019).

From an economic perspective, growth continues to serve as a significant – though increasingly debated – metric for assessing progress, especially in developed economies. According to Lei Pan and Vinod Mishra (2018, p. 661), "the interplay between the stock market and the real economy is crucial in the various channels through which financial markets drive economic growth". Lazonick (2017) argues for an expanded understanding of the stock market, viewing it not merely as a mechanism for profit but as a space that also encompasses functions such as control, creation, combination, and compensation.

Moreover, sentiment plays a powerful – and sometimes underappreciated – role in shaping economic outcomes. Morck et al. (1990) highlighted this dynamic by examining the stock market crash of October 1987. They discovered that corporate insiders actively purchased shares of their own companies during the crisis, recognising that the crash was driven not by changes in fundamentals but by shifts in market sentiment. As they noted: "The insiders quite correctly saw no change in fundamentals and attributed the crash to a sentiment shift. The thrust of the evidence is that stock prices respond not only to news, but also to sentiment changes" (Morck et al., 1990, p. 160).

These perspectives underscore that progress is not a simple linear march forward. It is a multidimensional concept that intertwines technological capability, human relationships, identity, skills development, and economic dynamics – all unfolding in the context of societal values and uncertainties. Yet in a world of rapid technological shifts, geopolitical tensions, and global crises, progress is no longer just about growth or social reform. It is about strategic adaptability – the capacity of individuals, firms, and nations to anticipate disruptions, respond creatively to emerging challenges, and redefine competitive advantages. This notion of adaptability forms the backbone of this book, which seeks to explore how modern economies transform under pressure and how strategic actors recalibrate their decisions to secure resilience and competitiveness. At the core of this adaptability lies what we define as *econothinking*: a mindset that integrates economic implications into decision-making, balances short-term choices with long-term impacts, and pursues outcomes that align business profitability with societal well-being and global competitiveness.

Such adaptability is nowhere more evident than in the digital sphere. Digital transformation exemplifies how technological change both disrupts existing structures and offers new strategic opportunities. From today's perspective, it is clear that digital transformation has become one of the most defining trends shaping our understanding of progress and modern development. Digitalisation touches every aspect of human life, reshaping economic structures, social relationships, and the way individuals perceive opportunities for self-fulfilment. Nie and Erbring (2000) offer early insight into how the Internet began to shape human interactions, while Kiesler et al. (1984) look beyond the efficiency and technical capabilities of computer communication technologies, providing a deeper understanding of their psychological, social, and cultural significance. These early perspectives foreshadow the profound ways digital transformation has come to influence society.

The COVID-19 pandemic accelerated the adoption of digital solutions at an unprecedented pace, creating unforeseen opportunities for scaling up alternative approaches to social and economic life (Hantrais et al., 2021). Researchers have also shown how the ethics of artificial intelligence have become a primary concern for government regulation, and how features enabling smart cities to act as productivity drivers did not necessarily provide advantages during the pandemic.

The *Digital Society Index 2019* introduced a Maslow-inspired hierarchy for the digital age, illustrating how digitalisation intersects with fundamental human needs (Dentsu Aegis Network, 2019):

- *Basic needs* – access to digital tools and trust in data;
- *Psychological needs* – improved health, well-being, and quality of life through digital technologies;
- *Self-fulfilment needs* – digital empowerment and utilisation;
- *Societal needs* – confidence in digital's potential to improve society.

Yet, a global survey of over 43,000 people revealed that less than half (49%) believe their basic digital needs – such as access to quality digital infrastructure and trust in responsible data use – are being met (Dentsu Aegis Network, 2019). This finding echoes Manfred Max-Neef's framework of fundamental human needs, which identified universal needs consistent across cultures and eras. Max-Neef cautioned that poorly aligned satisfiers – particularly in consumer-driven systems – can alienate societies and impede meaningful development (Max-Neef, 2010). This perspective offers a foundation for examining how digital transformation, industry shifts, and work adaptations address or fail to address these needs in contemporary contexts.

Aligned with Max-Neef's principles, Lu et al. (2022) proposed a human-centric approach to Industry 5.0, where manufacturing systems prioritise worker well-being over pure efficiency. Their *Industrial Human Needs Pyramid* mirrors the hierarchy of needs, emphasising empathy-driven human-machine collaboration. This shift recognises the connection between technological progress and the fulfilment of human needs at cognitive, social, and self-actualisation levels. Similarly, Zhang and Chen (2024) explored the digital transformation of human resource management, emphasising how digital tools can enhance employee selection, training, and development.

However, they also warned of potential negative consequences during transitions between old and new systems, echoing Max-Neef's concerns about misaligned satisfiers in rapidly changing environments.

The narrative of digital transformation has been widely explored, particularly in the context of remote and hybrid work models. Studies such as Sokolic (2022), Grzegorczyk et al. (2021), Babapour Chafi et al. (2022), and Kraus et al. (2023) highlight how workplace flexibility can enhance autonomy, productivity, and work-life balance, while also raising challenges like weakened workplace relationships and the need for fair policies to avoid disparities between remote and on-site workers. The "new normal" shaped by COVID-19 has reshaped labour markets, with Vyas (2022) emphasising trends of acceleration and remodelling in flexible work arrangements, and Juchnowicz and Kinowska (2021) noting the vital role of digital tools for maintaining well-being and workplace connections. Faruque et al. (2024) extend these insights to small businesses, pointing to benefits in flexibility and cost-effectiveness, yet also highlighting communication challenges. Dahlke et al. (2021) frame these shifts as crisis-driven innovations requiring systemic responses. These studies illustrate that digital transformation and new work practices are more than technological changes – they reflect strategic recalibrations essential for aligning competitiveness with human well-being and societal values. They underscore that true resilience and sustainable success depend on integrating technological advances into strategies that meet fundamental human needs. Yet, this also raises a crucial question: *are human needs currently being met on a global scale?* From an economic perspective, the stock market provides one lens for evaluating the alignment between investment strategies and modern human needs (Figure 2.1). In this context, an optimally structured investment portfolio might serve as a practical response to these shifting priorities – balancing profitability and risk with societal and individual well-being. As we examine how digitalisation reshapes societies and economies, we are inevitably led to question how markets – including financial markets – respond and adapt. The stock market, as both a reflection and driver of strategic sentiment, becomes a powerful indicator of how modern economies balance profitability, resilience, and human-centric progress. This is precisely where strategic adaptability manifests in economic decision-making, linking individual, corporate, and national strategies in a complex global landscape.

2.2 Strategic Portfolio Design: Aligning Markets with Human Needs

2.2.1 Methodological Framework for Portfolio Construction

Constructing an optimal investment portfolio becomes both a technical and strategic exercise, linking market behaviour with the deeper drivers of progress and economic thinking, and aiming to achieve a balance between

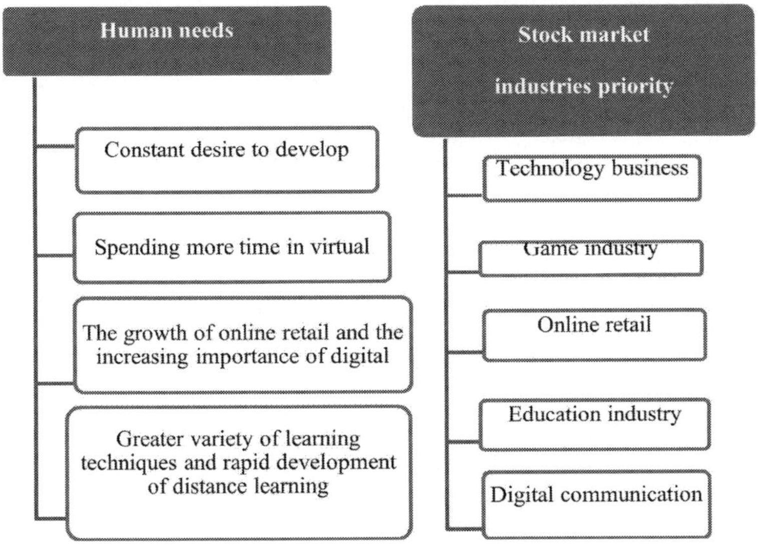

Figure 2.1 Human Needs and Investment Strategies.

Source: Own elaboration.

profitability and risk while being guided by contemporary human needs and current market trends. To simplify our approach, we begin by defining key human needs and identifying major trends. Using a list of trending stock tickers (which naturally varies depending on the specific date of the analysis) and examining cumulative return dynamics, we identify the leading performers across three consecutive market clusters. We then proceed to optimise the investment portfolio based on these leaders. In the context of the stock market, we assume that an optimal investment portfolio – one that strikes a suitable balance between risk and return – can serve, particularly in developed markets, as a financial reflection of modern human priorities and needs. The Sharpe Ratio calculated for the resulting portfolio serves as an indicator of how effectively the portfolio aligns with these goals. While the Sharpe Ratio is the primary metric used to assess portfolio efficiency, our analysis also incorporates alternative performance measures such as the Treynor Ratio, Sortino Ratio, Calmar Ratio, and Maximum Drawdown. These additional metrics provide a more comprehensive understanding of portfolio behaviour under diverse market conditions, especially during periods of extreme volatility.

The next stage involves calculating the optimal portfolio weights for individual industries. By combining top-performing stocks from one industry with the leading companies from other sectors, we create a cross-industry, diversified optimal portfolio. This approach allows us to exploit synergies between sectors, mitigate sector-specific risks, and create portfolios that are more resilient to economic shocks and structural market changes. Following this, we compare the investment priorities revealed through our stock market analysis with the critical human skills identified earlier in this chapter. The approach we use, known as the Efficient Frontier method (illustrated in Figure 2.2), evaluates all possible portfolio combinations based on their risk and return characteristics. In practical terms, we aim to locate the tangency point between the Capital Allocation Line and the Efficient Frontier, which represents the most efficient portfolio. This portfolio configuration maximises the expected return for a given level of risk – or, conversely, minimises risk for a specified target return.

In addition to mean-variance optimisation, we explore utility-maximisation methods, aligning portfolio strategies with specific investor risk preferences and long-term objectives. This dual approach ensures that portfolio construction reflects both quantitative efficiency and qualitative strategic goals.

Additionally, to capture the dynamic nature of market trends, we analyse portfolio performance over different time horizons, including both long-term periods (up to ten years) and shorter time frames of six months. This temporal perspective allows us to identify emerging trends, sector-specific cycles, and periods of heightened volatility.

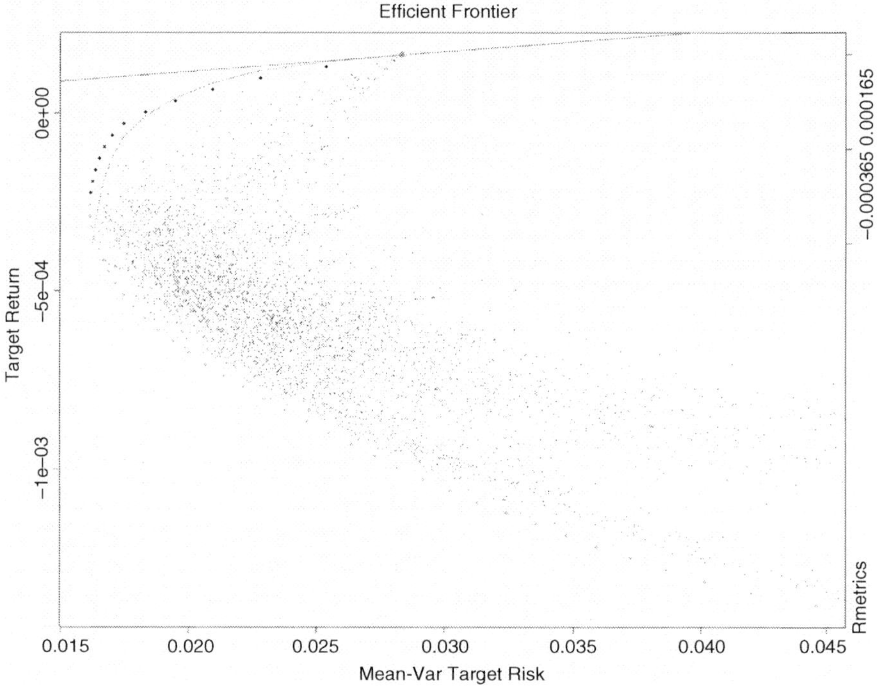

Figure 2.2 Efficient Frontier: Mapping Optimal Portfolios for Risk and Profitability.

Source: Own elaboration based on the PortfolioAnalytics, fPortfolio, and PerformanceAnalytics packages in R.

Our next part comprises several tasks:

- Identify the leaders within three consecutive clusters based on a list of trending tickers (characterised by upward or downward trend on a defined slope), and optimise the corresponding investment portfolios;
- Construct an investment portfolio consisting of the first 25 companies classified under the "technology" sector and determine the optimal portfolio allocation;
- Construct an investment portfolio consisting of the first 25 companies classified under the "real estate" sector and determine the optimal portfolio allocation;
- Construct an investment portfolio consisting of the first 25 companies classified under the "energy" sector and determine the optimal portfolio allocation;
- Compare the Sharpe Ratios of the optimised portfolios for these sectors, and then create a joint optimal portfolio #1, incorporating the best-performing assets from each;
- Build an optimal investment portfolio composed of the 19 most prominent companies in the "education" sector;
- Integrate the top companies from the education portfolio into joint portfolio #1, forming joint portfolio #2, and compare key indicators (annual return, annual volatility, Sharpe Ratio);
- Construct the optimal portfolio for companies in the gaming industry and integrate its top assets into joint portfolio #2, resulting in joint portfolio #3;
- Compare the performance and characteristics of joint investment portfolios #1, #2, and #3;
- Test the robustness of optimised portfolios under various crisis scenarios, including the COVID-19 pandemic, geopolitical conflicts, and trade wars, to assess how different macroeconomic shocks influence risk-return profiles.

2.2.2 *Industry-Specific Portfolio Analysis*

The sample used for cluster analysis was taken on a specific date in January 2022. Naturally, the components would vary for other time periods, although the set of analysed industries remain unchanged. Based on the list of trending tickers and corresponding share price movements, we categorised companies into three clusters: leading performers, average performers, and those that are "catching up". For this analysis, all data were sourced directly from Yahoo Finance using the Python yfinance package. It is important to note that some of these companies might no longer be active in the market or may have lost their leadership status since the time of data collection.

Table 2.1 Trending Stock Clusters Based on Cumulative Return

Clusters	*I*	*II*	*III*
Range of firms	ROKU, ARKK, 3690. HK, BTC-USD, ISPO, DBX, CPTN, ANGH, PLTR, TSLA, RDFN	1024.HK, SHAK, PARA, GOOGL, FB, ETH-USD, CRM, COST, MELI, 9988.HK, COIN	ZM, MSFT, VRTX, HOOD, INTC, YM=F, LTHM, GOOGL
Leaders*	TSLA, BTC-USD, ROKU, 3690.HK	ETH-USD, MELI, COST	MSFT, GOOGL, ZM

Source: Own elaboration based on data from Yahoo Finance Trending Tickers.

*Leaders were identified through analysis of cumulative returns.

As shown in Table 2.1, the leading companies in terms of cumulative return include:

- *Communication services* – Roku, Inc. (ROKU), Zoom Video Communications, Inc. (ZM), Alphabet, Inc. (GOOGL), and Microsoft Corporation (MSFT);
- *Software infrastructure* – Microsoft Corporation (MSFT);
- *E-commerce* – Mercado Libre, Inc. (MELI) and Meituan (3690.HK).

It is important to note that two cryptocurrencies – Bitcoin USD (BTC-USD) and Ethereum USD (ETH-USD) – appear among the leading performers, highlighting the role of emotional rather than purely pragmatic factors in investment decisions. Such investments often stem from superficial analyses rather than thorough fundamental assessments. Figures 2.3–2.5 present a graphical illustration of this case over time, allowing us to observe a shift in trends beginning in 2020. The top-performing companies are labelled alongside their corresponding cumulative return curves.

The next step in our study involved calculating the weights for an optimal investment portfolio and assessing its Sharpe Ratio, which serves as an indicator of the best trade-off between annual return and risk. This optimisation was performed using the Efficient Frontier method (Table 2.2). All the models in our analysis cover the period from January 1, 2013, to January 30, 2022. We intentionally chose this time frame to exclude the impact of the Russian–Ukrainian war and related sanctions, which have disrupted logistics chains, influenced market dynamics, and affected access to technology. The resulting portfolio includes key industries such as software applications (Cepton Inc. – CPTN), communication services (ROKU, MSFT, ZM), and online retail (Meituan – 3690.HK). The calculated Sharpe Ratio of 1.9 (Table 2.2) is sufficiently high to conclude that the portfolio is well-balanced and reasonable from an investment perspective. We also explored how the same portfolio might perform with adjustments for delisted or renamed assets during the most turbulent period anticipated in 2025 – a time potentially marked by

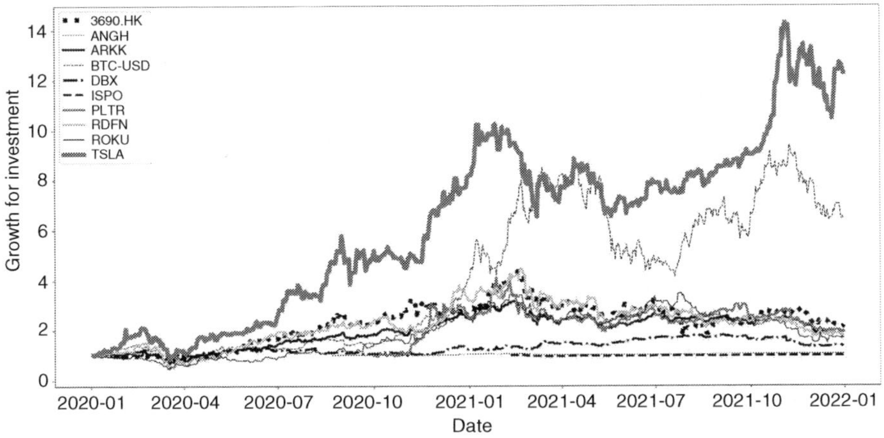

Figure 2.3 Performance Trends of Top Companies in Cluster I.

Source: Own elaboration based on data from Yahoo Finance (n.d.b). Results were obtained using Python packages numpy, matplotlib.pyplot, and yfinance reflecting cumulative returns.

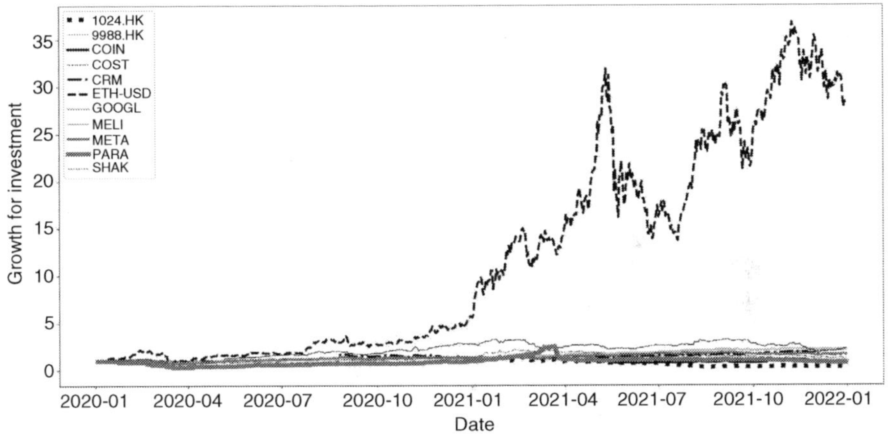

Figure 2.4 Performance Trends of Top Companies in Cluster II.

Source: Own elaboration based on data from Yahoo Finance (n.d.b). Results were obtained using Python packages numpy, matplotlib.pyplot, and yfinance reflecting cumulative returns.

the collapse of traditional economic cooperation models, logistical disruptions, and so-called "tariff wars". Under such conditions, while profitability and risk levels differ substantially, the portfolio still achieves a higher Sharpe Ratio, albeit with reduced diversification. Notably, investments in online commerce platforms in South America (SA) or consultancy services for real estate transactions in the US and Canada emerge as optimal assets offering

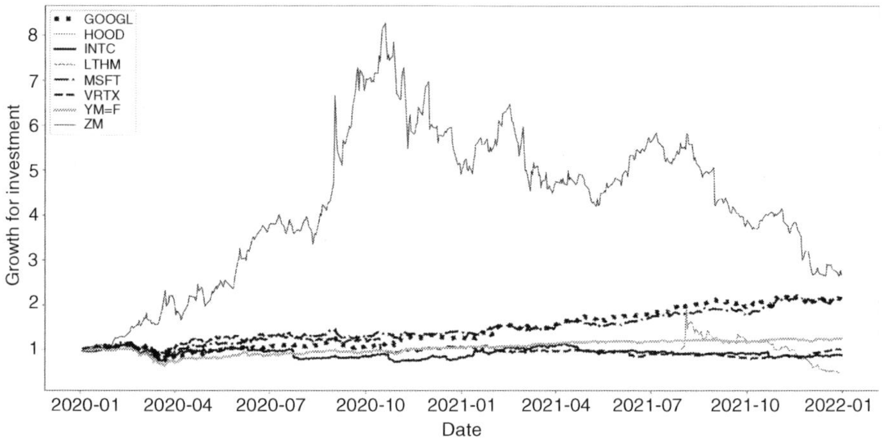

Figure 2.5 Performance Trends of Top Companies in Cluster III.

Source: Own elaboration based on data from Yahoo Finance (n.d.b). Results were obtained using Python packages numpy, matplotlib.pyplot, and yfinance reflecting cumulative returns.

an acceptable balance between profitability and risk. During the longer and ongoing period of the Russian–Ukrainian war (Table 2.2), we also observed increased investor interest in online platforms, stocks, exchange traded funds (ETFs), and commodities like gold (via platforms such as Robinhood). Additionally, biotechnology has attracted attention, driven by its role in fighting specific diseases and providing reliable, verified information, with companies like Palantir playing a notable role. A clear trend has also emerged, revealing that interest in digital communication, digital payments, and digital money remains strong despite geopolitical and market turbulence. Whether for renting, buying, selling, trading, conducting business negotiations, or decision-making and consulting, digital platforms have become an essential solution.

To deepen our analysis, we conducted a structured assessment based on tickers retrieved from Yahoo Finance Markets for three sectors: technology, real estate, and energy (Table 2.3). From this dataset, we selected the top 25 companies (as of January 2022) as potential components of optimal portfolios. The results indicate that the technology sector is the most promising, achieving a Sharpe Ratio of 1.55, an expected annual return of 45.5%, and an annual volatility of 28.0%. This portfolio is also the most homogeneous, making it the most competitive among the three sectors. In contrast, the optimal portfolio for the energy sector comprises only two companies (CNQ and VLO), highlighting its lower diversity. We hypothesise that expanding the initial portfolios in these three industries with companies from the education sector may positively influence the overall Sharpe Ratio. Consequently, we selected education-related stocks not only from the US market but also globally, drawing from a pool of 250 prominent education companies.

Table 2.2 Optimal Investment Portfolio Allocations Under Different Market Conditions (2013–2025)

Scenario	*Period*	*Key Stocks With Positive Weights*	*Expected Annual Return (%)*	*Annual Volatility (%)*	*Sharpe Ratio*
Pre-February 2022	January 1, 2013, to January 30, 2022	CPTN (0.68175), COST (0.14991), TSLA (0.0483), MSFT (0.05457), BTC-USD (0.02967), 3690.HK (0.0262), ZM (0.00701), ROKU (0.00254)	17.6	8.2	1.90
Mid-term period (2022–2025)	February 24, 2022, to May 17, 2025	COST (0.38775), VRTX (0.26234), PLTR (0.25324), BTC-USD (0.03817), HOOD (0.0368), META (0.02171)	30.7	23.6	1.30
2025 Market disruptions	February 20, 2025, to May 17, 2025	MELI (0.92461), RDFN (0.07539)	81.6	36.8	2.22

Source: Own elaboration based on data retrieved from Yahoo Finance and computed using Python packages: pypfopt, pypfopt.efficient_frontier, matplotlib.pyplot, numpy. Only assets with non-zero weights are displayed for clarity.

Note: Table presents only assets with non-zero weight coefficients in the optimal portfolio. However, the analysis included a significantly broader universe of assets across various industries and regions. All assets, including those assigned zero weights, were evaluated as potential components of the portfolio.

Table 2.3 Optimised Portfolios Across Key Industries

Industry	*Key Holdings (Non-Zero Weights Only)*	*Expected Annual Return (%)*	*Annual Volatility (%)*	*Sharpe Ratio*
Technology	MSFT (0.27689), NVDA (0.3966), AVGO (0.16325), AMD (0.01821), SONY (0.11274), NOW (0.02891), INFY (0.0034)	45.5	28.0	1.55
Real estate	EQIX (0.03965), SPG-PJ (0.12615), CBRE (0.06384), SBAC (0.1763), EXR (0.59405)	20.3	18.0	1.02
Energy	CNQ (0.07873), VLO (0.92127)	14.5	37.9	0.33
Education	BHA.F (0.22054), 0CG.F (0.04375), GKD.F (0.12651), LTG.L (0.1567), 300559. SZ (0.04868), 7912.T (0.14877), BFAM (0.15606), CHGG (0.0065), LOPE (0.09249)	17.3	17.3	0.99
Gaming	9697.T (0.38768), T1TW34.SA (0.06831), EGLX.TO (0.08527), ZNGA (0.02646), SE (0.43228)	53.4	35.8	1.44

Source: Results obtained using Python packages pypfopt, pypfopt.efficient_frontier, matplotlib. pyplot, and numpy, based on Yahoo Finance data (January 1, 2013, to January 30, 2022) and the 250 Global Education Stocks dataset.

Note: Only holdings with non-zero portfolio weights are presented in the table for clarity. However, the optimisation process included a significantly broader set of assets from each industry, ensuring a comprehensive analysis. Full results available upon request.

Our selection criteria included factors such as originality, the range of services offered, and the duration of each company's presence in the market (Table 2.3).

2.2.3 *Cross-Industry and Joint Portfolios*

The elements of the optimal portfolio for the first three industries became the basis for Joint portfolio #1. It includes Microsoft Corporation (MSFT), NVIDIA Corporation (NVDA), Broadcom Inc. (AVGO), Advanced Micro

Devices, Inc. (AMD), Sony Group Corporation (SONY), ServiceNow, Inc. (NOW), Infosys Limited (INFY), Equinix, Inc. (EQIX), and Simon Property Group, Inc. (SPG-PJ). These companies represent software applications, the software infrastructure industry, and a group of semiconductor producers. As seen in Table 2.4, the Sharpe Ratio in this case is even higher than for the technology industry alone (1.66 compared to 1.55). Although such a market is characterised by slightly lower profitability than pure "technology", it shows reduced risk. At the same time, Joint portfolio #1 demonstrates a stronger Sharpe Ratio than the corresponding portfolios focused only on one industry (Table 2.3).

The next step was to expand Joint portfolio #1 by including companies from the "education" sector, resulting in Joint portfolio #2, which achieved a Sharpe Ratio of 1.76. These new elements include Bright Horizons Family Solutions Inc. (BHA.F), Grand Canyon Education, Inc. (GKD.F), Learning Technologies Group plc (LTG.L), Chengdu Jiafaantai Education Technology Co. (300559.SZ), and Dai Nippon Printing Co., Ltd (7912.T). These companies create bridges between work and home life, making education more accessible worldwide. The market clearly signals that investing in this sector is optimal, given the ratio of risk to return. Together with technology, this sector offers one of the best combinations for building an optimal portfolio.

Traditionally, creating an optimal portfolio involves combining alternative assets such as real estate, commodities, or private equity. However, our study took a different approach: we manipulated sector weights simultaneously, considering societal priorities and shifting economic interests. One area that had not yet received sufficient attention in our analysis was the process of virtualisation. We decided to address this gap by examining companies in the gaming industry. We analysed approximately two dozen market leaders to identify those with the strongest potential contribution to the optimal portfolio. As shown in Table 2.3, the gaming sector alone yields a Sharpe Ratio of 1.44, lower than Joint portfolio #1. However, when the gaming industry – represented here by companies like Japanese Capcom (9697.T) and Singaporean Sea (SE), both active in electronic gaming and multimedia – was added to Joint portfolio #2, the Sharpe Ratio increased further to 1.87.

Therefore, the results summarised in Table 2.4 highlight significant differences in the performance and risk characteristics of the constructed portfolios. Joint portfolio #1, primarily built around technology and infrastructure companies, achieves the highest expected annual return of 37.4%, albeit with higher volatility of 21.3%. This portfolio reflects a dynamic yet riskier investment strategy driven by growth-oriented sectors. Joint portfolio #2, enriched with education sector companies, demonstrates a slightly lower expected annual return of 32.4%. However, it benefits from noticeably reduced volatility (17.2%), suggesting a more stable investment profile. The increase in the Sharpe Ratio from 1.66 to 1.76 underscores the stabilising influence of the education sector on the overall portfolio. Interestingly, the inclusion of

Table 2.4 Comparative Results of Optimised Investment Portfolios

Portfolio	*Main Holdings (Non-Zero Weights Only)*	*Expected Annual Return (%)*	*Annual Volatility (%)*	*Sharpe Ratio*
Joint portfolio #1	MSFT (0.14115), NVDA (0.2903), AVGO (0.08885), AMD (0.01219), SONY (0.05328), NOW (0.01193), SPG-PJ (0.06488), EXR (0.33742)	37.4	21.3	1.66
Joint portfolio #2	MSFT (0.10016), NVDA (0.22437), AVGO (0.06988), AMD (0.0059), SONY (0.02586), NOW (0.00281), SPG-PJ (0.03786), EXR (0.24501), BHA.F (0.14165), GKD.F (0.05298), LTG.L (0.03512), 300559.SZ (0.01331), 7912.T (0.04509)	32.4	17.2	1.76
Joint portfolio #3	MSFT (0.07537), NVDA (0.19757), AVGO (0.06572), AMD (0.00364), SONY (0.0062), SPG-PJ (0.03698), EXR (0.22877), BHA.F (0.13755), GKD.F (0.03484), LTG.L (0.02116), 300559.SZ (0.00823), 9697.T (0.15181), SE (0.03218)	33.7	17.0	1.87

Source: Results were obtained using Python packages pypfopt, pypfopt.efficient_frontier, matplotlib.pyplot, and numpy, based on data from Yahoo Finance (January 1, 2013, to January 30, 2022).

Note: Table presents only assets with non-zero portfolio weights for clarity. Each optimisation included a broader universe of companies from multiple industries (e.g., technology, real estate, education, and gaming industry). Full results, including assets with zero weights, are available upon request.

gaming industry stocks in Joint portfolio #3 raises the Sharpe Ratio even further, to 1.87 – the highest result in this analysis. Despite maintaining a solid expected annual return of 33.7%, this portfolio also offers the lowest volatility among the three (17.0%). This indicates that although the gaming sector alone may have less impressive metrics, it can significantly enhance overall portfolio performance when combined strategically with other sectors. Taken together, these findings suggest that diversification across strategically selected industries not only improves portfolio resilience but also creates opportunities for superior risk-adjusted returns. Notably, the inclusions of sectors like education and gaming help reduce volatility while maintaining strong profitability, underscoring the value of interdisciplinary thinking in investment strategy design.

2.2.4 *Portfolio Robustness Across Crisis Scenarios*

Understanding that the period we initially chose for analysis (up to February 2022) reflects a relatively stable context compared to later turbulent times, we decided to re-test the same optimised investment portfolio – excluding companies that have since disappeared from the market – across four different crisis scenarios:

- the current period of "tariff wars";
- the period of the Russian–Ukrainian war;
- the Russian–Ukrainian war including weapon producers; and
- the COVID-19 pandemic (Table 2.5).

We reaffirm our core assumption: it is methodologically acceptable to apply the same optimised portfolio – derived from 2013 to 2025 data – as a benchmark for testing performance in these different crisis periods. This consistency enables meaningful comparisons of how portfolios behave under different geopolitical and economic stressors.

From the results in Table 2.5, several key insights emerge:

- Virtualisation, networking, wireless communications, and education remain strong priorities for investors across all scenarios, consistently appearing among top-ranked industries.
- A new, significant trend has emerged in the form of investments in high-quality weapon production, especially evident when analysing the Russian–Ukrainian war period. Incorporating weapon producers into the portfolio increased the expected annual return from 36.5% to 85.5%, albeit at a higher volatility (24.5%).
- The "tariff wars" scenario demonstrates the highest expected annual return of 49.9% and a strong Sharpe Ratio of 2.89, indicating an attractive risk-return trade-off during periods driven by economic nationalism and supply chain realignments. Interestingly, the top-ranked sectors here

Table 2.5 Performance of the Optimised Investment Portfolio Under Different Crisis Scenarios

Scenario	*Main Holdings (Non-Zero Weights Only)*	*Expected Annual Return (%)*	*Annual Volatility (%)*	*Sharpe Ratio*	*Leading Industries*
Tariff Wars	9697.T (0.17414), MSFT (0.00139), SBAC (0.45652), SE (0.06362), SPG-PJ (0.20773), T1TW34.SA (0.0966)	49.9	17.3	2.89	1 Wireless communication 2 Real estate investment 3 Gaming 4 Software interactive entertainment
Russian–Ukrainian War (to June 2025)	7912.T (0.02039), 9697.T (0.28819), AVGO (0.15138), GKD.F (0.2156), LOPE (0.20391), NVDA (0.07412), SPG-PJ (0.01441), T1TW34.SA (0.01885), VLO (0.01316)	36.5	18.6	1.96	1 Gaming 2 Automotive parts 3 Education 4 Semiconductors 5 Networking
Russian–Ukrainian War (with weapons industry added)	9697.T (0.18688), AVGO (0.12574), GKD.F (0.07759), LOPE (0.08918), NVDA (0.03365), RHM.DE (0.46529), SPG-PJ (0.02167)	85.5	24.5	3.50	1 Weapon and ammunition 2 Gaming 3 Semiconductors 4 Education
Pandemic Period	7912.T (0.16353), 9697.T (0.46836), CNQ (0.21886), EXR (0.00059), GKD.F (0.00275), NVDA (0.1459)	48.5	24.6	1.97	1 Gaming 2 Oil and gas internationally 3 Automotive parts 4 Networking

Source: Own elaboration using Python packages pypfopt, pypfopt.efficient_frontier, matplotlib.pyplot, and numpy, based on data from Yahoo Finance.

Note: Table reports only assets with non-zero portfolio weights for clarity. Each scenario was evaluated on a broader set of stocks and financial instruments, many of which ultimately received zero allocation after optimisation. Full results are available upon request.

were wireless communication, real estate investment, gaming, and software interactive entertainment.

- Even in the pandemic scenario, the portfolio achieved a robust expected return of 48.5% with a Sharpe Ratio of 1.97, suggesting that technological and digital sectors maintained resilience and profitability during health crises.

These findings confirm that our strategic approach of manipulating portfolio composition based on societal priorities proves viable across vastly different contexts. Despite significant geopolitical upheavals, core investment themes – especially those tied to digitalisation, communication, and education – remain resilient and profitable. Yet, today's investment environment differs substantially from the pre-2022 world, when international law, stable economic ties, and the inadmissibility of forceful solutions were upheld at least at the level of public discourse. Now, even this fragile equilibrium has been disrupted, justifying the inclusion of new sectors such as defence manufacturing in investment strategies.

Using the tools of optimal portfolio construction and cumulative return analysis, we now shift our attention to two time frames: the past six months, and the more turbulent last ten years. To explore this, we refer to the clusters identified earlier in this study. Gaming, even amid geopolitical and economic uncertainty, has not only retained popularity but in many ways has also intensified its role in the market (Figure 2.6, Table 2.6). Although there are some fluctuations, the overall trend remains robust. After the pandemic,

Figure 2.6 Cumulative Return Trends for the Gaming Sector.

Source: Results achieved based on numpy, matplotlib.pyplot, and yfinance packages of Python as a reflection of cumulative return.

Table 2.6 Optimal Portfolios in Gaming and Education Sectors (Comparison of Last Six Months and Last Ten Years)

Sector	*Period*	*Main Holdings (Non-Zero Weights)*	*Expected Annual Return (%)*	*Annual Volatility (%)*	*Sharpe Ratio*
Gaming	Last 6 months	CCOEF (0.17309), NTDOY (0.23448), OTGLY (0.28429), TTWO (0.30814)	89.4	22.9	3.81
	Last 10 years	CCOEF (0.14685), ESPO (0.26731), NTDOY (0.13029), SE (0.05577), TTWO (0.39979)	20.0	23.7	0.76
Education	Last 6 months	ATGE (0.86025), COE (0.05053), LOPE (0.08922)	113.6	36.6	3.05
	Last 10 years	ATGE (0.09639), BFAM (0.08195), LOPE (0.82166)	13.8	28.3	0.42

Source: Own elaboration using Python packages pypfopt, pypfopt.efficient_frontier, matplotlib.pyplot, and numpy, based on data from Yahoo Finance (n.d.a).

Note: Only holdings with non-zero portfolio weights are displayed for clarity. Full optimisations included additional companies. Gaming data as of June 2025. Company details: Capcom Co. (CCOEF) develops games worldwide; EA publishes games for multiple platforms; Nintendo manufactures entertainment products globally; CD Projekt (OTGLY) specialises in digital distribution. Adtalem Global Education (ATGE) focuses on healthcare-related education and stable financial returns.

as seen in the cumulative return graph, global interest in online learning has logically receded to its pre-pandemic levels around 2019 (Figure 2.7). We initially assumed that, due to deliberate challenges facing American universities – including funding cuts, visa restrictions for foreign students, and political pressures in 2025 – the education sector might show weaker performance. Yet, the reality is more nuanced. While traditional education has indeed struggled, the dominance of online education businesses remains evident. After a surge during the pandemic, this segment has stabilised back at 2019 levels, suggesting that virtual learning has become a permanent component of the educational ecosystem rather than a temporary phenomenon.

From Table 2.6, it's clear that the gaming sector stands out as a resilient asset class. In the last six months, the gaming-focused portfolio achieved an exceptionally high expected annual return of 89.4% and a Sharpe Ratio of 3.81, despite elevated volatility. In contrast, over the last decade, the same sector delivered a lower yet respectable expected annual return of 20.0% with a Sharpe Ratio of 0.76. This stark difference underscores the sector's current dynamism and its potential role as an emotional escape for consumers, substituting for travel or mass events increasingly limited by geopolitical tensions and social unrest. Positive signals also emerge from the automation

Figure 2.7 Cumulative Return Trends for the Education Sector.

Source: Results were achieved based on numpy, matplotlib.pyplot, and yfinance packages of Python as a reflection of cumulative returns.

Notes: Company summaries: Adtalem Global Education (ATGE, USA) specialises in healthcare education. Bright Horizons Family Solutions (BFAM, USA) provides childcare and education services. 51Talk (COE, Singapore) offers online language education. EDU (China) provides private education services. Grand Canyon Education (LOPE, USA) focuses on online and campus-based education. STRA (USA) delivers post-secondary education. TAL (China) provides tutoring services.

sector. Despite challenges like tariff barriers, required investments in fixed assets, and changing logistics networks, automation companies continue to show a solid upward trend (Figure 2.8). Nevertheless, short-term declines in early 2025, visible in the downward slope in Figure 2.8, should be a matter of concern for policymakers. These may be early indicators of a slowdown in long-term growth, emphasising the importance for businesses to remain committed to their chosen strategic directions despite volatility. As for education, the sector's global presence, including significant participation from Chinese firms, supports the broader trends identified earlier in this book. However, as seen in Table 2.6, there's a substantial difference between the short-term and long-term optimal portfolios. Notably, Adtalem Global Education (ATGE) has emerged as a standout performer, focusing on healthcare-related education and strategic stock buybacks (see more: Investor's Business Daily, n.d.). This specialisation has shielded the company from geopolitical risks, demonstrating how niche focus can yield resilience in turbulent times.

While risk management remains crucial, it's important to note that risk measures such as the Sharpe Ratio are particularly volatile in the early months of 2025. This volatility calls for alternative metrics like utility maximisation to ensure that portfolio strategies align with long-term goals rather than short-term market turbulence (Figure 2.9). However, transitioning entirely to a utility-focused approach would imply a reduced reliance on traditional

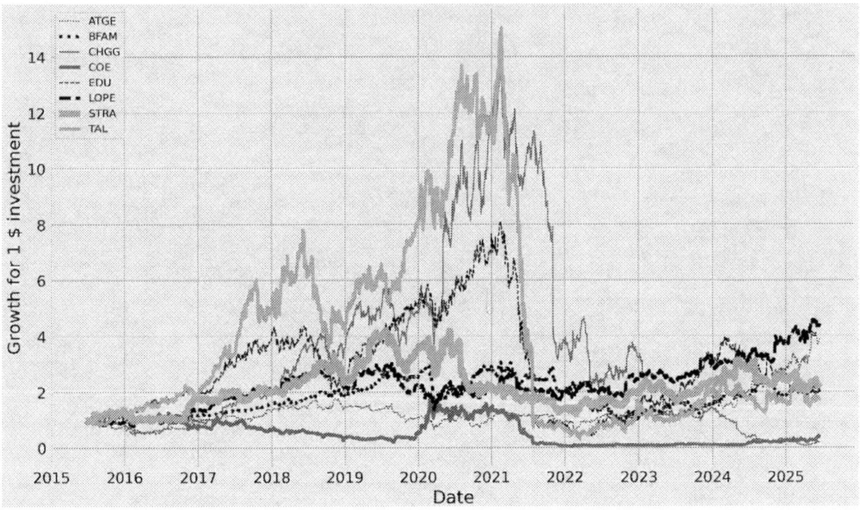

Figure 2.8 Cumulative Return Trends for the Automation Sector.

Source: Results were achieved based on numpy, matplotlib.pyplot, and yfinance packages of Python as a reflection of cumulative return.

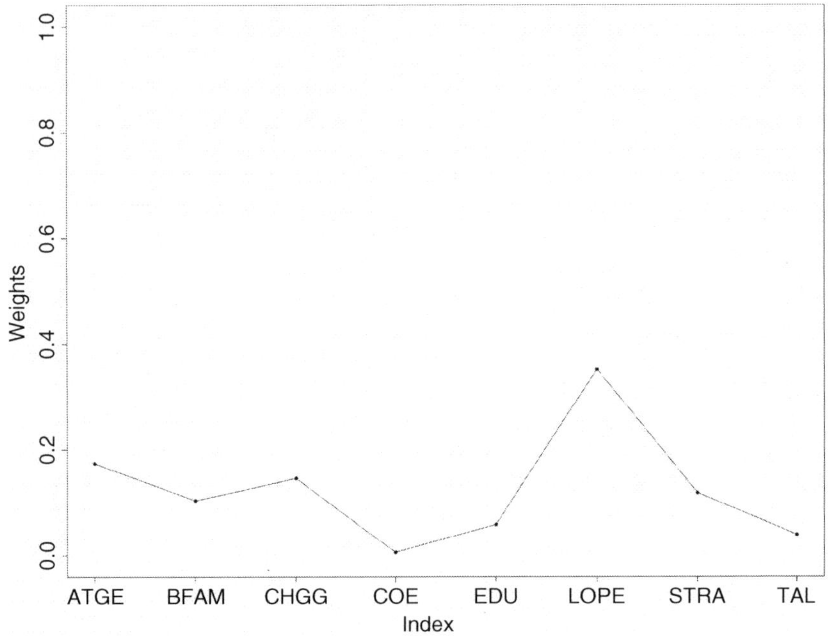

Figure 2.9 Utility Maximisation Versus Sharpe Ratio: Strategic Perspectives for 2025.

Source: Results were achieved based on PortfolioAnalytics of R.

stock markets, potentially undermining fundamental mechanisms of capital allocation and corporate governance.

Despite its analytical power, the optimal portfolio method remains somewhat underestimated. This scepticism is understandable, particularly in markets without the depth or liquidity of developed stock exchanges. When a market includes only a few dozen listed companies and several indices, drawing generalisable conclusions is risky and often unwarranted. Moreover, markets are highly susceptible to manipulation. Price movements can be influenced not only by fundamental performance but also by political statements, celebrity endorsements, or even misinformation campaigns – leaving small investors particularly vulnerable. However, there was a remarkable moment during the COVID-19 pandemic when stock markets in developed economies became a genuine mirror of society's evolving needs. Social priorities temporarily outweighed pure price manipulation. Maison et al. (2021) highlighted the central challenges of this period: "limitations of direct contact with people, restrictions on movement and travel, change in active lifestyle, boredom and monotony, and finally uncertainty about the future". Thus, to identify industry trends, the behaviour of individual companies, and the resilience of long-term strategies against external shocks, there is a clear need for continuous optimisation over short time horizons, paired with comparisons to longer-term historical results. In response to the unique crises of recent years – from the pandemic, to geopolitical conflicts, to economic fragmentation – it becomes relevant to test an all-encompassing portfolio that reflects both traditional financial assets and emerging alternative investments.

For this purpose, new Optimal Cross-Industry Portfolios were constructed (Table 2.7), combining:

- *Traditional financial assets* – Crude Oil (CL=F), Gold (GC=F), Silver (SI=F), EUR/USD (EURUSD=X), U.S. Treasury Yield 10 years (^TNX);
- *Digital assets and cryptocurrencies* – CMC Crypto 200 Index (^CMC200)[1], Bitcoin (BTC-USD), Ethereum (ETH-USD), Tether (USDT-USD), USD Coin (USDC-USD), Solana (SOL-USD), Binance USD (BUSD-USD);
- *Equities across sectors* – BNP (basic materials), AMZN (consumer cyclical), XOM (energy), BRK-A (financial services), UPS (industrials), AAPL, MSFT (technology), NEE (utilities), JNJ (healthcare), WMT (e-commerce, retail).

The inclusion of diverse asset classes aimed to capture the multidimensional drivers of modern market dynamics, including energy shifts, digital transformation, and geopolitical tensions.

The pandemic reshaped portfolio structures (Table 2.7), elevating companies like UPS amid booming e-commerce and home deliveries. Gold (GC=F) maintained its traditional role as a safe haven, particularly during politically turbulent periods such as the Trump-era tariff wars. Cryptocurrencies

Table 2.7 Optimal Cross-Industry Portfolios During Crisis Periods (Pandemic and Geopolitical Shifts)

Scenario	*Main Holdings (Non-Zero Weights)*	*Expected Annual Return (%)*	*Annual Volatility (%)*	*Sharpe Ratio*
Pandemic (2020–2023)	ETH-USD (0.1306), GC=F (0.11632), SOL-USD (0.16708), UPS (0.26928), XOM (0.20493), ^TNX (0.1118)	37.0	34.0	1.03
Pandemic → Geopolitical Conflict (2020–2022)	BRK-A (0.15264), ETH-USD (0.06081), GC=F (0.23772), MSFT (0.14853), SOL-USD (0.20447), WMT (0.0752), XOM (0.01224), ^TNX (0.1084)	38.0	29.6	1.21
War & Early 2025 Volatility (2022–2025)	GC=F (0.30117), ^TNX (0.3158), MSFT (0.09149), WMT (0.16253), BRK-A (0.08193), BTC-USD (0.0104)	22.2	12.2	1.65

Source: Results were achieved using Python packages: yfinance, pypfopt, matplotlib.pyplot, and numpy.

Note: Table includes only assets with non-zero portfolio weights for readability. Original optimisations analysed a broader set of assets.

retained investor interest, driven both by speculation and their utility for cross-border transactions. Meanwhile, exposure to the energy sector persisted despite a temporary slowdown in the global transition towards renewables due to supply shocks and geopolitical tensions. As geopolitical dynamics shifted with the Russian–Ukrainian conflict, investor behaviour became more cautious, emphasising resilience and stability. Gold allocations increased further, while technology equities, such as Microsoft, continued to benefit from digital transformation trends, particularly cloud adoption driven by remote work.

Over two years of full-scale war and into early 2025, global financial markets underwent significant structural shifts (Table 2.7). Confidence in U.S. Treasury bonds weakened, evidenced by declining portfolio weights allocated to ^TNX, while gold and select commodities attracted higher allocations due to concerns over currency stability, inflation, and geopolitical risk. Gold's share in optimal portfolios rose markedly, underscoring its enduring role as a store of value. Simultaneously, traditional consumer sectors like Walmart (WMT) maintained significant allocations, reflecting the resilience of consumer demand even under macroeconomic stress.

These observations affirm that, while diversification remains crucial, optimal portfolios must continuously adapt to shifting geopolitical, economic, and technological landscapes.

Notable examples from the analyses include:

- UPS, gaining weight during the pandemic thanks to the logistics boom driven by e-commerce growth;
- Gold, consistently emerging as a safe haven across various crises;
- Cryptocurrencies, remaining relevant as alternative stores of value despite volatility;
- Technology equities, exemplified by Microsoft, maintaining prominence amid ongoing digitalisation and structural changes in business operations.

Crucially, there is no universal optimal portfolio. Its composition varies widely based on an investor's knowledge, sector exposure, risk tolerance, and strategic interests. The war in Ukraine has deeply disrupted global markets – not only through direct impacts on regional businesses but also via broader effects such as sanctions, shifts in global logistics, and commodity price volatility. This underscores the book's central thesis: in modern economic environments, strategic adaptability is not optional but essential for survival.

2.2.5 *Alternative Performance Metrics and Broader Strategic Implications*

While the Sharpe Ratio remains the classic tool for assessing investment portfolios, alternative performance measures offer a richer understanding of market dynamics, especially during turbulent periods. One of these alternatives is the Treynor Ratio, which, unlike the Sharpe Ratio, accounts specifically for systematic risk by relating excess returns to market beta. An analysis of selected Chinese real estate developers across two contrasting periods – 2022–2024 and November 2024 to April 2025 – demonstrates how rapidly risk-return profiles can shift in response to external pressures (Table 2.8). For example, Shanghai Zhangjiang Hi-Tech Park Development Co. enjoyed a solid Treynor Ratio of 3.97 during the earlier period, only to plunge into negative territory in the subsequent months. This stark reversal underscores the importance of monitoring sector-specific vulnerabilities, particularly in markets as fragile as Chinese real estate.

Beyond the Treynor Ratio, further insights emerge when examining other risk-adjusted metrics such as the Sortino Ratio, which focuses exclusively on downside volatility, the Maximum Drawdown (MAXDD), which reveals the worst peak-to-trough loss, and the Calmar Ratio, which relates returns to maximum drawdowns. Even the familiar Sharpe Ratio, while widely respected, may fail to capture tail risks that become visible only through these complementary measures.

Table 2.8 Treynor Ratios for Selected Chinese Real Estate Companies

Company	*Treynor (2022–2024)*	*Treynor (November 2024–April 2025)*
China World Trade (600007.SS)	2.65	−0.16
Kunwu Jiuding Investment Holding Co. (600053.SS)	0.41	−1.02
Shanghai Chinafortune Co., Ltd. (600621.SS)	1.14	−0.46
Shanghai Zhangjiang Hi-Tech Park Development Co., Ltd. (600895.SS)	3.97	−0.13

Source: Results calculated using Python's yfinance and numpy.

Note: Current RFR (risk-free rate) = 1.66%; RFR = 2.3% for 2022–2024.

Table 2.9 summarises these indicators for individual assets during early 2025. Gold and the EUR/USD currency pair stood out as safe havens, maintaining solid results across nearly all risk-adjusted measures, while cryptocurrencies like Bitcoin and Ethereum exhibited poor downside protection and significant volatility. Traditional equities such as Berkshire Hathaway demonstrated moderate resilience, further confirming their reputation as defensive holdings. This convergence across different ratios suggests that triangulating results from multiple indicators is essential for robust decision-making.

Despite differences in methodology, these diverse approaches consistently identify certain winners. Gold, cryptocurrencies, and the financial services sector emerge as prominent investment leaders during the volatile months of early 2025. Such findings affirm that the core methodology used in this study – employing Python's pypfopt.efficient_frontier package – provides robust analytical depth for evaluating strategic choices under uncertainty.

Yet the significance of optimal portfolio analysis extends far beyond traditional investing. The insights derived from these models hold value for policymakers, business leaders, and educators alike. In today's interconnected world, understanding financial market signals influences political strategies, career planning, and the development of educational programmes that align with market needs. As explored in Chapter 1, building and analysing investment portfolios has become akin to designing virtual worlds – both involve anticipating future events, responding to emerging signals, and aligning decisions with personal or institutional values.

Thus, portfolio optimisation serves as more than a financial tool. It offers a lens through which we can examine how societies adapt to shocks, how individuals weigh risk against reward, and how emerging trends reshape the fabric of modern economies. Even amid periods of high volatility and geopolitical tension, one message remains clear: strategic adaptability demands a multifaceted understanding of risk, opportunity, and the forces that shape our economic future.

Table 2.9 Comparative Risk-Adjusted Metrics for Selected Assets (January–May 2025)

Ticker	*Sortino*	*Ticker*	*Sharpe*	*Ticker*	*Maxdd*	*Ticker*	*Calmar*
EURUSD=X	2.365917	GC=F	1.69496	USDC-USD	-0.00049	GC=F	5.524663
GC=F	2.024973	EURUSD=X	1.480981	USDT-USD	-0.00207	EURUSD=X	4.735384
BRK-A	0.827786	BRK-A	0.830833	BUSD-USD	-0.01937	BRK-A	2.582989
MSFT	0.648275	NEE	0.486869	EURUSD=X	-0.03624	NEE	1.1296
NEE	0.631228	MSFT	0.452034	GC=F	-0.06742	MSFT	0.855628
WMT	0.530741	WMT	0.43631	BRK-A	-0.08638	WMT	0.760315
SI=F	0.255628	SI=F	0.273429	JNJ	-0.12725	SI=F	0.690377
JNJ	0.180317	JNJ	0.198893	^TNX	-0.14079	JNJ	0.667834
BTC-USD	-0.04569	BTC-USD	-0.03042	NEE	-0.15822	USDT-USD	0.113349
XOM	-0.13348	XOM	-0.14071	XOM	-0.16053	BTC-USD	0.110604
AAPL	-0.22058	AAPL	-0.19113	Port	-0.16311	XOM	0.044847
PLD	-0.36115	PLD	-0.354	SI=F	-0.16566	BUSD-USD	-0.09651
^TNX	-0.66022	^TNX	-0.45275	MSFT	-0.20557	AAPL	-0.10742
Port	-0.81992	Port	-0.53211	WMT	-0.21928	PLD	-0.23505
AMZN	-0.82938	AMZN	-0.61483	CL=F	-0.24271	USDC-USD	-0.26934
ETH-USD	-0.95787	ETH-USD	-0.61977	PLD	-0.26992	Port	-0.2854
SOL-USD	-1.08577	SOL-USD	-0.73396	BTC-USD	-0.27235	^TNX	-0.32033
GOOGL	-1.29201	GOOGL	-1.08356	GOOGL	-0.29806	AMZN	-0.5934
UPS	-1.30598	UPS	-1.52997	AAPL	-0.30223	ETH-USD	-0.76409
CL=F	-1.76591	CL=F	-1.57108	AMZN	-0.30877	SOL-USD	-0.99402
BUSD-USD	-1.82538	BUSD-USD	-1.8578	UPS	-0.31575	GOOGL	-1.07624
USDT-USD	-9.80328	USDT-USD	-7.18077	ETH-USD	-0.55842	UPS	-1.55854
USDC-USD	-37.3177	USDC-USD	-23.8233	SOL-USD	-0.58983	CL=F	-1.63756

Source: Results were based on yfinance, numpy, pandas, and matplotlib.pyplot. All calculations were performed in Python.

This analysis underscores a critical insight: no single metric captures all dimensions of market risk or opportunity. The interplay of diverse measures enriches our understanding of how assets behave under stress. Moreover, these insights reach far beyond finance:

- Political campaigns can interpret market signals to refine rhetoric and policy agendas.
- Educators can design curricula that anticipate technological and labour market shifts.
- Entrepreneurs can align new ventures with emerging societal and economic trends.

Ultimately, portfolio analysis is not merely about investing capital – it's a powerful tool for anticipating and navigating change across all domains of society.

2.3 Market Dynamics and Strategic Actors in Emerging Economies

2.3.1 Analytical Framework for Assessing Emerging Capital Markets

The pandemic-related restrictive measures have prompted a re-evaluation of the role of stock exchanges as market mechanisms. While stock markets in developed countries are characterised by robust oversight, thorough analysis, daily monitoring of changes, and well-developed financial tools, emerging markets face more complex challenges. In these markets, actors must navigate decisions between listing shares on major global exchanges, developing their domestic capital markets, managing the burden of government debt, or pursuing some combination of these strategies. Given the weakness of social and market institutions, alternative sources of capital are often underdeveloped or perceived as difficult to access in predominantly oligarchic societies. For example, in the banking sectors of such economies, the majority of loans are frequently distributed among co-owners or related parties, while lending to small businesses is not a priority. Under these conditions, zombie banking – where banks survive only due to government support, either explicit or implicit – becomes not the exception but the norm.

In many cases, the stock markets of developing countries receive insufficient domestic attention, limiting their capacity to compete internationally and attract foreign investment. This, in turn, affects the overall competitiveness of these nations on the global economic stage. While it is sometimes argued that the absence of accessible capital markets enables local oligarchs to maintain monopolistic positions, it also means that privatisation processes remain confined to a limited group. Genuine transformation in such societies arises not merely from macroeconomic adjustments but primarily from institutional reforms. There is hope that this vision – underpinning the post-Washington Consensus – will continue to gain broader support, not only within the academic community but also among policymakers and practitioners. In this context, the stock markets in SA (particularly Brazil and Argentina) and Central and Eastern Europe (notably Poland, the Czech Republic, and Hungary) hold particular significance. Although the Polish stock market has recently attained developed market status, it is recognised that its transformation processes remain incomplete.

The success of these markets in aligning with global standards can directly influence the economic competitiveness of their respective countries. Well-functioning stock markets enhance investor confidence, resulting in greater capital inflows, increased innovation, and sustained economic growth – all critical factors for maintaining or improving a country's position in the global economy.

Within the scientific discourse, there is an extensive body of literature examining stock markets broadly, as well as studies focused on specific regions such as SA and Central, Southern, and Eastern Europe (e.g., Batten et al., 2014; Bubbico et al., 2017; EYGM, 2020; Gea et al., 2023; Guidi & Ugur, 2014; Syriopoulos & Roumpis, 2009; Simões et al., 2012; Syllignakis & Kouretas, 2011; Zaimović & Arnaut Berilo, 2015; Zaimović et al., 2017).

Argentina's stock market has historically exhibited pronounced volatility, driven by recurrent economic and political crises. A notable episode occurred during the 1998 crisis, when share prices rose unexpectedly – not due to domestic economic strength but because investors converted Argentine peso-denominated shares into U.S. dollars through American Depositary Receipts (ADRs), effectively safeguarding their assets in more stable markets (Melvin, 2003). Despite such financial mechanisms, Argentina's domestic market remains shallow, with low market capitalisation relative to GDP, and continues to rely heavily on North American financial channels for external financing (Harmilapi, 2012; OECD, 2019). The crises of 2001–2002 inflicted significant damage on market confidence and performance, and subsequent recovery has been driven mainly by revitalising existing firms rather than new market entries. Persistent low liquidity is compounded by the widespread practice of cross-listings; in 2017, nine of Argentina's ten most actively traded firms were also listed abroad via ADRs or Global Depositary Receipts (GDRs).

In contrast, Brazil's stock market demonstrates substantial development in infrastructure and financial instruments, despite a complex regulatory and operational environment. Conducting business in Brazil remains challenging, due to frequent regulatory changes and a multi-layered tax system at federal, state, and municipal levels (TFM, 2022). Nonetheless, market reforms have driven significant growth in capitalisation and diversified financial instruments available to investors (Nyasha & Odhiambo, 2013). Recent research highlights the growing importance of sentiment analysis in guiding investment strategies, with evidence that such approaches can outperform traditional models like random walks or simple buy-and-hold tactics (De Oliveira Carosia et al., 2021). Costa et al. (2022) further observed that the Brazilian stock market responded dynamically to both local and global COVID-19 developments, with variations in intensity and timing as the pandemic evolved. However, persistent challenges remain: Brazilian markets continue to exhibit lower liquidity compared to developed markets, a limited number of listed companies, and high ownership concentration, which restricts opportunities for equity financing (Crisóstomo et al., 2020). Despite these obstacles, firms with robust growth prospects continue to pursue equity issuance, indicating both structural constraints and adaptive potential.

Central and Eastern European (CEE) stock markets, while modest in scale from a pan-European perspective, offer valuable insights into financial development amid economic transformation. According to Wiśniewski (2017), these markets, though expanding and gradually converging towards Western European standards, continue to face structural limitations, including restricted market scale, modest globalisation, and aging infrastructure. Before the pandemic, the European Investment Bank identified substantial investment potential in the CEE region, particularly in research and development, education, transport, and energy infrastructure (Bubbico et al., 2017). Yet challenges persist, exemplified by Poland's complex tax environment and the rising influence of state ownership in key economic sectors. While practices such as enhanced audit oversight, inspired by American regulatory frameworks, may improve market confidence, excessive state intervention risks inefficiency and diminished market dynamism. Balancing public sector involvement with private market development remains a central issue in shaping the future of CEE financial markets.

Therefore, these regional cases underscore the heterogeneous nature of emerging stock markets while highlighting common themes such as the critical role of institutional frameworks, the importance of cross-border financial mechanisms, and the necessity for strategic adaptability in navigating global financial integration. Nonetheless, significant questions remain. Are traditional tools from developed markets suitable for emerging economies? How has the pandemic reshaped these markets? And crucially, how can these markets evolve to protect small investors while simultaneously enhancing national competitiveness through improved market efficiency and global integration? Understanding corporate strategies in these contexts is essential for answering these questions and forecasting future developments.

We propose the following main hypotheses:

H1. Both SA and CEE countries successfully place shares on their domestic stock markets as well as on major global exchanges, pursuing a diversification strategy.

H2. Both regions' markets are well integrated with leading global stock markets, making them relatively predictable for foreign investors.

H3. CEE markets offer lower returns but also present less risk compared to SA markets, enhancing their appeal to conservative investors.
H4. Domestic portfolios are often characterised by high returns driven by the dominance of a few key companies. Removing these leading firms significantly reduces profitability, whereas "foreign portfolios" do not exhibit such pronounced dependence on individual market leaders.

In our empirical analysis, we employ widely used Python packages, including numpy, pandas, matplotlib, and yahoo_fin (although similar functionality is available via y_finance). For price prediction (based primarily on close or adjusted prices), we apply Linear Regression (LR), Support Vector Regression (SVR), Random Forest (RF), Gradient Boosting (GB), and other machine learning techniques. In our view, the five-factor Fama–French model remains the most relevant tool for institutional analysis and strategy assessment in this context. We deliberately chose long-established strategies commonly used in developed markets to examine the degree of institutional disconnection – or adaptability – present in developing markets. However, our findings indicate that for many companies, a significant portion of the model's factors turn out to be statistically insignificant. Portfolio optimisation in our study relies on the Sharpe Ratio, as previously discussed in the context of the Efficient Frontier (via Python's pypfopt package). As several earlier studies have shown, utility-maximisation approaches tend to yield a similar result, which is why we narrowed the list of methods employed in our analysis (see Hurnyak & Struk, 2024). We also use the data of yahoo.finance setting the ticker of the respective company into the Python code. In most models, these are daily statistics for the last seven to ten years. In order to accomplish the Fama–French model, we draw on Kenneth R. French's Data Library for the necessary statistics pertaining to emerging markets. The components of indices were taken from Investing.com (n.d.). By analysing these stock markets and their trends, our study also explores how improvements in national market efficiency and alignment with international standards can enhance the global competitiveness of these countries, particularly in attracting foreign investment and fostering long-term economic stability.

2.3.2 *Portfolio Construction and Cumulative Returns*

Is it feasible to apply classic tools like the Fama–French model to investigate markets characterised by low levels of disclosure? De Peña et al. (2010) examined the validity of small minus big (SMB) and high minus low (HML) as risk factors and found evidence supporting the use of this model in the Spanish capital market. Jin and Shaojun (2014) analysed the applicability of the Fama–French three-factor model in the Chinese stock market and concluded that it could explain more than 93% of the variation in portfolio returns for Chinese A-shares. Deng et al. (2013) proposed a portfolio optimisation framework designed to select portfolios with the largest worst-case-scenario Sharpe Ratios. They noted that traditional Sharpe Ratio estimates, when based on limited historical return data, are prone to estimation errors. Annaert et al. (2011) constructed a market-weighted return index for the largest stocks listed on the Brussels Stock Exchange. Their findings supported the empirical practice of focusing analysis on the largest stocks as a proxy for assessing the market as a whole. The subsequent research incorporates all of these ideas and methodological approaches. Meanwhile, our performance analysis focuses on stock portfolios composed of components from main stock indices. Daily statistics for each share are retrieved using the appropriate Python packages, based on the company's ticker symbol. The portfolios examined in this study include: Argentinian, Brazilian, CEE, ARG, BR in Europe, BR in USA, and CEE in West Europe (Table 2.10).

Even within the Brazilian sample (Figure 2.10), we already observe a clear segmentation of the market into obvious leaders and a trailing majority. A few stocks display rapid cumulative growth, forming visible outliers above the main cluster of trajectories, while the majority of stocks exhibit more modest performance clustered around lower growth levels. This pattern suggests that in the Brazilian market, constructing an optimally diversified portfolio may be challenging, as substantial performance is often concentrated in a small group of companies. Such concentration increases the portfolio's sensitivity to the performance of a few dominant firms. Moreover, Figure 2.10 shows that Brazilian equities experienced pronounced peaks between 2020 and 2021, likely driven by pandemic-induced market

Table 2.10 Main Argentinian, Brazilian, and CEE Portfolios

Argentinian	*Brazilian*	*CEE*
GAMI.BA, BOLT.BA, CGPA2.BA, CAPX.BA, CADO.BA, 'TRAN. BA,DGCU2.BA, DYCA. BA, EDSH.BA, BHIP. BA, FIPL.BA, HARG. BA, PAMP.BA, POLL. BA, RIGO.BA, RIO.BA, TECO2.BA, TGNO4. BA, 'INVJ.BA	ABEV3.SA, CRFB3.SA, AZUL4.SA, BBSE3.SA, COGN3.SA, CYRE3. SA, FLRY3.SA, LWSA3.SA, VIVT3.SA, ELET3.SA, CMIG4.SA, LIGT3.SA, OIBR4.SA, PETR3.SA, CSNA3.SA, C2AC34.SA	DNP.WA, JSW.WA, KRU.WA, OPL.WA, PKN. WA, IFI.WA, CCE.WA, SGN.WA, CEZ.PR, CZG.PR, MONET.PR, TABAK.PR, TOMA.PR, PEN. PR,EMAN.PR, 4IG.BD, AKKO.BD, ALTEO.BD, ANY.BD, UBM.BD
ARG, BR in EUROPE	**BR in USA**	**CEE in WEST EUROPE**
B4W.F, C3TA.F, CD8. SG, TEO.F, FXMA.F, KE0A.F, 4XZ.F, TSPA.F	ABEV, BBSEY, AZUL, BBDO, COGNY, CYRBY, VIV, VALE, WEGZY, BTOW	SFB1.F, 8PL2.F, SP9.F, 1VY.F, KGHA.F, 9Y2.F, 1RY.F, 6PG.MU, PKY1.F, BZI.F

Source: Own elaboration based on historical data from Yahoo Finance (n.d.a).

Note: Tickers are shown instead of full company names. The portfolios include companies for which historical data are available, drawn from the components of WIG20 (Poland), PX (Czech Republic), Budapest SE (Hungary), S&P Merval (Argentina), and Bovespa (Brazil).

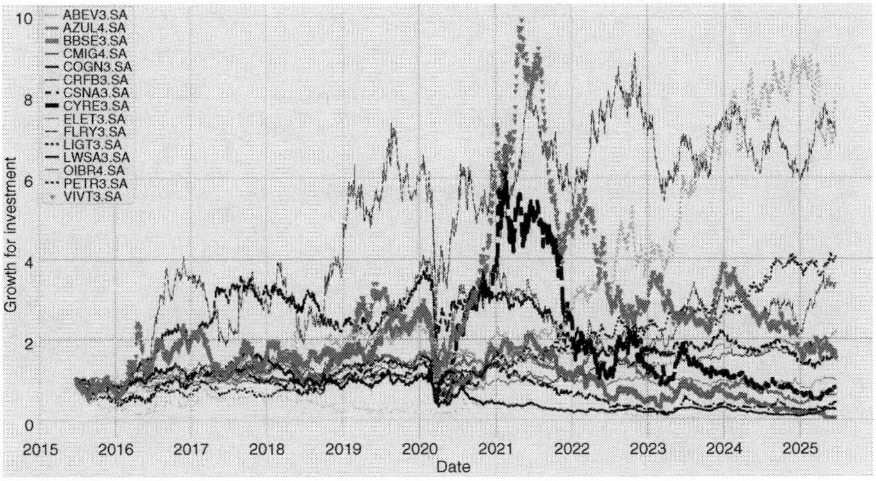

Figure 2.10 Cumulative Return on SA Stock Markets (Portfolio "Brazilian").

Source: Own elaboration based on historical data from Yahoo Finance (n.d.a). Results were obtained using the Python packages numpy, matplotlib.pyplot, and yfinance, reflecting cumulative returns.

speculation and subsequent corrections. For example, some lines on the chart reach high spikes before returning to the overall trend channel. This indicates the presence of short-lived rallies, potentially tied to market overreactions or sector-specific booms (such as commodities).

Turning to Figure 2.11, the CEE market exhibits a different structure. While the majority of equities show relatively stable and lower cumulative growth, a few stocks – represented by sharply rising lines from mid-2024 onward – significantly outperform the rest. This upward divergence reflects emerging winners in the region, possibly linked to sector-specific gains such as technology, energy, or industries adapting successfully to geopolitical shifts. Interestingly, the CEE market, despite being impacted by the pandemic, shows less pronounced volatility spikes than Brazil. The cumulative curves appear smoother overall, suggesting lower market turbulence or a more cautious investor response during crisis periods. This stability may reflect the influence of the region's increasing integration with the EU, which offers a stabilising institutional framework. The period of uncertainty caused by the Trump administration's tariff wars between March and May 2025 appears not to have seriously disrupted the CEE market (Figure 2.11). Possibly, due to frequent announcements and postponements of planned measures, market participants did not fully believe that such a rupture in traditional economic ties would materialise. However, isolated spikes are visible in the CEE trajectories from mid-2024 onward, suggesting that certain stocks benefited disproportionately during times of uncertainty, perhaps due to being perceived as safer investments or due to sector-specific tailwinds.

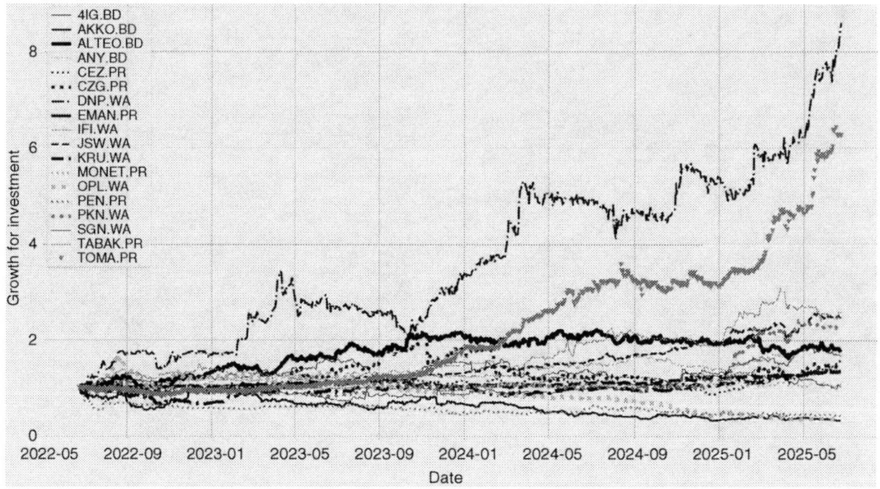

Figure 2.11 Cumulative Return on CEE Stock Markets (Portfolio "CEE").

Source: Own elaboration based on historical data from Yahoo Finance (n.d.a). Results were obtained using the Python packages numpy, matplotlib.pyplot, and yfinance, reflecting cumulative returns.

Figure 2.12 depicts cumulative return trajectories for individual stocks in Argentina's market (Portfolio "Argentinian"), revealing both notable growth episodes and sharp reversals over the period analysed. A few companies, like CAPX.BA and HARG.BA, exhibit steep growth curves, reflecting their outsized influence on overall market performance. However, most stocks cluster at much lower return levels, indicating a highly concentrated market where diversification is difficult. Volatility is pronounced, especially between 2023 and 2025, corresponding with Argentina's macroeconomic instability marked by hyperinflation, currency depreciation, and shifting investor sentiment. Peaks and subsequent declines in several stocks during this time mirror speculative surges followed by corrections, typical in markets with fragile institutions and low investor confidence. External shocks and local policy changes also play significant roles; for instance, the early 2023 rally appears linked to optimism over governmental reforms, while declines in late 2023 and into 2025 reflect renewed caution amid worsening inflation and political uncertainty. The impact of inflation is critical: the 220% inflation rate in 2025 not only eroded purchasing power but also distorted equity valuations, resulting in nominal price increases that may not represent real economic gains when measured in stable currencies like the U.S. dollar. Investors thus face the dual challenge of interpreting nominal returns in light of severe macroeconomic distortions. Overall, Figure 2.12 illustrates Argentina's market as one driven by a few dominant firms, high inflation, and significant institutional risk, highlighting the need for caution and underscoring the limited diversification benefits available to foreign investors.

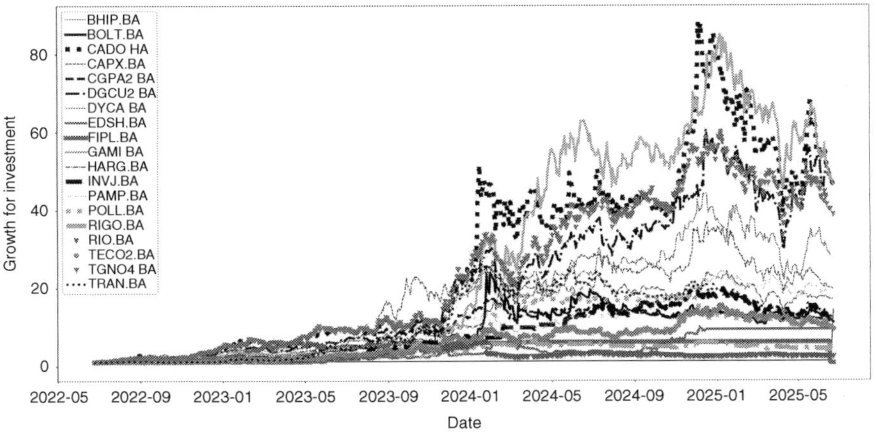

Figure 2.12 Cumulative Return on Argentinian SE (Portfolio "Argentinian").

Source: Own elaboration based on historical data from Yahoo Finance (n.d.a).

Notes: Results were obtained using the Python packages numpy, matplotlib.pyplot, and y_finance to compute and visualise cumulative returns. Information on the profitability of the Merval Index in U.S. dollars is available at: https://estadisticasbcra.com/en/merval_in_usd.

The influence of inflation on the Merval Index (S&P MERVAL Index) in Argentina is significant, particularly during the period from 2023 to 2025, when the inflation rate reached 220% in 2025. Inflation has directly affected corporate earnings, consumer spending, and investment decisions – factors that are critical for stock market performance. Historical inflation data for Argentina can be found at: https://www.statista.com/statistics/316750/inflation-rate-in-argentina/.

Therefore, analysis of cumulative returns across all examined markets reveals a significant impact of the pandemic. This period was marked by an initial steep drop followed by rapid rebounds for certain stocks, indicating heightened volatility and investor sentiment swings during the pandemic crisis. These findings indicate that while all markets faced pandemic-related disruptions, their capacity for recovery and the pattern of cumulative returns differ significantly. The Brazilian market stands out for its high volatility and concentrated leadership effects, whereas the CEE market appears more stable, albeit still dependent on a few outperforming equities for cumulative growth. Such insights are crucial for investors seeking to design portfolios that balance exposure to high-growth sectors with resilience against systemic shocks.

2.3.3 *Risk Maps, Fama–French Modelling, and Machine Learning Approaches*

The risk maps presented in Figures 2.13 and 2.14 provide valuable insights into the volatility patterns and market responses of the Brazilian and CEE stock markets over the analysed period. In Figure 2.13, it is evident that the Brazilian market exhibits pronounced spikes in daily simple returns,

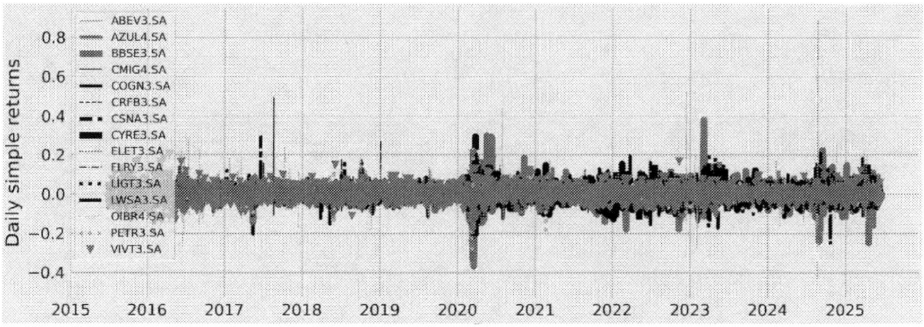

Figure 2.13 Risk Map of the Brazilian Stock Market (Portfolio "Brazilian").

Source: Own elaboration based on historical data from Yahoo Finance (n.d.a). Results were obtained using the Python packages numpy, matplotlib.pyplot, and yfinance.

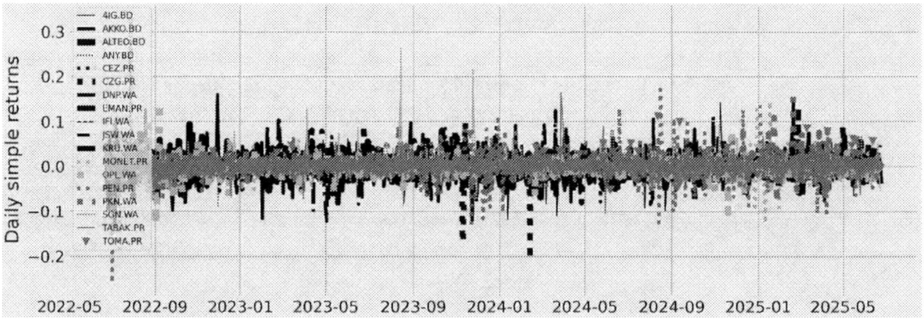

Figure 2.14 Risk Map of the CEE Stock Markets (Portfolio "CEE").

Source: Own elaboration based on historical data from Yahoo Finance (n.d.a). Results were obtained using the Python packages numpy, matplotlib.pyplot, and yfinance.

reflecting periods of heightened volatility. Particularly notable are the fluctuations observed during the COVID-19 pandemic, as well as the first quarter of 2025, when the combined effects of renewed tariff wars and logistics disruptions significantly increased market turbulence. Specific Brazilian companies, such as B2W Digital and Locaweb, faced considerable challenges in adapting to restrictive pandemic measures, which translated into sharp movements in their stock prices.

By contrast, the CEE market, illustrated in Figure 2.14, demonstrates a more stable volatility profile throughout much of the observed period. While 2020 stands out as a notably riskier year for the CEE region – likely due to the onset of the pandemic – the subsequent periods show relatively lower volatility compared to Brazil. Importantly, the risk maps suggest that the CEE market did not react as strongly to external shocks such as the Russian–Ukrainian war or the global tensions surrounding the renewed tariff disputes in early 2025. The only significant disturbance visible for the CEE market appears during the initial months following the Russian aggression, where localised volatility spikes can be observed.

Given the substantial institutional differences between these regions, it is difficult to draw broader conclusions solely based on the obtained portfolio compositions. It is undeniable that certain markets in SA and CEE have demonstrated impressive performance in specific portfolios, largely driven by one or two dominant companies. However, when companies from these markets attempt to enter the American or Western European markets, the differences in the weights of optimal portfolio components become far less pronounced. The Sharpe Ratio, as a measure of how an equity investment performs relative to the return on a risk-free asset, provides valuable insights. Yet, given the significant institutional differences across these markets, it remains impossible to derive absolute conclusions solely from such analysis. Nonetheless, these findings allow us to compare the underlying nature and composition of the portfolios.

Disregarding institutional disparities for a moment – particularly given that CEE markets are now integrated into the EU business environment – several notable trends emerge. It appears that the entry of CEE companies into Western European markets has been less profitable and significantly riskier than operations in their domestic markets. Consequently, a company may be a recognised leader in its home market yet remain relatively unknown – or a "dark horse" – in neighbouring markets, ultimately influencing both risk perceptions and pricing. The higher profitability observed for Brazilian and Argentine firms in U.S. and European stock markets can be attributed to certain institutional factors discussed earlier in the review (see also Tables 2.11 and 2.12).

Brazilian and Argentine companies operating in Western European markets face the challenge of balancing higher profitability with elevated risk levels. Nevertheless, their Sharpe Ratios remain more attractive than those of the Brazilian domestic market, although still significantly lower than those of the Argentine market. The exceptionally high Sharpe Ratio observed for the Argentine portfolio could be partly explained by the model's reliance solely on numerical factors, which can be problematic in markets characterised by unstable institutional environments and high inflation expectations – particularly when it comes to risk assessment beyond mere calculations of standard deviation.

If the objective is to derive more comparable figures, placing greater emphasis on portfolio utility maximisation rather than purely numerical optimisation appears to be a more suitable approach for such cases.

The Fama–French method enables the integration of institutional analysis into our research framework (Table 2.13) and provides a concise description of potential investment strategies. The probability values associated with the F-statistic essentially indicate whether the model is appropriate in each specific case. For this analysis, monthly data spanning the past five years (up to May 15, 2023) were utilised. An exception is Locaweb (LWSA3.SA), for which data were available only for a three-year period, rendering the method

Table 2.11 The Comparative Portfolio Analysis on the Local Markets

PORTFOLIO	*BRAZIL*	*ARGENTINA*	*CEE*
	CMIG4.SA (0.05945), PETR3.SA (0.17974), C2AC34.SA (0.7608)	GAMI.BA (0.01716), CGPA2.BA (0.05492), CAPX. BA (0.06304), DGCU2.BA (0.00363), EDSH.BA (0.27297), FIPL.BA (0.06758), HARG. BA (0.25535), PAMP.BA (0.03086), POLL.BA (0.05693), RIGO.BA (0.08066), RIO.BA (0.07843), TGNO4.BA (0.00858), INVJ.BA (0.0099)	DNP.WA (0.12057), IFI.WA (0.12713), CCE.WA (0.0059), SGN.WA (0.00199), CEZ.PR (0.03245), CZG.PR (0.29215), TABAK.PR (0.07851), TOMA.PR (0.04487), PEN.PR (0.02486), EMAN.PR (0.0355), 4IG.BD (0.08181), AKKO.BD (0.02866), ALTEO.BD (0.10082), ANY.BD (0.02475)
METRIC	*BRAZIL*	*ARGENTINA*	*CEE*
Expected annual return	18.6%	71.9%	40.8%
Annual volatility	21.0%	13.7%	14.1%
Sharpe Ratio	0.79	5.09	2.75
Priorities	Exploration, production, and selling oil and gas in Brazil and internationally; hydroelectric, wind, and solar energy; distribution infrastructure; IT management; and cybersecurity services.	Computer services, electric utilities, building materials, forestry and food products, construction, household goods, general mining, farming.	Information technology services; renewable utilities; aerospace and defence industries.

Source: Own elaboration based on historical data from Yahoo Finance.

Note: Table presents only holdings with non-zero portfolio weights for clarity. Results achieved using Python packages pypfopt, pypfopt.efficient_frontier, matplotlib.pyplot, and numpy.

inapplicable in that instance. Data on emerging markets were sourced directly from Kenneth French's Data Library.

This procedure proves suitable for all the markets included in our study, confirming their integration into the global financial system and offering strategic insights for external investors. Notably, the highest-performing companies identified within the CEE portfolios exhibited significantly lower

Table 2.12 The Comparative Portfolio Analysis on the Foreign Markets

Portfolio	*Main Holdings (Non-Zero Weights Only)*	*Expected Annual Return (%)*	*Annual Volatility (%)*	*Sharpe Ratio*
CEE in EU	SFB1.F (0.55061) PKY1.F (0.44939)	22.5	34.7	0.59
Brazil in USA	CYRBY (0.08628) WEGZY (0.91372)	33.5	54.3	0.58
Argentina and Brazil in EU	B4W.F (0.08122) C3TA.F (0.45003) FXMA.F (0.46876)	92.8	43.8	2.07

Source: Own elaboration based on historical data from Yahoo Finance.

Note: Table presents only holdings with non-zero portfolio weights for clarity. Results achieved using Python packages pypfopt, pypfopt.efficient_frontier, matplotlib.pyplot, and numpy.

Table 2.13 Result of Fama–French Analysis

Company Ticker	*Adj R^2*	*Prob. (F)*	*Mkt – Rf (sign.)*	*Durbin-Watson*
ALUA.BA	0.162	0.01	1.39 (0.002)	1.955
TRAN.BA	0.149	0.01	1.4 (0.007)	2.22
MIRG.BA	0.425	$8.9*10^{-7}$	2.5 (0.000)	1.831
EDN.BA	0.233	0.001	1.54 (0.000)	2.13
LWSA3.SA	*Available only 13 monthly observations*			
BTOW3.SA	0.117	0.03	1.25 (0.08)	1.364*
VIVT3.SA	0.01	0.358	-	-
TABAK.PR	0.138	0.02	0.3 (0.007)	2.07
MONET.PR	0.49	$1.2*10^{-6}$	0.89 (0.000)	2.045
AKKO.BD	–0.04	0.78	-	-
ANY.BD	0.121	0.03	0.25 (0.005)	1.844

Source: Results were achieved based on numpy, pandas, pandas_datareader, and yfinance packages of Python, own elaboration based on historical data from Yahoo Finance (n.d.a).

* Durbin-Watson coefficient is outside permissible limits.

risk than the overall market (*Mkt – Rf* < 1), while the leading firms in the SA portfolios were considerably riskier than the market average (*Mkt – Rf* > 1). This finding partially supports our hypothesis H3. Only one company, B2W DIGITAL (BTOW3.SA), displayed excessive autocorrelation, which may compromise the model's reliability in that specific case. Overall, the results indicate that the classic Fama–French approach remains feasible for conducting long-term strategic analyses and is broadly consistent with methodologies applied in developed markets. However, achieving comprehensive analysis across the maximum number of criteria – without artificially forcing data convergence – proved challenging. This underscores the need for the development and adoption of new analytical tools.

Machine learning methods have proven to be valuable tools for analysing business predictability, particularly in financial markets where complex,

Table 2.14 Predictability of Market Returns Based on R^2 Coefficient Across Machine Learning Models (Confidence Levels: 80%, 20%)

Company Ticker	R^2 *(Applied Method)*
C2AC34.SA	0.515 (svr), 0.32 (enet), 0.266 (ridge), 0.405 (lr)
PETR3.SA	0.89 (rf), 0.889 (gb), 0.889 [svr (rbf)]
CMIG4.SA	0.909 (svr (rbf)), 0.931 (rf), 0.918 (gb)
CSNA3.SA	0.849 (rf), 0.842 (gb), 0.83 (lasso), 0.825 (svr (rbf))
GAMI.BA	0.956 (rf), 0.944 (lasso), 0.944 (lr), 0.939 (svr (rbf))
CGPA2.BA	0.948 (rf), 0.941 (gb), 0.933 (svr (rbf)), 0.864 (enet)
CAPX.BA	0.969 (gb), 0.925(enet), 0.925 (lr), 0.988 (svr(rbf))
HARG.BA	0.99 (rf), 0.987 (enet), 0.991 (svr (rbf))
4IG.BD	0.934 (lr), 0.951 (svr (rbf)), 0.958 (rf), 0.934 (lasso)
EMAN.PR	0.382 (lr), 0.363 (svr (rbf)), 0.658 (rf), 0.382 (lasso)
IFI.WA	0.935 (lr), 0.984 (svr (rbf)), 0.988 (rf), 0.935 (lasso)
SGN.WA	0.934 (lr), 0.948 (rf), 0.946 (gb), 0.934 (lasso)
ALTEO.BD	0.97 (lr), 0.985 (svr (rbf)), 0.99 (rf), 0.97 (lasso)
CEZ.PR	0.908 (lr), 0.951 (svr (rbf)), 0.947 (gb), 0.908 (lasso)
DNP.WA	0.936 (lr), 0.956 (svr (rbf)), 0.955 (gb), 0.936 (lasso)
PEN.PR	0.675 (lr), 0.723 (svr (rbf)), 0.806 (gb), 0.67 (lasso)

Source: Own elaboration.

Note: R^2 denotes the coefficient of determination, indicating the proportion of variance explained by each model. Results were obtained using Python libraries including numpy, pandas, scikit-learn (e.g., Decision Tree Regressor, Linear Regression, Ridge, Lasso, Elastic Net, Support Vector Regression [SVR], Random Forest Regressor, Gradient Boosting Regressor), matplotlib. pyplot, and yfinance. Data were divided into training and testing subsets, with approximately 80% used for training and 20% for testing.

nonlinear relationships often exist among variables. In this study, several algorithms were employed to estimate the coefficient of determination (R^2) for each company, as shown in Table 2.14. These algorithms include:

- *RF* – an ensemble learning method that constructs multiple decision trees and aggregates their predictions, effectively capturing nonlinear interactions and reducing overfitting;
- *SVR* – a technique that finds a hyperplane in a high-dimensional space, useful for handling outliers and capturing complex patterns;
- *GB* – a sequential ensemble approach that builds models iteratively, focusing on the residuals of previous predictions to improve accuracy.
- *LR* – a fundamental technique modelling the relationship between variables under the assumption of linearity;
- *Ridge, Lasso, and Elastic Net* – regularised linear models that introduce penalties to reduce overfitting and handle multicollinearity among predictors.

The analysis relied on splitting data into training and testing subsets to evaluate predictive accuracy, thereby ensuring that the models could generalise beyond the observed data. The diversity of methods enables a robust assessment of the underlying predictability of stock prices, as each algorithm possesses unique strengths in capturing different data characteristics.

Notably, the results indicate that most companies in the analysed portfolios exhibit relatively high R^2 values across several models (Table 2.14). For example, PETR3.SA achieved R^2 values exceeding 0.88 under multiple methods, suggesting highly predictable price dynamics, possibly reflecting the systematic influence of macroeconomic and sector-specific factors in Brazil's energy sector. Similarly, stocks such as HARG.BA and ALTEO.BD demonstrate consistently strong predictability, indicating the presence of stable patterns in their price behaviour. However, there are companies where predictability appears more modest. For instance, C2AC34.SA shows lower R^2 values across all methods, pointing to greater volatility or weaker model fit, perhaps due to company-specific events or lower market liquidity. These differences are critical for strategic decision-making. Firms with high predictability may be better candidates for algorithmic trading or systematic investment strategies, while those with lower predictability could be subject to more speculative dynamics, requiring alternative risk management approaches.

Moreover, the feasibility of applying advanced machine learning methods demonstrates that the markets studied – despite institutional differences – share structural features with developed markets, where data-driven models are already a core part of financial analysis. The results further suggest that even in emerging markets, systematic patterns can be detected, although caution is warranted due to potential institutional volatility and external shocks. Thus, Table 2.14 not only confirms the technical possibility of price prediction but also hints at the existence of underlying market strategies or behavioural rules driving stock movements. This reinforces the argument that machine learning models are not mere statistical tools but can offer insights into the strategic dynamics of financial markets.

While applying machine learning methods, we encountered several challenges related to the predictability of stock prices. One of the most significant issues was the occurrence of negative-adjusted prices for certain SA companies, which hindered the effectiveness of specific models and necessitated either additional data cleaning or the exclusion of affected tickers. Moreover, not all models were suitable for every company; as seen in Figure 2.15, some stocks were analysed using only a subset of algorithms, reflecting either technical constraints or the unsuitability of certain methods for particular data characteristics.

Figure 2.15 illustrates the results of short-term price predictions for selected stocks based on multiple machine learning algorithms. The models applied include SVR, RF, GB, Decision Tree Regressor (TREE), and classical linear techniques such as Ridge, Lasso, and Elastic Net regressions. For each stock, daily price forecasts were generated for up to 50 days ahead, based on

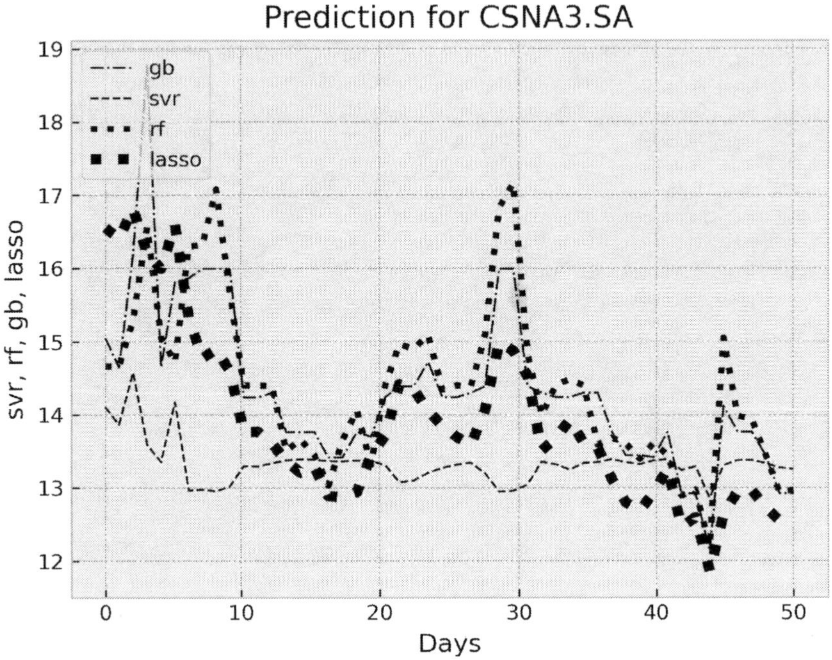

Figure 2.15 Predicted Price Trajectories Based on Machine Learning Models.

Source: Own elaboration based on historical data from Yahoo Finance. Results were achieved based on numpy Pandas, sklearn.tree (Decision Tree Regressor), sklearn.linear_model (Linear Regression), sklearn.model_selection (train_test_split), sklearn.svm (SVR), matplotlib.pyplot, sklearn.pipeline (make_pipeline), sklearn.linear_model (Ridge, Lasso, Elastic Net), and sklearn.ensemble (Random Forest Regressor, Gradient Boosting Regressor) packages of Python.

historical data up to May 2023. The graphs reveal considerable variability in predictive performance across companies and methods. Some stocks, such as CAPX.BA and PETR3.SA, exhibit relatively stable prediction paths with lower volatility across different models. In contrast, other stocks, including CSNA3.SA and SGN.WA, display significant divergence among predictions, indicating either lower model reliability or heightened market uncertainty for those cases.

Additionally, the generally low R^2 values observed for certain companies (as shown in Table 2.14) indicate limited predictive power and raise questions about the practical applicability of machine learning models for individual stock price forecasting, particularly in markets characterised by institutional instability or low liquidity. Nevertheless, despite these limitations, the machine learning methods employed provide valuable insights into market dynamics, highlighting stocks with higher predictability and identifying those where price behaviour remains largely stochastic. Such insights are crucial for constructing optimal investment portfolios and for developing informed trading strategies.

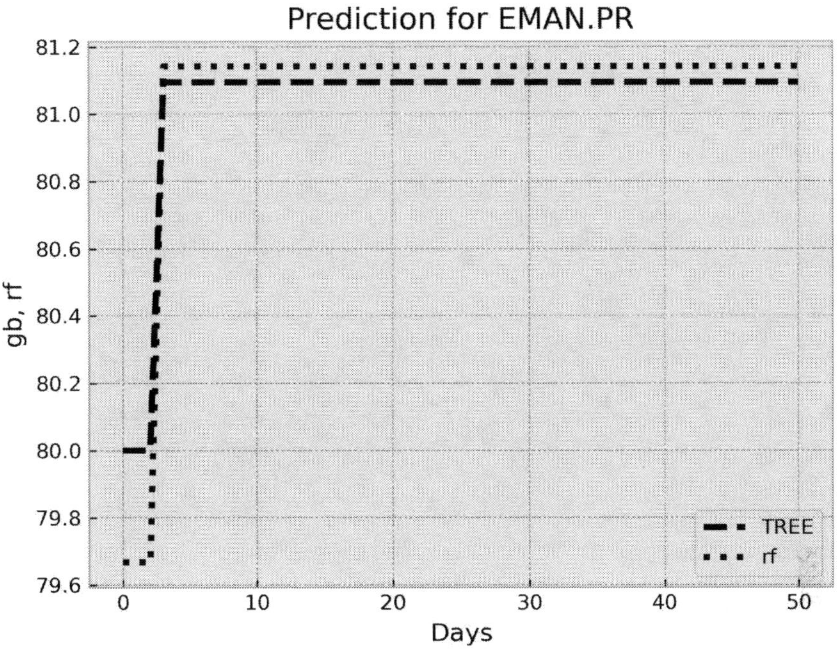

Figure 2.15 (Continued)

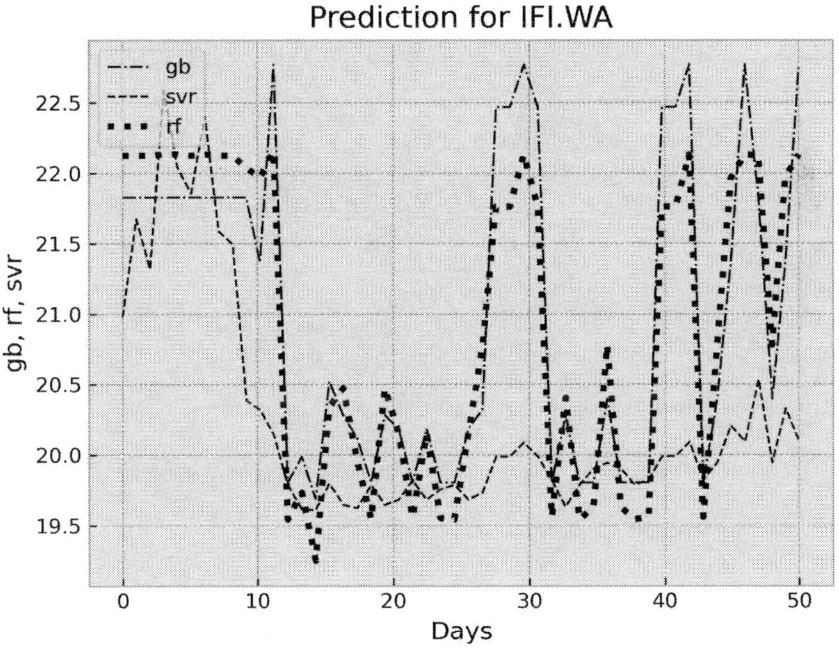

Figure 2.15 (Continued)

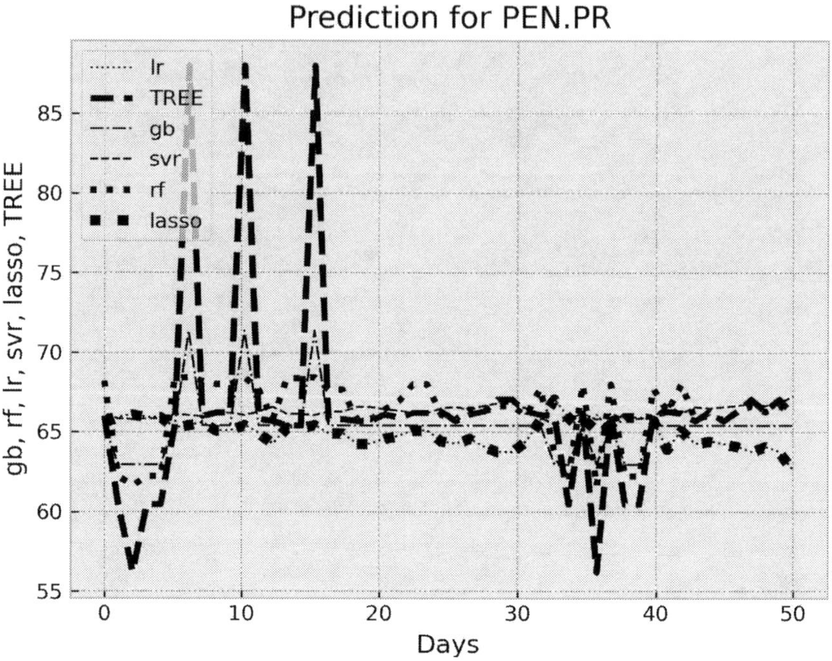

Figure 2.15 (Continued)

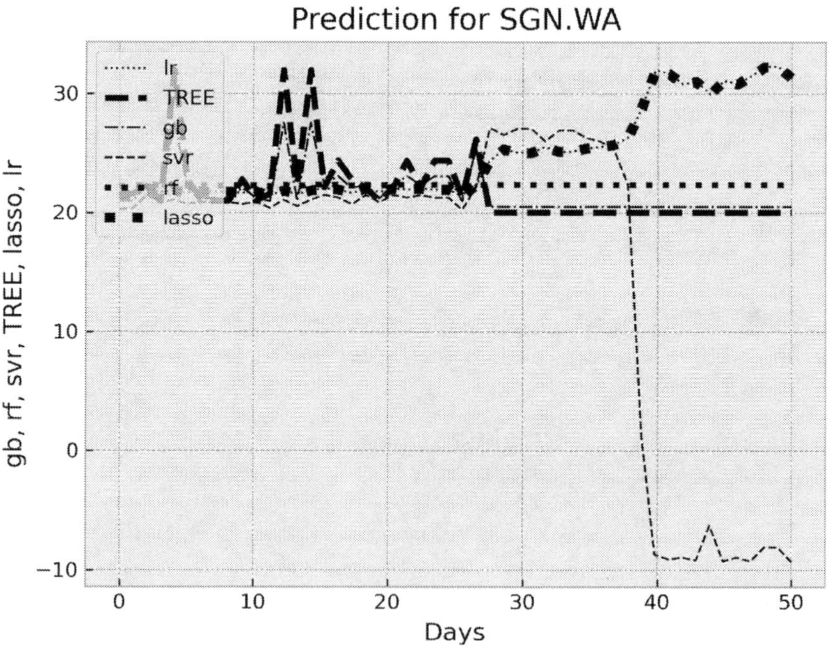

Figure 2.15 (Continued)

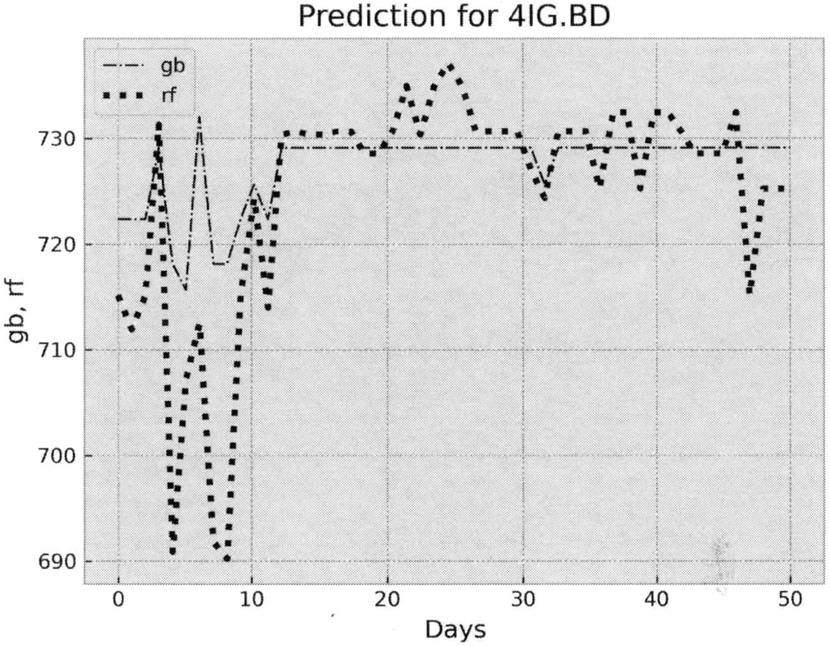

Figure 2.15 (Continued)

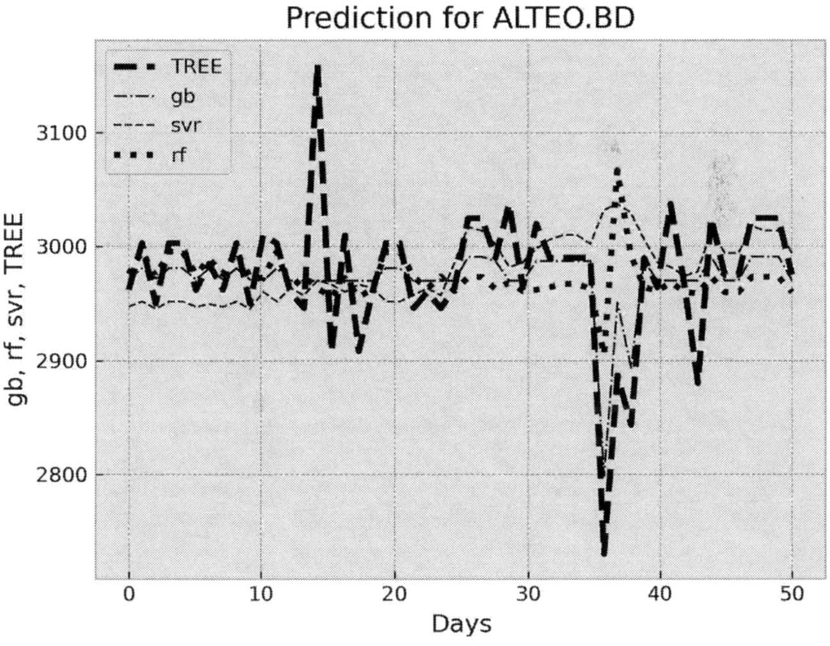

Figure 2.15 (Continued)

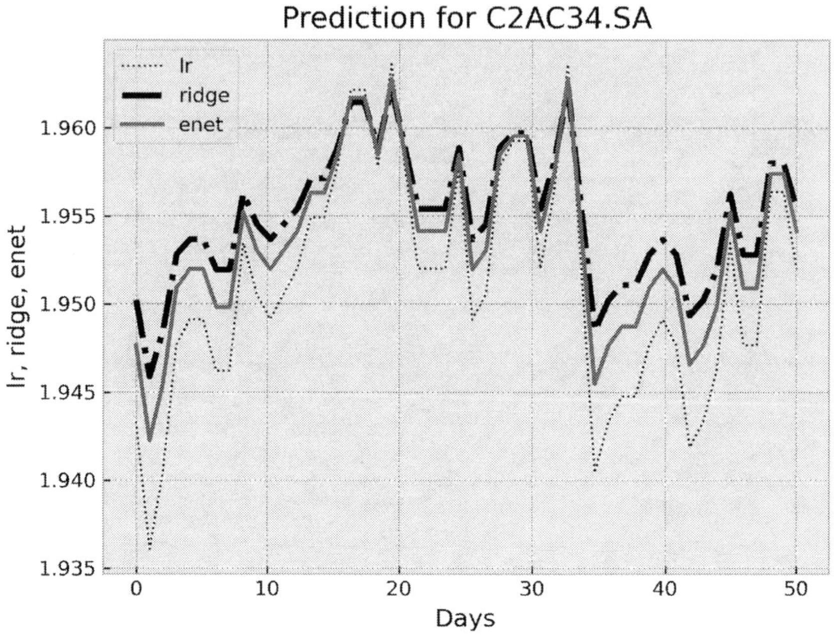

Figure 2.15 (Continued)

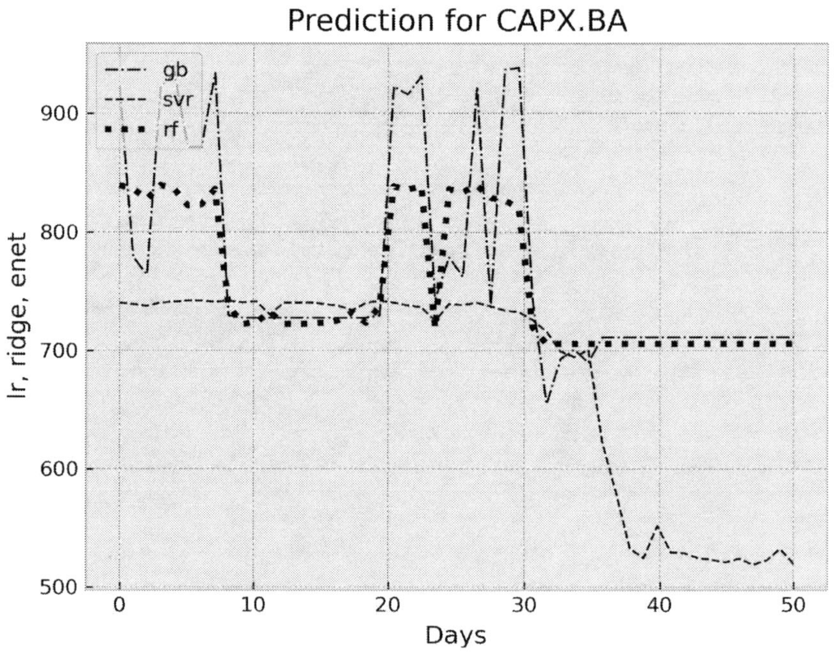

Figure 2.15 (Continued)

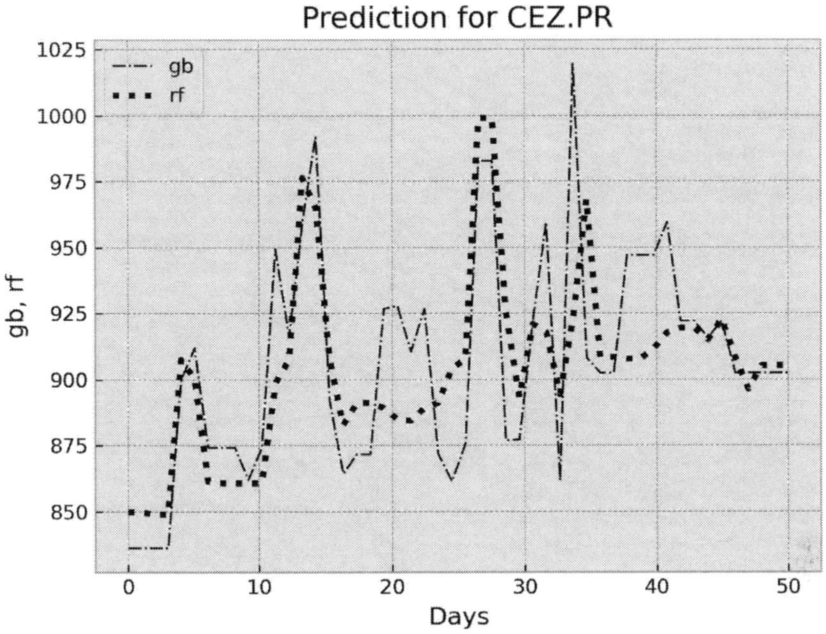

Figure 2.15 (Continued)

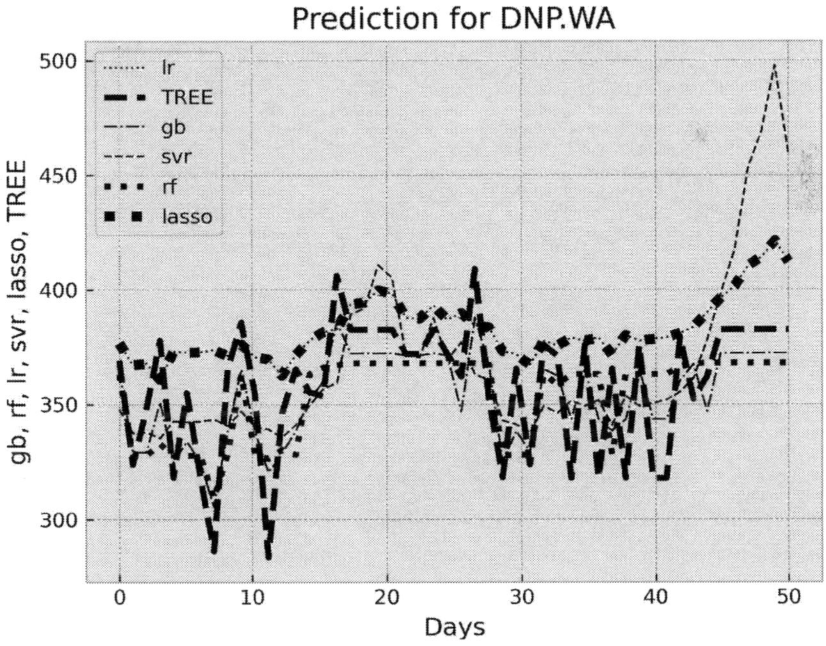

Figure 2.15 (Continued)

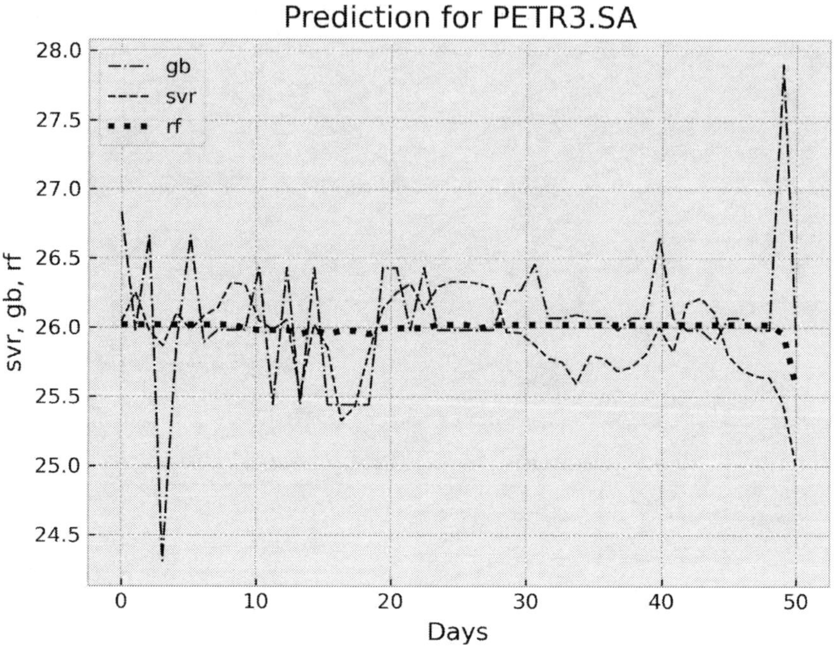

Figure 2.15 (Continued)

The application of price prediction methods has revealed both clear failures, as seen in the case of CSNA3.SA (Companhia Siderúrgica Nacional), and the practical applicability of commonly used approaches for other companies (Figure 2.15). Daily statistics of the adjusted closing price for the past five years were collected for this analysis. In certain instances, different methods yielded significantly divergent results, even with similar R^2 values, which can be attributed to data quality issues and the unsuitability of specific models when handling negative values. Despite these limitations, most companies across all examined markets exhibit a visible trend of stabilisation during the analysed period.

2.4 Key Takeaways and Closing Reflections

The COVID-19 pandemic has profoundly reshaped the economic landscape, accelerating digital adoption and redefining the relationship between markets, investors, and technology. As physical interactions dwindled, digital solutions became a vital lifeline, enabling individuals, businesses, and entire economies to maintain continuity through remote operations, e-commerce, and virtual services. This transformation is reflected in the significant growth of sectors such as telecommunications, software, robotics, and digital communication channels.

In this study, we combined two complementary analytical approaches. Firstly, we identified leading companies through cumulative return dynamics, categorising them into three market clusters to capture trend differentiation. Secondly, we applied the Efficient Frontier method to determine optimal portfolio allocations, evaluating the associated Sharpe Ratios to balance expected returns against investment risk. Our analysis demonstrates that industries closely aligned with societal needs – such as technology, gaming, digital communication, and education – consistently exhibit strong investment potential. This relationship between market dynamics and human-centric trends is reflected in Table 2.15, highlighting how shifting social priorities translate into tangible financial strategies.

Our research highlights that beyond sector-specific insights, significant geographical dynamics shape emerging stock markets, particularly in SA and CEE. Companies from these regions increasingly seek participation both in domestic markets and on global exchanges, reflecting ambitions for broader integration. Yet, many portfolios remain heavily dependent on a few dominant firms, creating concentration risks and complicating diversification. This pattern is especially visible in SA, where removing key firms can severely impact returns, while CEE markets, though less volatile, still contend with modest profitability and structural challenges.

Institutional frameworks are crucial in shaping these market realities. Developed markets offer transparency and predictability, whereas emerging markets face higher volatility and institutional weaknesses. Still, progress is evident. Our findings confirm growing integration of SA and CEE markets into the global financial system, consistent with an econothinking perspective that sees economic decisions as intertwined with broader systemic forces. Tools like the Fama–French model and machine learning techniques prove valuable here, though their reliability declines in contexts marked by poor data quality and fragile institutions. Even so, these models continue to yield useful insights when applied with sensitivity to local conditions.

Table 2.15 Human-Centric Drivers Reflected in Market and Investment Responses

Human Needs	*Market Reaction*
Constant desire to raise the level of technology into daily life	Presence of technology firms in optimal portfolios and clustering results
Spending increasing time in virtual environments	Gaming companies featuring in optimal portfolios
Growing demand for diverse learning methods and rapid development of distance education	Education businesses included in optimal portfolios
Rise of online retail and the increasing role of digital communication	Internet retailers and communication services consistently appearing in optimal portfolios, trending tickers, and clustering results

Source: Own elaboration.

A central theme in our analysis is strategic adaptability. Modern economies no longer merely respond to technological and social change but actively shape it, guided by the understanding that financial and geopolitical developments are deeply interconnected. This reflects econothinking in practice – a mindset recognising that economic strategies must align with wider societal and geopolitical contexts. The convergence of technological innovation, digitalisation, and evolving societal needs demands constant recalibration of investment approaches. Businesses and policymakers alike must balance short-term performance with long-term sustainability and social impact.

Geopolitical and institutional contexts remain critical influences. Recent years have brought new risks, such as weakened international norms, disruptions in logistics, and selective trade barriers. Countries with modernised, transparent financial systems are better positioned to withstand such shocks and maintain competitiveness. For CEE nations, further alignment with Western regulatory standards remains crucial, while regions lagging in reforms risk diminishing relevance in global finance.

Digitalisation creates new growth opportunities but also demands institutional evolution to sustain competitiveness. The optimal portfolios identified in our study reflect not only financial performance but also how markets align with broader economic, geopolitical, and social dynamics – a perspective shaped by econothinking. This underscores that strategic adaptability is essential, not merely advantageous, for maintaining competitiveness in a complex global environment.

The pandemic further accelerated changes in investor focus, bringing technology and digital services to the forefront. Yet key questions persist: should emerging markets prioritise expanding global presence or strengthen domestic markets for sustainable investment? Our findings suggest that improving national market efficiency and institutional capacity offers a resilient path forward that weighs both economic and societal impacts.

While CEE markets structurally resemble developed markets more closely than those in SA, they continue to lag in profitability, whereas SA markets remain highly sensitive to the performance of individual firms, underscoring the need for greater diversification and strategic foresight.

Accordingly, the modernisation of financial markets plays a pivotal role in national competitiveness. Well-regulated, transparent stock markets attract foreign capital, foster innovation, and support sustainable growth. Prioritising sectors like technology and renewable energy can strengthen both individual firms and broader economic resilience. Yet ongoing geopolitical tensions and shifting global dynamics demand continuous vigilance and strategic agility. For emerging markets, the challenge lies not only in managing volatility but also in aligning institutions and strategic priorities with the rapid transformations of a digital, interconnected world. In this context, strategic adaptability grounded in econothinking remains essential for turning uncertainty into sustainable competitive advantage.

Note

1 This cryptocurrency index comprises the volume-weighted average price ("VWAP") on the top 200 cryptocurrencies except for Bitcoin and stablecoins, by market capitalization, in USD. A Stablecoin is a type of cryptocurrency where the value of the digital asset is supposed to be pegged to a reference asset, which is either fiat money, exchange-traded commodities (such as precious metals or industrial metals), or another cryptocurrency. The term "fiat" is a Latin word that is often translated as "it shall be" or "let it be done". Thus fiat currencies only have value because the government maintains that value; there is no utility to fiat money in itself.

References

Annaert, J., Buelens, F., Cuyvers, L., De Ceuster, M., Deloof, M., & De Schepper, A. (2011). Are blue chip stock market indices good proxies for all-shares market indices? The case of the Brussels Stock Exchange 1833–2005. *Financial History Review, 18*(3), 277–308. https://doi.org/10.1017/S0968565011000187

Babapour Chafi, M., Hultberg, A., & Bozic Yams, N. (2022). Post-pandemic office work: Perceived challenges and opportunities for a sustainable work environment. *Sustainability, 14*(1), Article 294. https://doi.org/10.3390/su14010294

Batten, J. A., Szilagyi, P. G., & Wong, M. C. S. (2014). Stock market spread trading: Argentina and Brazil stock indexes. *Emerging Markets Finance & Trade, 50* (Suppl. 3), 61–76.

Bubbico, R. L., Gattini, L., Gereben, Á., Kolev, A., Kollár, M., & Slacik, T. (2017). *Wind of change: Investment in Central, Eastern and South Eastern Europe*. European Investment Bank.https://www.eib.org/attachments/efs/economics_study_wind_of_change_investment_in_cesee_en.pdf

Costa, A., da Silva, C., & Matos, P. (2022). The Brazilian financial market reaction to COVID-19: A wavelet analysis. *International Review of Economics & Finance, 82*, 13–29. https://doi.org/10.1016/j.iref.2022.05.010

Crisóstomo, V. L., Pinheiro, B. G., & Nakamura, W. T. (2020). Ownership concentration and share issue: Evidence from Latin America. *Brazilian Review of Finance, 18*(4). https://doi.org/10.12660/rbfin.v18n4.2020.81194

Dahlke, J., Bogner, K., Becker, M., Schlaile, M. P., Pyka, A., & Ebersberger, B. (2021). Crisis-driven innovation and fundamental human needs: A typological framework of rapid-response COVID-19 innovations. *Technological Forecasting and Social Change, 169*, Article 120799. https://doi.org/10.1016/j.techfore.2021.120799

de O. Carosia, A. E., Coelho, G. P., & da Silva, A. E. A. (2021). Investment strategies applied to the Brazilian stock market: A methodology based on sentiment analysis with deep learning. *Expert Systems with Applications, 184*, Article 115470. https://doi.org/10.1016/j.eswa.2021.115470

de Peña, F. J., Forner, C., & López-Espinosa, G. (2010). Fundamentals and the origin of Fama-French factors: The case of the Spanish market. *Czech Journal of Economics and Finance, 60*(5), 426–446.

Deng, G., Dulaney, T., McCann, C. J., & Wang, O. (2013). Robust portfolio optimization with value-at-risk adjusted Sharpe ratio. *Journal of Asset Management, 14*(5), 293–305. https://doi.org/10.2139/ssrn.2146219

Dentsu Aegis Network. (2019). *Digital society index 2019: Human needs in a digital world.* https://www.dentsu.com/cn/en/news-releases/digital-world

EYGM. (2020). *Divesting in turbulent times: How European companies can manage divestments through the COVID-19 pandemic (2020 Global Corporate Divestment Study)*. https://www.ey.com/content/dam/ey-unified-site/ey-com/en-gl/insights/strategy-transactions/documents/ey-divestment-study-2020-highlights.pdf

Faruque, M. O., Talukder, T., Pranto, M. N., Debnath, A., & Sultana, S. (2024). The rise of remote work and its impact on small businesses. *American Journal of Industrial and Business Management, 14*, 869–890. https://doi.org/10.4236/ajibm.2024.146044

Gea, C., Klotzle, M. C., Vereda, L., & Pinto, A. C. F. (2023). Pricing uncertainty in the Brazilian stock market: Do size and sustainability matter? *SN Business & Economics, 3*(25). https://doi.org/10.1007/s43546-022-00400-5

Grzegorczyk, M., Mariniello, M., Nurski, L., & Schraepen, T. (2021). Blending the physical and virtual: A hybrid model for the future of work. *Bruegel Policy Contribution, 14*. https://www.econstor.eu/handle/10419/251067

Guidi, F., & Ugur, M. (2014). An analysis of South-Eastern European stock markets: Evidence on cointegration and portfolio diversification benefits. *Journal of International Financial Markets, Institutions and Money, 30*, 119–136. https://doi.org/10.1016/j.intfin.2014.01.007

Hantrais, L., Allin, P., Kritikos, M., Sogomonjan, M., Anand, P. B., Livingstone, S., Williams, M., & Innes, M. (2021). COVID-19 and the digital revolution. *Contemporary Social Science, 16*(2). https://doi.org/10.1080/21582041.2020.1833234

Harmilapi, P. (2012). Features and functions of stock market: Argentina. *SSRN*. https://doi.org/10.2139/ssrn.2123534

Hurnyak, I., & Struk, O. (2024). Prioritization of the IT sector in the CEE stock markets: Investment policies, trends and hidden gems. *Comparative Economic Research. Central and Eastern Europe, 27*(3), 23–45. https://doi.org/10.18778/1508-2008.27.20

International Science Council. (2020). *Conversations on rethinking human development*. https://doi.org/10.24948/2020.09

Investing.com. (n.d.). World indices. *Investing.com*. Retrieved June 21, 2025, from https://www.investing.com/indices/world-indices

Investor's Business Daily. (n.d.). Adtalem Global Education thrives in stock market under Trump administration. *Investor's Business Daily*. https://www.investors.com/research/the-new-america/adtalem-global-education-stock-market-trump/

Jin, X., & Shaojun, Z. (2014). The Fama-French three factors in Chinese stock market. *China Accounting and Finance Review, 16*(2), 210–227. https://doi.org/10.2139/ssrn.2367908

Joynes, C., Rossignoli, S., & Fenyiwa Amonoo-Kuofi, E. (2019). *21st century skills: Evidence of issues in definition, demand and delivery for development contexts (K4D Helpdesk Report)*. Institute of Development Studies.

Juchnowicz, M., & Kinowska, H. (2021). Employee well-being and digital work during the COVID-19 pandemic. *Information, 12*(8), Article 293. https://doi.org/10.3390/info12080293

Kiesler, S., Siegel, J., & McGuire, T. W. (1984). Social psychological aspects of computer-mediated communication. *American Psychologist, 39*(10), 1123–1134. https://doi.org/10.1037/0003-066X.39.10.1123

Kraus, S., Ferraris, A., & Bertello, A. (2023). The future of work: How innovation and digitalization re-shape the workplace. *Journal of Innovation & Knowledge, 8*(4), Article 100438. https://doi.org/10.1016/j.jik.2023.100438

Lazonick, W. (2017). The functions of the stock market and the fallacies of shareholder value. *Institute for New Economic Thinking Working Paper Series, 58*. https://doi.org/10.2139/ssrn.2993978

Lu, Y., Zheng, H., Chand, S., Xia, W., Liu, Z., Xu, X., Wang, L., Qin, Z., & Bao, J. (2022). Outlook on human-centric manufacturing towards Industry 5.0. *Journal of Manufacturing Systems, 62*, 612–627. https://doi.org/10.1016/j.jmsy.2022.02.001

Maison, D., Jaworska, D., Adamczyk, D., & Affeltowicz, D. (2021). The challenges arising from the COVID-19 pandemic and the way people deal with them. *Plos One, 16*(10), Article e0258133. https://doi.org/10.1371/journal.pone.0258133

Max-Neef, M. (2010). Development and human needs. In A. L. St. Clair (Ed.), *Development ethics* (pp. 49–75). Routledge. https://doi.org/10.4324/9781315258003-14

Melvin, M. (2003). A stock market boom during a financial crisis? ADRs and capital outflows in Argentina. *Economics Letters, 81*(1), 129–136.

Morck, R., Shleifer, A., Vishny, R. W., Shapiro, M., & Poterba, J. M. (1990). The stock market and investment: Is the market a sideshow? *Brookings Papers on Economic Activity, 1990*(2), 157–215. https://doi.org/10.2307/2534506

Nie, N. H., & Erbring, L. (2000). Internet and society: A preliminary report. Stanford Institute for the Quantitative Study of Society.

Nyasha, S., & Odhiambo, N. M. (2013). The Brazilian stock market development: A critical analysis of progress and prospects during the past 50 years. *Risk Governance and Control: Financial Markets & Institutions, 3*(3), 7–15. https://doi.org/10.22495/rgcv3i3art1

OECD. (2019). *Equity market development in Latin America: Argentina*. OECD Publishing.

Pan, L., & Mishra, V. (2018). Stock market development and economic growth: Empirical evidence from China. *Economic Modelling, 68*, 661–673.

Ruzzeddu, M. (2022). Ascribed identities in the global era: A complex approach. *Contemporary Social Science, 17*(1). https://doi.org/10.1080/21582041.2021.1933157

Simões, M. D., van Aduard de Macedo-Soares, T. D. L., Klotzle, M. C., & Pinto, A. C. F. (2012). Assessment of market efficiency in Argentina, Brazil and Chile: An event study of mergers and acquisitions. *Brazilian Administration Review, 9*(2). https://doi.org/10.1590/S1807-76922012000200007

Simpson, J. A., & Weiner, E. S. C. (1989). *The Oxford English dictionary*. Clarendon Press.

Sokolic, D. (2022). Remote work and hybrid work organizations. In *78th International Scientific Conference on Economic and Social Development — Aveiro*. https://www.esd-conference.com/upload/book_of_proceedings/Book_of_Proceedings_esdAveiro2022_Online.pdf#page=208

Syllignakis, M. N., & Kouretas, G. P. (2011). Dynamic correlation analysis of financial contagion: Evidence from the Central and Eastern European markets. *International Review of Economics & Finance, 20*, 717–732. https://doi.org/10.1016/j.iref.2011.01.006

Syriopoulos, T., & Roumpis, E. (2009). Dynamic correlations and volatility effects in the Balkan equity markets. *Journal of International Financial Markets, Institutions and Money, 19*(4), 565–587. https://doi.org/10.1016/j.intfin.2008.08.002

TMF Group (2022). *Global Business Complexity Index 2022*. https://www.tmf-group.com/en/news-insights/publications/2022/global-business-complexity-index

Vyas, L. (2022). New normal at work in a post-COVID world: Work–life balance and labor markets. *Policy and Society, 41*(1), 155–167. https://doi.org/10.1093/polsoc/puab011

Wiśniewski, P. (2017). The competitiveness of Central and Eastern European (CEE) financial markets. *SSRN*. https://doi.org/10.2139/ssrn.2920897

Xingfu, W., & Siming, L. (2020). Rethinking progress today. *Yearbook for Eastern and Western Philosophy, 2019*(4). https://doi.org/10.1515/yewph-2020-0017

Yahoo Finance. (n.d.a). Markets. *Yahoo*. Retrieved June 21, 2025, from https://finance.yahoo.com/markets/

Yahoo Finance. (n.d.b). Trending tickers. *Yahoo*. Retrieved May 20, 2025, from https://finance.yahoo.com/trending-tickers/

Zaimović, A., & Arnaut Berilo, A. (2015). Risk diversification between stock markets in Germany and Bosnia and Herzegovina. *South East European Journal of Economics and Business, 9*(1), 30–36. https://doi.org/10.2478/jeb-2014-0003

Zaimović, A., Arnaut-Berilo, A., & Mustafic, A. (2017). Portfolio diversification in the South-East European equity markets. *South East European Journal of Economics and Business, 12*(1), 126–135. https://doi.org/10.1515/jeb-2017-0010

Zhang, J., & Chen, Z. (2024). Exploring human resource management digital transformation in the digital age. *Journal of Knowledge Economy, 15*, 1482–1498. https://doi.org/10.1007/s13132-023-01214-y

3 National Strategy and Global Competitiveness

Economic Insights for Policymakers

3.1 Geopolitical Games, Strategic Choices, and National Resilience

In an era defined by profound geopolitical upheavals, technological disruption, and shifting global alliances, the concept of national competitiveness extends far beyond mere economic indicators. It encompasses the strategic behaviour of states as they navigate a complex international environment marked by both cooperation and rivalry. Modern geopolitics operates as a dynamic arena where decisions are not made in isolation but are deeply interwoven with historical patterns, perceived threats, and the evolving configurations of global power. The interplay between geopolitics and national economic strategies has become particularly salient in recent years, as events such as the Russian–Ukrainian war, U.S.–China tensions, and global supply chain realignments have exposed the fragility of interdependence and the resurgence of economic nationalism (Bremmer, 2022; World Bank, 2025). In this context, states face the dual imperative of ensuring security and maintaining economic vitality, often requiring them to adopt strategies that blend cooperation with calculated defection – a phenomenon well captured by the frameworks of game theory. Meanwhile, financial markets, frequently viewed as mere reflections of economic fundamentals, have proven themselves to be sensitive barometers of geopolitical dynamics. Patterns observed in equity markets, shifts in portfolio compositions, and sectoral realignments offer valuable clues about a country's strategic priorities and resilience. Such market-based signals can help scholars and policymakers discern whether nations are pursuing paths of openness and multilateralism or retreating into self-reliance and protective economic measures (OECD, 2023a; Naughton, 2021).

This part seeks to bridge these perspectives by integrating insights from both game-theoretic modelling and empirical financial data. Through the lens of strategic games such as the Chicken Game, the Stag Hunt, and the Prisoner's Dilemma, we examine how states calibrate their actions under uncertainty and risk. At the same time, by analysing optimal stock portfolios across different geopolitical periods, we reveal how strategic priorities

DOI: 10.4324/9781003660194-3

materialise in economic structures and sectoral investments. Taken together, these analytical tools illuminate the fundamental link between a nation's geopolitical posture and its economic competitiveness, highlighting how strategic choices ripple through both diplomatic relations and financial markets.

Against this backdrop, the following sections explore how various countries, notably China and Japan, have navigated these turbulent waters, adjusting their strategic behaviour and economic configurations in response to shifting geopolitical pressures. In doing so, we aim to illustrate that national competitiveness in the 21st century cannot be understood purely in terms of GDP figures or trade balances but must be analysed as a multidimensional phenomenon where security, strategy, and economic policy converge.

When facing situations involving repeated actions – known in game theory as repeated games – it becomes possible to simplify a state's strategic choices for each specific type of problem. Drawing on the heuristics and historical behaviours exhibited by states in handling past crises, we attempt here to project such behavioural patterns into potential strategies for interacting with Ukraine in the context of countering external aggression. The proposed strategies for each country are indicated in the notes accompanying the tables below. It must be stressed that the choice of such strategies is inherently ambiguous. Each set of strategies corresponds to a particular scenario of events. Under different circumstances, states may behave differently, influenced significantly by the human factor – particularly, the personal attitudes and decisions of whoever holds executive power at the time.

3.1.1 *Risky Environment: The Chicken Game and State Strategies*

It is logical to choose the Chicken Game as a model when discussing the Russian–Ukrainian war. The deepening of this conflict could carry catastrophic consequences for the entire region. At the same time, opting out of the war entails medium-term costs that differ for each side – for Russia, primarily reputational costs, including the suspension of imperial ambitions and the risk of explosive internal instability, and for Ukraine, even more painfully, the possible temporary loss of territory and the subjugation of part of its population under cruel occupation. Engagement in the conflict resembles being "on the road" in a game of chicken: refusing to continue amounts to leaving the road and accepting the status of the "chicken". For either side, this decision would likely be accompanied by significant military and political repercussions, and potentially the effective victory of the opponent. Naturally, this is a simplification, since for Ukraine the conflict is existential, while for Russia it revolves around the pursuit of imperial goals. On the other hand, the US government's focus on cooperation with SpaceX, the manufacturer of a number of launch vehicles, suddenly becomes hostage to the personal relationship between the president and the entrepreneur. Nonetheless, with appropriate caveats, this framework offers a useful analytical lens.

Table 3.1 Risky Environment: Ranking of Winners in Chicken Game

Game = Chicken, Turns = 300, Noise = 0.1	*Game = Chicken, Turns = 10, Noise = 0.1*	*Game = Chicken, Turns = 50, Noise = 0.1*
Bush Mosteller, Hard Tit For Tat, Resurrection, Tit For Tat, GTFT, Generic Memory Two Player, Cooperator, Generic Memory One Player, Handshake, Cycler CCCCCD, Cycler DDC, Collective Strategy, Cycler CCCDCD	GTFT, Resurrection, Tit For Tat, Hard Tit For Tat, Generic Memory Two Player, Cooperator, Cycler CCCCCD, Bush Mosteller, Cycler CCCDCD, Generic Memory One Player, Handshake, Collective Strategy, Cycler DDC	Hard Tit For Tat, Bush Mosteller, Resurrection, Tit For Tat, GTFT, Generic Memory Two Player, Cooperator, Handshake, Generic Memory One Player, Cycler CCCCCD, Cycler CCCDCD, Cycler DDC, Collective Strategy

Source: Own elaboration based on outcomes from the Axelrod tournament simulations.

Notes: EU = Collective Strategy; Kazakhstan = Hard Tit For Tat; Hungary = Cycler DDC; Poland = Cycler CCCDCD; France = GTFT (Generous Tit For Tat); Germany = Resurrection; Great Britain = Handshake; India = Bush Mosteller; USA = Memory Two Player; China = Cycler CCCCCD; Türkiye = Cooperator; Russia = Memory One Player; Ukraine = Tit For Tat.

Special attention is given to the Bush Mosteller strategy, where the probability of choosing cooperation (C) or defection (D) is updated dynamically based on a stimulus reflecting the gain or loss from the previous move's payoff.

Within this risky environment, different states have adopted strategies shaped by their national interests, political cultures, and historical experiences (Table 3.1). Ukraine, for example, behaves in line with a Tit For Tat strategy – responding in kind to Russian aggression while maintaining the possibility of cooperation when aggression subsides. This mirrors Ukraine's need to defend itself firmly while avoiding unnecessary escalation. Russia, meanwhile, follows a Memory One Player approach, characterised by adapting decisions based on previous outcomes rather than fixed rules, reflecting its tendency towards unpredictability and tactical shifts in response to costs or changing circumstances. The United States exhibits behaviour akin to the Generic Memory Two Player strategy, taking into account not only bilateral dynamics with Russia and Ukraine but also the broader implications for global alliances and strategic balance. The European Union, with its tradition of seeking collective action and consensus, fits the Collective Strategy model, emphasising coordination among diverse member states despite occasional internal disagreements.

France's early attempts at mediating peace through prolonged negotiations reflect a Generous Tit For Tat (GTFT) approach – one that initially leans towards cooperation but remains prepared to retaliate if provoked repeatedly. Germany, on the other hand, has often sought ways to reset relationships despite crises, embodying the Resurrection strategy, where cooperation resumes even after conflict. The United Kingdom operates in line with a Handshake strategy, starting with cooperative gestures but prepared to defend its interests firmly when necessary. Poland's firm yet sometimes provocative stance in regional security aligns with a Cycler CCCDCD strategy, reflecting a repeated pattern of cooperation interspersed with moments of defection – visible in Warsaw's strong advocacy for decisive Western support for Ukraine and occasional criticisms of perceived Western hesitation. Kazakhstan, balancing carefully between Russia and the West, reflects a Hard Tit For Tat stance, showing cautious cooperation but ready to respond firmly if its sovereignty feels threatened. Hungary, meanwhile, exhibits a Cycler DDC approach, oscillating between periods of defection and cooperation, consistent with its often-contrarian position within the EU regarding Russia policy. Türkiye's diplomatic balancing act – maintaining dialogue with both Russia and the West, while playing the role of mediator – fits well with the Cooperator strategy, seeking benefits through engagement with all sides. China's behaviour aligns with the Cycler CCCCCD approach, maintaining extended periods of cooperation with the broader international community, punctuated by occasional calculated defection, allowing it to subtly test Western resolve without overtly siding with Russia. India, finally, exemplifies the Bush Mosteller strategy, adapting its level of cooperation or defection dynamically based on the results of previous engagements – reflecting its careful, pragmatic navigation between maintaining ties with Russia and deepening its relationships with Western partners.

These varied strategies (Table 3.1) underscore that the Russian–Ukrainian war is not merely a bilateral clash but a complex network of shifting calculations, historical legacies, and national priorities. The Chicken Game captures this reality well, highlighting the dangers of mutual escalation and the delicate signalling each state must perform to balance risk, reputation, and strategic interests. It is interesting to observe how these theoretical strategies – many of which emerged as winners in Robert Axelrod's repeated games tournament – correspond with real-world diplomatic behaviour. Variations of Tit For Tat, in particular, appear especially suitable for high-stakes, iterative conflicts where nations seek to protect themselves while leaving open the possibility of de-escalation.

3.1.2 *Joint Hunting Scenario: The Stag Hunt and the Challenges of Cooperation*

In contrast to the confrontational dynamics modelled by the Chicken Game, the Stag Hunt Game represents a setting where mutual cooperation offers the greatest rewards, but where hesitation, mistrust, or divergence in goals can quickly lead to suboptimal outcomes for all involved. This game is an apt metaphor for peace negotiations or joint ventures between states: success depends on shared trust and alignment towards a common goal.

In the Stag Hunt, the Cooperator strategy emerges as the long-term winner, especially in scenarios involving many repeated interactions – as demonstrated in the simulations extending to 300 turns (Table 3.2). The logic

Table 3.2 Two Possible Equilibria of Nash: Ranking of Winners in Stag Hunt Game

Game = Stag Hunt, Turns = 10, Noise = 0.1	*Game = Stag Hunt, Turns = 50, Noise = 0.1*	*Game = Stag Hunt, Turns = 300, Noise = 0.1*
Generic Memory Two Player, Cooperator, Tit For Tat, GTFT, Cycler CCCCCD, Generic Memory One Player, Hard Tit For Tat, Cycler CCCDCD, Resurrection, Bush Mosteller, Handshake, Collective Strategy, Cycler DDC	Cooperator, Generic Memory Two Player, GTFT, Cycler CCCCCD, Tit For Tat, Resurrection, Cycler CCCDCD, Bush Mosteller, Generic Memory One Player, Hard Tit For Tat, Handshake, Collective Strategy, Cycler DDC	Cooperator, Generic Memory Two Player, Cycler CCCCCD, GTFT, Tit For Tat, Resurrection, Cycler CCCDCD, Generic Memory One Player, Bush Mosteller, Hard Tit For Tat, Handshake, Collective Strategy, Cycler DDC

Source: Own elaboration based on outcomes from the Axelrod tournament simulations.

is clear: when all parties consistently choose to cooperate, they secure the highest mutual payoff. In geopolitical terms, this can be likened to two primary pathways towards peace: a ceasefire along existing front lines or a full-fledged peace agreement negotiated through diplomacy. Both outcomes require not merely the absence of aggression, but genuine alignment of interests and mutual confidence that cooperation will be honoured. However, as of June 2025, no such alignment was evident in the Russian–Ukrainian context. Despite periodic statements suggesting openness to negotiation, Russia's declarations were cloaked in conditions and demands aimed at eliminating perceived fictional sources of conflict. Such conditions – often broad and shifting – made genuine cooperation unattainable. The Russian stance highlighted a central challenge of the Stag Hunt Game: cooperation can only emerge when both sides clearly commit to a shared objective and believe that the other party will not defect. This strategic complexity is further illustrated by negotiations hosted in Türkiye. While these sessions generated considerable media attention and superficial gestures towards peace, there was virtually no substantive convergence in negotiating positions. Despite the presence of mediators and external actors seeking to bridge gaps, the fundamental interests of the two primary belligerents remained irreconcilable. In Stag Hunt terms, the absence of a clear, shared "stag" – i.e., a goal that both sides could jointly pursue – doomed these talks to stalemate.

What makes the Stag Hunt Game particularly insightful is how it underscores the limitations of relying solely on a state's past behaviours or traditional strategic inclinations. Whereas historical patterns might help predict behaviour in simpler or more bipolar conflicts, modern geopolitical confrontations are increasingly fragmented. States are driven by a web of overlapping interests, alliances, domestic political considerations, and external pressures. Even longstanding behavioural patterns can become unreliable guides when new variables disrupt the strategic calculus.

The results of the Axelrod tournament simulations, summarised in Table 3.2, shed light on which strategies might theoretically thrive in such an environment. Unsurprisingly, the Cooperator strategy dominates the rankings in long-term games. Alongside Cooperator, strategies such as Generic Memory Two Player also perform well. The GTFT strategy, which tempers retaliatory actions with occasional forgiveness, likewise ranks highly. These dynamics in the Stag Hunt Game mirror the strategic tendencies already described for the major players in the Chicken Game scenario. While the underlying strategic inclinations of each state remain broadly consistent across different games, the effectiveness of these strategies varies depending on the specific context. In the Stag Hunt context, the success of even cooperative strategies hinges on mutual trust and shared objectives – conditions notably absent in the Russian–Ukrainian negotiations as of mid-2025. Therefore, these strategies illuminate why even in a game designed to favour cooperation, like the Stag Hunt, sustained peace remains elusive when trust is absent and strategic objectives diverge. The fragmented interests and complex calculations of modern actors make the establishment of a shared goal – the proverbial stag – increasingly difficult. Until such convergence emerges, even repeated diplomatic overtures risk stalling in mutual suspicion and misaligned incentives. Thus, the Stag Hunt model not only underscores the theoretical conditions for peace but also exposes why, despite numerous negotiations and shifting tactical signals, the Russian–Ukrainian war persists without resolution. As of mid-2025, the geopolitical environment remains one where cooperation, though theoretically optimal, continues to be undermined by profound strategic discord.

3.1.3 Strategic Dynamics Under Mistrust and Asymmetry: Lessons from Game Theory

If we turn our attention to the world modelled by the Prisoner's Dilemma, the outcomes and strategic dynamics differ markedly from those in the Chicken or Stag Hunt Game. In the short term, stability and consistency – embodied in long-cycle behavioural patterns – tend to yield success. However, as interactions extend into the medium and long term, the advantage shifts towards strategies rooted in bipolarity and strategic alliances, where major players balance cooperation and confrontation to secure their interests (Table 3.3). This observation resonates with John Nash's original conception of equilibrium for the Prisoner's Dilemma, which rightly perceives the world as a place where mutual mistrust and cautious cooperation define interactions. Yet, the geopolitical landscape in 2025 looks significantly different. Modern digital societies, characterised by rapid, multi-channel interactions and interconnected economies, no longer neatly fit the classic notion of isolated "prisoners" locked in bilateral negotiations. Nevertheless, considering a hypothetical return to older modes of political and economic behaviour provides valuable insights into strategic decision-making under conditions of fundamental mistrust and institutional fragility.

Table 3.3 The World of "Prisoners": Ranking of Winners

Game = Prisoner's Dilemma, Turns = 10, Noise = 0.1	*Game = Prisoner's Dilemma, Turns = 50, Noise = 0.1*	*Game = Prisoner's Dilemma, Turns = 300, Noise = 0.1*
Cycler CCCCCD, Generic Memory Two Player, Cooperator,GTFT, Cycler CCCDCD, Resurrection, Generic Memory One Player, Tit For Tat, Bush Mosteller, Hard Tit For Tat, Cycler DDC, Handshake, Collective Strategy	Generic Memory Two Player, Cooperator, Cycler CCCCCD, Cycler CCCDCD, GTFT, Tit For Tat, Bush Mosteller, Generic Memory One Player, Resurrection, Hard Tit For Tat, Cycler DDC, Handshake, Collective Strategy	Generic Memory Two Player, Cooperator, Cycler CCCCCD, GTFT, Cycler CCCDCD, Tit For Tat, Generic Memory One Player, Resurrection, Bush Mosteller, Cycler DDC, Hard Tit For Tat, Handshake, Collective Strategy

Source: Own elaboration based on outcomes from the Axelrod tournament simulations.

Table 3.3 presents the rankings of strategies in the Prisoner's Dilemma under various game lengths. The leading strategies across all time horizons tend to blend memory, flexibility, and cautious cooperation. The Generic Memory Two Player strategy consistently ranks at the top, demonstrating the effectiveness of recalling past interactions and adjusting behaviour accordingly. Likewise, the Cooperator strategy remains competitive, especially over longer timeframes, indicating that sustained cooperation can be advantageous – provided mutual trust can be established. By contrast, strategies like Tit For Tat, once celebrated for their simplicity and effectiveness, fare poorly in this environment. In a world defined by deep suspicion, eroded associativity, and weak international institutions, rigid retaliation leaves little room for strategic manoeuvring or diplomatic recovery, explaining its lower rankings in these simulations. This landscape underscores why traditional American foreign policy, with its inclination towards managing bipolar relations (whether in balancing Russia or, increasingly, negotiating with China), can appear effective over the medium and long term. Under the logic of the Prisoner's Dilemma, maintaining clear alliances and predictable partnerships offers stability and leverage in an otherwise uncertain environment.

Yet, the Prisoner's Dilemma alone cannot fully capture the intricacies of contemporary geopolitics. Each strategic game – whether the Chicken Game, the Stag Hunt, or the Prisoner's Dilemma – highlights different facets of international relations. In reality, global affairs often represent a complex hybrid of these dynamics, making definitive conclusions about which model best describes the global arena in mid-2025 inherently difficult and ultimately a matter for political scientists and policymakers.

An additional layer of complexity arises when considering the asymmetric distribution of power on the global stage. Conceptualising this distribution as an Asymmetric Subordinate Game offers insight into how states divide into those genuinely empowered to shape international norms and those compelled to adapt. Figure 3.1, derived from simulations of this asymmetric game, vividly illustrates these dynamics. In such scenarios, dominant players employ strategies that combine patience and cyclical engagement, carefully choosing moments to cooperate or defect based on evolving circumstances.

China's strategic behaviour exemplifies this cyclical patience. Often described metaphorically as "watching the fire from the opposite shore", China tends to adopt a wait-and-see approach, avoiding immediate interventions until conditions align optimally with its interests. This is strategically mirrored in high-performing cyclic strategies like Cycler CCCCCD, which blend periods of cooperation with calculated, limited defections designed to probe vulnerabilities or test red lines without severing cooperative relationships altogether. Notably, Tit For Tat emerges as an absolute loser in this model of geopolitical competition, reinforcing the notion that the world of 2025 demands strategies far more nuanced than simple reciprocal responses. Effective statecraft now hinges on the capacity to assess risk levels, allocate resources judiciously, and sustain influence over extended time horizons.

Taken together, our models – the Prisoner's Dilemma, the Chicken Game, the Stag Hunt, and the Asymmetric Subordinate Game – collectively illustrate that strategic flexibility and calibrated responses are critical. Different time horizons and contexts necessitate different dominant strategies. This underscores a central lesson for contemporary geopolitics: there is no single, universally superior strategy. Instead, successful navigation

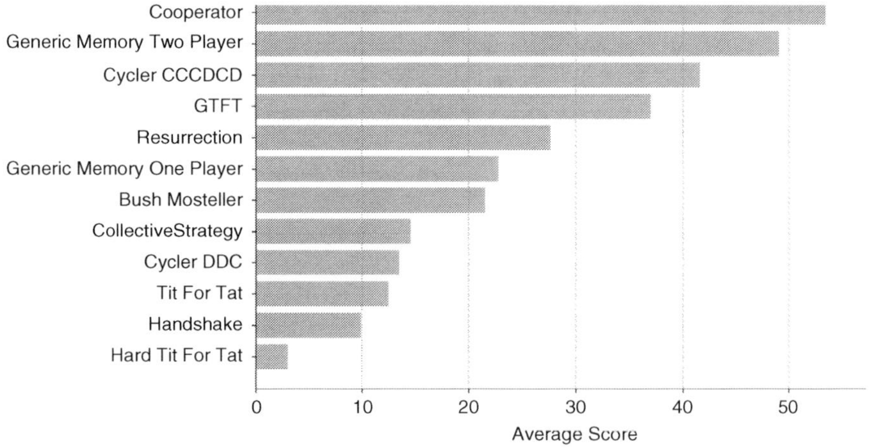

Figure 3.1 Strategic Performance in the Asymmetric Subordinate Game Reflecting 2025 Power Dynamics.

Source: Own elaboration by using Python packages.

of international relations requires dynamic adaptation, informed by both historical experience and real-time signals from an increasingly complex and interconnected world. The most critical factor in developing effective strategies lies in accurately assessing the inherent risk levels in any given situation and determining the availability of the influence and resources required to sustain a chosen course over the long term. As our findings indicate, employing different strategic approaches is not merely permissible but rational, depending on the time horizon and specific geopolitical context under consideration.

3.1.4 Economic Signatures of Strategy: Portfolio Composition Under Geopolitical Shifts

While strategic games provide valuable insights into how nations navigate geopolitical risks and alliances, it is equally crucial to examine how these strategic choices manifest in the economic sphere. Financial markets often serve as a sensitive barometer of geopolitical tensions, revealing how states translate security concerns, industrial priorities, and technological ambitions into concrete economic actions. Equity markets, in particular, can reflect the economic signatures of national strategies, showing where governments and investors alike anticipate future risks and opportunities. Thus, to complement the game-theoretic analysis, the following section explores how geopolitical dynamics shape the composition of optimal stock portfolios, focusing on the cases of China and Japan across different geopolitical contexts (Table 3.4). Notably, the period between February and May 2025 was marked by heightened geopolitical uncertainty, including renewed tariff threats and partial decoupling of longstanding economic partnerships (World Bank, 2025). Against this backdrop, the optimal portfolio structures in both Chinese and Japanese equity markets shifted significantly, mirroring their distinct national strategies (Roubini, 2022).

During this turbulent early 2025 period, China's optimal portfolio achieved an exceptionally high expected annual return of 79.1%, coupled with moderate volatility of 18.8%, yielding a Sharpe Ratio of 4.22 (Table 3.4). However, this strong performance reflected a marked concentration in industries aligned with national strategic goals (OECD, 2023b). Chinese portfolios were heavily weighted towards sectors deemed vital for national security, technological self-sufficiency, and industrial resilience. Core holdings included AECC SCI AND TECH, involved in aircraft engine development and emblematic of China's ambitions for self-reliance in advanced manufacturing and defence technologies (Kendall-Taylor et al., 2020); Air China, reflecting the geopolitical significance of connectivity and logistics for initiatives such as the Belt and Road (Rolland, 2020); and the Agricultural Bank of China, highlighting the enduring role of state-owned banks in maintaining financial stability and policy implementation (Naughton, 2021). ADD Industry's presence underscores the strategic relevance of automotive and industrial supply chains,

Table 3.4 Optimal Stock Portfolios for China and Japan During Different Geopolitical Contexts

Country	*Period*	*Expected Annual Return (%)*	*Annual Volatility (%)*	*Sharpe Ratio*	*Selected Companies & Industries*
China	February–May 2025	79.1	18.8	4.22	AECC SCI AND TECH (aircraft engines), Air China (airlines), Agricultural Bank of China (banking), ADD Industry (vehicle components)
China	2013–2022	17.6	30.0	0.52	Angel Yeast (packaged foods), AECC Aviation Power (aerospace), Agricultural Bank of China (banking), Advanced Micro-Fabrication Equipment (semiconductors)
Japan	February–May 2025	96.8	23.5	4.13	Daiichi Sankyo (pharma), CyberAgent (digital media), Aeon (retail), Chubu Electric Power (energy)
Japan	2013–2022	41.9	27.9	1.43	Advantest (semiconductors), Daiichi Sankyo (pharma), Ajinomoto (food), Dai-ichi Life Holdings (insurance)

Source: Own elaboration.

Note: Data reflect optimal portfolios calculated for China and Japan in two distinct geopolitical periods: the years before the Russian–Ukrainian war (2013–2022) and the period of heightened geopolitical tensions from February to May 2025, including trade disruptions and shifting alliances. Expected returns, volatility, and Sharpe Ratios are derived from historical price data sourced from Yahoo Finance and reflect theoretical portfolio optimisation results, not investment recommendations.

particularly amid fears of Western decoupling (US-China Economic and Security Review Commission, 2023).

In contrast, Japan's optimal portfolio during the same period displayed an even higher expected annual return of 96.8%, with volatility at 23.5% and a Sharpe Ratio of 4.13 (Table 3.4). This Japanese portfolio leaned strongly towards sectors associated with consumer welfare, technological innovation, and societal infrastructure – a pattern consistent with Japan's economic strategies (METI, 2024). Key Japanese holdings included Daiichi Sankyo, underscoring the importance of pharmaceuticals and healthcare exports (JETRO, 2023); CyberAgent, reflecting Japan's vibrant digital economy and the global appeal of its cultural industries (Fukuyama, 2022); Aeon, symbolising deep regional integration through retail operations in Japan, China, and ASEAN nations (World Bank, 2024); and Chubu Electric Power, indicative of Japan's ongoing emphasis on energy diversification and security following the lessons of the Fukushima disaster (IEA, 2023).

A retrospective look at the period before the Russian–Ukrainian war (2013–2022) highlights how relative geopolitical stability shaped different investment dynamics (Table 3.4). During this decade, Japan's optimal portfolio achieved an expected annual return of 41.9%, with volatility of 27.9% and a Sharpe Ratio of 1.43. Holdings in this period reflected Japan's steady emphasis on technology and consumer-oriented industries. Companies such as Advantest signalled Japan's leading role in semiconductor testing equipment, crucial for technological sovereignty (SIA, 2022), while Ajinomoto represented strengths in food sciences and biotechnology, echoing Japan's global consumer brand presence. The presence of Dai-ichi Life Holdings highlighted the demographic and social dimensions of Japan's economic fabric (METI, 2022).

Conversely, China's pre-war portfolio was notably more conservative, with an expected annual return of 17.6%, volatility of 30.0%, and a modest Sharpe Ratio of 0.52. The composition included companies like Angel Yeast, reflecting stable domestic consumption; AECC Aviation Power, emphasising the enduring strategic focus on defence technologies; and Advanced Micro-Fabrication Equipment, foreshadowing China's ambitions in achieving semiconductor self-sufficiency (CSIS, 2023). These more restrained figures align with structural transitions underway in China's economy during that decade, balancing rapid growth with emerging vulnerabilities (Naughton, 2021).

Taken together, these findings reveal how geopolitics and financial markets intersect. Japan has consistently directed its economic focus towards sectors that directly enhance quality of life, technological progress, and international cooperation, consistent with its geopolitical identity as a democratic, innovation-driven economy (OECD, 2023a). China, in contrast, has demonstrated an increasingly strategic consolidation around industries critical for national security, technological independence, and economic resilience, particularly during periods of crisis (Li, 2021; Rolland, 2020). The sharp increase in Sharpe Ratios in early 2025 underscores heightened market concentration on domestic priorities and reduced tolerance for geopolitical risk, reflecting broader global trends of geopolitical fragmentation and shifting alliances (Bremmer, 2022; World Bank, 2025). This analysis reinforces that stock markets, while financial in nature, serve as highly sensitive indicators of national strategic priorities and geopolitical fault lines. For policymakers and investors alike, changes in optimal portfolio structures offer a crucial lens through which to anticipate economic resilience, industrial policy directions, and the evolving dynamics of global competitiveness (see OECD, 2023a; World Bank, 2025).

3.2 Multidimensional Cluster Analysis and the Landscape of National Competitiveness

The preceding analysis underscored how geopolitical tensions and strategic decision-making profoundly shape national trajectories, influencing both political behaviour and economic structures. Game-theoretic models such as the Chicken Game, Stag Hunt, and Prisoner's Dilemma illustrate that state strategies are neither uniform nor static, but evolve in response to shifting risks, alliances, and opportunities. Simultaneously, evidence from financial markets reveals how these strategic choices manifest in concrete economic patterns, offering valuable signals about national priorities and resilience. Yet to fully understand national competitiveness in the 21st century, it is essential to move beyond individual games or market signals and examine the multidimensional realities that underpin state strategies. Competitiveness is shaped not only by geopolitical manoeuvres but also by how nations invest in innovation, manage environmental challenges, and foster social cohesion. While traditional economic metrics such as GDP remain central to assessing national performance, there is growing recognition that sustainable development and geopolitical competitiveness depend on a broader set of factors. Strategic planning at the national level increasingly integrates diverse indicators, encompassing not only the scale of economic output but also how resources are allocated, how environmental impacts are managed, and how societies perceive their own well-being.

This part takes a multidimensional perspective on national strategies, employing advanced cluster analysis to identify patterns across three critical domains: research and development (R&D) funding structures, carbon dioxide (CO_2) emission profiles, and indicators of subjective well-being. These dimensions capture the interplay between technological innovation, environmental sustainability, and social cohesion – three pillars widely regarded as essential for resilience and prosperity in the 21st century (see OECD, 2023a; UNDP, 2022). By systematically examining R&D funding profiles, we reveal how different models of innovation finance reflect broader strategic choices, ranging from market-driven approaches to state-led interventions. Analysis of CO_2 emissions offers insights into how countries balance economic growth with climate commitments, highlighting tensions and trade-offs inherent in sustainable development. Finally, exploring clusters based on happiness and related social indicators illustrates that societal progress extends far beyond material wealth, encompassing factors like institutional trust, social support, and perceived freedom. Understanding these strategic clusters provides valuable insights for policymakers, researchers, and international organisations seeking to navigate the complex challenges of the 21st century. The findings presented in this part aim to support more informed decisions, enabling nations to align their development trajectories with both global sustainability goals and the aspirations of their populations.

3.2.1 R&D Funding Profiles and Their Strategic Implications

Across the world, governments increasingly recognise that their economic strength and global influence depend heavily on investments in R&D. Innovations born in laboratories and research centres often become the driving force behind entire industries, helping countries stay competitive, create new jobs, and reduce dependency on foreign technology. However, it's not just the size of R&D spending that matters – it's equally important who is paying for it.

There are essentially two extremes in how nations fund R&D. One is a decentralised approach, where private companies and universities are the main investors. In such systems, research tends to be dynamic, closely linked to market demands, and more focused on civilian applications. This is typical of advanced economies where private businesses see R&D as a critical investment for future profits, and universities actively contribute to innovation.

At the other end of the spectrum is a centralised model, where the government controls most of the spending on R&D. While this can lead to large-scale, spectacular projects – such as national space programmes – it often means that the overall R&D ecosystem is less flexible, less innovative, and more vulnerable to political shifts. For example, Russia's once-renowned space programme has struggled in recent years, demonstrating the risks of relying too heavily on centralised control.

From a strategic point of view, nations have to decide which path to follow: should they prioritise business and academia? Should they rely primarily on government funding? Or should they aim for a balance among different funding sources?

The data behind this analysis comes from the OECD (2022a, 2022b). In the tables and figures, we use the following abbreviations:

- GERDP stands for Gross Domestic Expenditure on R&D as a percentage of GDP. Essentially, it measures how much of a country's economy is devoted to R&D.
- BERDP means Business Expenditure on R&D (also as a percentage of GDP). This shows how much the private sector is contributing to research efforts.
- HERDP represents Higher Education Expenditure on R&D, measuring how much universities and colleges invest in research.
- GOVERDP stands for Government Expenditure on R&D, capturing how much the state itself directly spends on research.
- PSERDP refers to Public Sector Expenditure on R&D, including spending by publicly funded institutions outside of direct government ministries (such as public hospitals, research centres linked to state-owned enterprises, and other non-market institutions).

- PS refers to the gross value added of the public sector, expressed in million US dollars (USD).
- The final "P" signals that it's expressed as a percentage of GDP, that is why, the figures are relative to the size of the economy (GDP), making it possible to compare small and large countries fairly.

To examine how different countries allocate resources to R&D, we collected data from the OECD covering various expenditure indicators across sectors. These figures provide the empirical foundation for our cluster analysis, allowing us to identify patterns of national R&D funding and their strategic implications. Table 3.5 presents these indicators for a broad set of countries, showing the relative share of R&D expenditure funded by business enterprises, higher education, government, and the broader public sector, all expressed as a percentage of GDP. In addition, the table includes the size of the public sector and the value added by manufacturing as a share of GDP, providing further context for each country's economic structure.

This dataset (Table 3.5) serves as the basis for our subsequent cluster analysis – a tool that groups countries together based on how similar they are across several factors – in this case, the different sources of R&D funding. Countries placed in the same cluster have similar funding structures and strategic approaches, while countries in different clusters are more distinct from each other. By comparing these clusters, we can better understand the strategic choices nations make in organising their research ecosystems and assess the implications for their competitiveness and innovation capacity.

First, we normalised all the data so that differences in the absolute size of economies wouldn't dominate the analysis. Without this step, large countries like the USA or China would automatically appear "important" just because of their sheer size, not because of how they allocate their R&D spending. We then used the NbClust library in the R programming environment to help determine how many clusters made the most sense statistically. Different mathematical criteria suggested different numbers of clusters. Nine methods suggested that dividing the world into just two clusters was optimal. Others proposed three, four, five, or even as many as ten clusters. Given these mixed signals, we decided to explore both a simple division into two clusters and a more detailed breakdown into six clusters. Each approach provides unique insights.

When we grouped countries into just two clusters, the world divided roughly as follows (Figure 3.2; Table 3.6):

- Cluster 1 includes countries like Germany, Finland, Austria, South Korea et al., where R&D spending is relatively high, and a significant share comes from business and academia. Governments still play a role, but they're not the dominant force.
- Cluster 2 includes countries like China, Chile, Slovak Republic, Türkiye, Mexico et al., where the government is the primary driver of R&D spending, and private-sector involvement is smaller.

Table 3.5 R&D Expenditure Indicators and Industrial Value Added by Country (2020)

Indicator	*GERDP*	*BERDP*	*HERDP*	*GOVERDP*	*PSERDP*	*PS (mln.)*	*VAE (% of GDP)*
Australia	2,19	1,23	0,58	0,24	0,86	1046	12,51
Austria	2,86	1,95	0,73	0,15	0,87	227	31,64
Belgium	2,24	1,52	0,52	0,18	0,7	395	35,03
Canada	1,69	0,88	0,65	0,15	0,8	1120	19,54
Chile	0,35	0,11	0,12	0,01	0,14	91	18,46
Czech Republic	1,88	1,01	0,52	0,35	0,86	147	39,39
Denmark	2,98	1,96	0,95	0,07	1,01	286	32,01
Estonia	2,19	1,26	0,7	0,2	0,91	27	33,22
Finland	3,55	2,44	0,77	0,32	1,09	187	33,78
France	2,29	1,48	0,47	0,31	0,78	1330	24,75
Germany	2,98	2,02	0,53	0,43	0,96	1525	26,64
Hungary	1,3	0,85	0,24	0,19	0,43	73	39,91
Iceland	2,61	1,38	0,69	0,46	1,15	25	36,55
Ireland	1,66	1,2	0,38	0,08	0,46	154	42,28
Israel	3,93	3,32	0,49	0,07	0,57	201	30,59
Italy	1,27	0,69	0,36	0,17	0,54	1087	20,08
Japan	3,35	2,57	0,45	0,29	0,74	889	14,79
South Korea	4,36	3,4	0,41	0,49	0,91	773	40,64
Luxembourg	1,46	1	0,18	0,28	0,46	17	58,89
Mexico	0,43	0,17	0,12	0,13	0,25	128	30,33
Netherlands	2,16	1,22	0,7	0,23	0,94	655	35,91
New Zealand	1,26	0,57	0,4	0,29	0,69	139	18,41
Norway	1,65	0,86	0,52	0,27	0,79	186	15,3
Poland	0,9	0,33	0,31	0,25	0,56	292	27,89
Portugal	1,5	0,7	0,58	0,1	0,68	297	32,41
Slovak Republic	0,82	0,34	0,28	0,2	0,48	26	44,35
Slovenia	2,63	1,99	0,29	0,34	0,64	47	34,4
Spain	1,3	0,69	0,36	0,25	0,61	1310	20,73
Sweden	3,41	2,31	0,92	0,16	1,09	416	33,62
Switzerland	2,87	2,17	0,88	0,02	0,9	429	28,47
Türkiye	0,92	0,42	0,4	0,1	0,51	233	21,79
United Kingdom	1,73	1,1	0,46	0,14	0,6	1856	17,31
United States	2,79	1,95	0,39	0,34	0,73	6001	11,29
China	1,98	1,51	0,15	0,32	0,47	3863	32,63

Source: Data on research and development (R&D) expenditure indicators are from OECD (2022a). Data on Value Added in Manufacturing (VAE) are from OECD (2022b).

Note: Indicators include Gross Domestic Expenditure on R&D (GERDP), Business Expenditure on R&D (BERDP), Higher Education Expenditure on R&D (HERDP), Government Expenditure on R&D (GOVERDP), Public Sector Expenditure on R&D (PSERDP), Gross Value Added of the Public Sector (PS) and Value Added in Manufacturing (VAE) as a percentage of GDP.

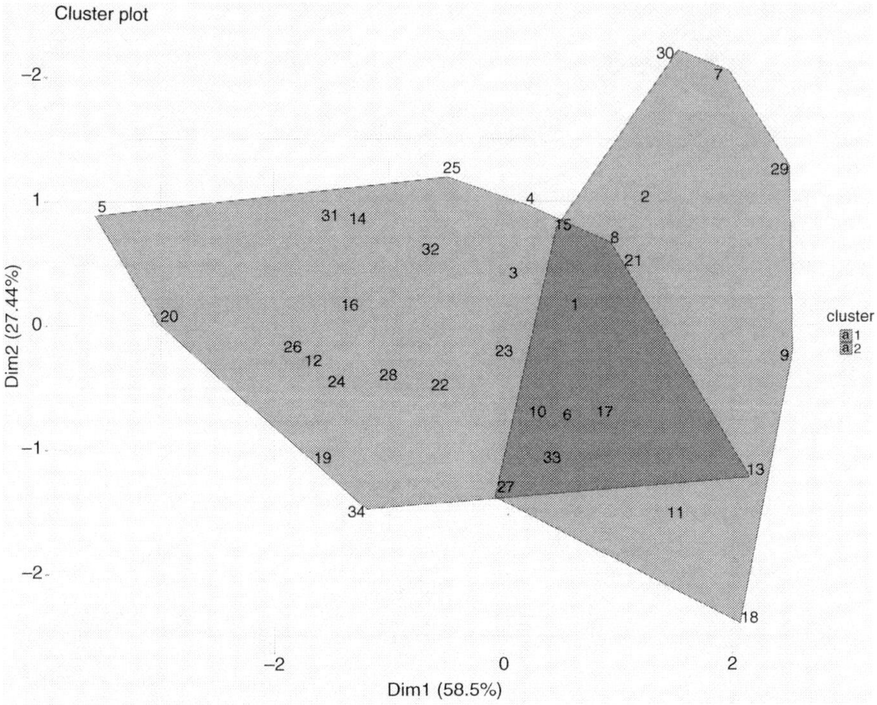

Figure 3.2 Two-Cluster Solution for Countries Based on R&D Investment Structure.

Source: Own elaboration using NbClust in R.

Notes: Results are based on k-means clustering of normalised R&D expenditure data from Table 3.5. The numbers displayed in the figure represent country codes. Clustering performed using the NbClust package in R, indicating two optimal groups reflecting centralised vs. decentralised innovation funding structures.

Table 3.6 Average Normalised Values of R&D Funding Indicators and Economic Variables for Two Clusters

Cluster	*GERDP*	*BERDP*	*HERDP*	*GOVERDP*	*PSERDP*	*GDPP*	*VAE*	*SD*
1	0.594	0.528	0.588	0.507	0.718	0.258	0.362	0.517
2	0.213	0.177	0.229	0.353	0.348	0.346	0.401	0.579

Source: Own calculations based on Table 3.5, using NbClust in R.

This essentially divides the world into economies where innovation is driven by decentralised, diverse players, and economies where the state orchestrates innovation centrally. Interestingly, the analysis revealed that Cluster 2 – despite lower business participation – achieved higher value added for business in certain circumstances. This might appear paradoxical. However, in economies with strong state intervention, the government can sometimes channel resources more effectively into targeted sectors. Yet, this advantage may not be sustainable due to risks like inefficiency, corruption, or geopolitical shocks. Thus, even highly innovative economies may belong to Cluster 2 when public-sector influence on R&D is substantial, highlighting that cluster membership reflects funding patterns rather than a simple measure of innovation capacity. Moreover, the caution here is that different countries calculate value added in diverse ways (e.g., Chinese GAAP differs from Western accounting standards), so comparisons must be interpreted carefully.

Dividing the world into six clusters paints a much more nuanced picture of how nations fund R&D. In Figure 3.3, we visualise the result of dividing 34 countries into six clusters using the k-means method. Each "cloud" shows one cluster of countries that share similar patterns in how they finance R&D.

These clusters reveal significant differences in how countries balance the contributions of business, government, higher education, and public-sector institutions. In some countries, private businesses and universities are the primary drivers of R&D investment, creating systems that are dynamic, market-oriented, and closely tied to technological trends. Sweden is an example

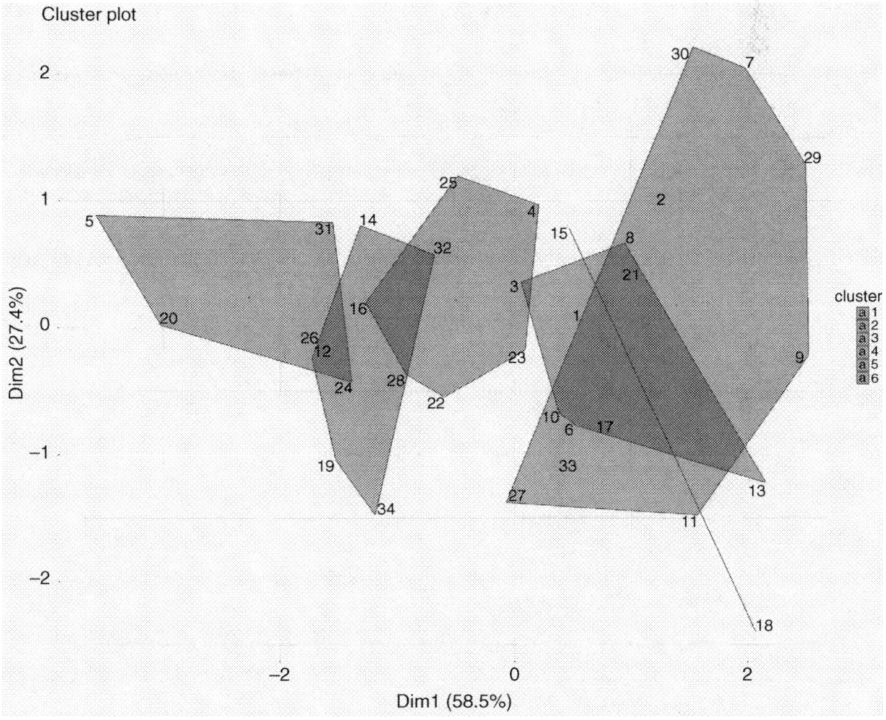

Figure 3.3 Six-Cluster Segmentation of Countries by R&D Funding Profiles.

Source: Own elaboration using NbClust in R.

Notes: Six-cluster segmentation was visualised using k-means algorithm on normalised indicators from Table 3.5. Countries represented by their assigned cluster centroids. Data sourced from OECD (2022a).

of this model, where innovation thrives on strong business engagement and academic research excellence. In other places, government remains the dominant force behind R&D spending. Here, research agendas often reflect national priorities, and large-scale public projects can shape entire industries. China exemplifies this approach, with significant state-led initiatives steering technological progress, although sometimes at the expense of flexibility and market responsiveness. A third group of countries operates on a more balanced model, where responsibility for funding R&D is shared relatively evenly among businesses, government, universities, and public-sector institutions. Japan and USA fall into this category, maintaining strong engagement from both private and public actors, which creates a diversified ecosystem for innovation. Beyond these broad distinctions, the six-cluster analysis shows even greater diversity. Some clusters gather countries with moderate, but well-distributed R&D spending across all sectors, offering stability but sometimes lacking the dynamism needed for global leadership. Others consist of nations with low overall investment in R&D, raising concerns about long-term competitiveness, despite sometimes strong industrial bases or relatively high living standards. Finally, certain clusters bring together countries where high public-sector and government involvement coexists with significant business investment, reflecting complex strategies to foster innovation while maintaining state influence.

Our next step was to calculate and analyse the cluster centres presented in Table 3.7. The numeric values in this table represent the average normalised scores for each indicator within a cluster. For example, Cluster 2 has the highest average values for business and higher education funding (BERDP and HERDP), suggesting strong private-sector and academic involvement in R&D. Countries like France and Germany exemplify this pattern, combining robust private investment with significant contributions from universities

Table 3.7 Average Normalised Values of R&D Funding Indicators and Economic Variables for Six Clusters

Cluster	*GERDP*	*BERDP*	*HERDP*	*GOVERDP*	*PSERDP*	*GDPP*	*VAE*	*SD*
1	0.442	0.395	0.375	0.470	0.524	0.136	0.255	0.759
2	0.713	0.678	0.812	0.175	0.741	0.297	0.420	0.473
3	0.377	0.272	0.556	0.494	0.689	0.299	0.286	0.379
4	0.239	0.224	0.181	0.370	0.314	0.239	0.737	0.498
5	0.141	0.121	0.120	0.317	0.244	0.611	0.314	0.520
6	0.754	0.669	0.578	0.865	0.879	0.298	0.486	0.500

Source: Own elaboration based on NbClust of R.

Notes: Values represent normalised cluster centroids rounded to three decimal places.

GERDP – Gross Domestic Expenditure on R&D as % of GDP; BERDP – Business Expenditure on R&D; HERDP – Higher Education Expenditure on R&D; GOVERDP – Government Expenditure on R&D; PSERDP – Public Sector Expenditure on R&D; GDPP – GDP per capita; VAE – Value Added in Manufacturing as % of GDP; SD – Standard deviation indicating variability around the cluster centroid.

and public research institutions. In contrast, Cluster 5 reflects nations with the lowest levels of R&D spending across all sectors. Yet, interestingly, some of these countries still achieve relatively high GDP per capita, indicating that economic prosperity does not automatically translate into significant R&D investment. Chile and Mexico are typical representatives of this group, where structural challenges or policy choices limit innovation spending despite broader economic development. Cluster 6 is characterised by high government and public-sector spending, and in some cases, significant business R&D investment as well. Countries like China and South Korea fall into this cluster, reflecting strong state involvement alongside dynamic private sectors. However, this group shows higher internal variability (standard deviation [SD]), indicating differing national strategies even under a broadly similar funding model.

To better understand these differences, we ranked the clusters according to how dominant each funding source is, as presented in Table 3.8. This ranking provides insight into the strategic orientation of each cluster:

- Cluster 1 exhibits moderate and balanced R&D funding across all sectors, with average internal variability (SD).
- Cluster 2 combines high levels of business, higher education, and public-sector R&D funding, while the government's direct role remains smaller. The lower SD in this cluster indicates that countries here form a relatively homogeneous group in their funding patterns.
- Cluster 3 has a balanced R&D profile but with a higher share of public-sector involvement.
- Cluster 4 stands out for lower overall R&D spending, yet these countries often record higher Value Added in Manufacturing (VAE). This suggests

Table 3.8 Ranking of Clusters by Dominant R&D Funding Sources

Cluster (e.g., State)	*Business Rank*	*Higher Education Rank*	*Government Rank*	*Public Sector Rank*
1 (incl. Australia)	3rd	4th	3rd	4th
2 (incl. France)	1st	1st	6th	2nd
3 (incl. Estonia)	4th	3rd	2nd	3rd
4 (incl. Hungary)	5th	5th	4th	5th
5 (incl. Chile)	6th	6th	5th	6th
6 (incl. China)	2nd	2nd	1st	1st

Source: Own elaboration.

Notes: Ranks indicate relative magnitude of R&D funding sourced from each sector, where 1 = highest and 6 = lowest, based on cluster centroids shown in Table 3.6.

The countries correspond to the six-cluster solution shown in Figure 3.3. However, cluster membership is determined by multidimensional distance to cluster centroids, not strictly by matching individual indicator levels. Therefore, some countries (e.g., France in Cluster 2) may seem less typical when compared to average values in Table 3.7. This is not a mistake but a normal feature of clustering results.

a strong industrial base capable of generating competitiveness despite limited research investment. However, the higher SD signals considerable diversity within this group, indicating that policy strategies might need to be tailored individually.

- Cluster 5 shows the lowest R&D expenditure levels across all sectors. Nevertheless, some countries within this group enjoy relatively high GDP per capita, underlining that wealth alone does not guarantee strong R&D engagement. The low SD suggests that this group is fairly consistent in its funding patterns.
- Cluster 6 is notable for significant government and public-sector investment and, in some cases, substantial business R&D. The higher SD reflects internal differences among these countries, pointing to varied strategic approaches to combining public and private innovation efforts.

These differences imply distinct strategic philosophies among nations (Table 3.9). This segmentation is critical because the mix of R&D funding sources influences not only the nature and direction of technological progress but also broader aspects such as economic resilience, capacity for crisis adaptation, and geopolitical leverage. The way countries allocate resources to R&D shapes their ability to remain competitive in a rapidly changing global environment. To better understand how these funding profiles connect to overall national competitiveness, Table 3.9 combines the R&D cluster classification with average rankings from the Legatum Prosperity Index (Legatum, 2023), the IMD World Competitiveness Ranking (IMD, 2023), and the Global Innovation Index (WIPO, 2023). These average ranks provide a comparative snapshot, highlighting how different funding models may correlate with broader economic and innovation performance on the global stage.

Therefore, Cluster 1 brings together countries with moderate R&D spending that is spread quite evenly across business, higher education, government, and public-sector sources. Such a balanced funding pattern hints at resilience and the ability to adapt to shocks, although many of these nations might still have untapped potential in areas like high-tech industries where private-sector investment could play a bigger role (OECD, 2023a; European Commission, 2022). Interestingly, these countries hold respectable positions in global standings – averaging around 21st to 23rd place across indices like the Legatum Prosperity Index, IMD Competitiveness Ranking, and Global Innovation Index. This suggests that while they may not be the world's absolute frontrunners, their diversified approach has ensured a solid footing in both economic and innovation terms. Yet, differences remain among them, reflecting unique national contexts that shape how each pursues competitiveness (Archibugi & Filippetti, 2018).

Cluster 2, on the other hand, gathers countries that lean strongly on business and higher education to fuel R&D, with comparatively less direct government funding. Here, innovation ecosystems are clearly driven by close partnerships between private industry, universities, and public research

Table 3.9 Average Competitiveness and Innovation Rankings of Countries Across R&D Clusters (2023)

Cluster	*Countries*	*Avg. Legatum Rank*	*Avg. IMD Rank*	*Avg. GII Rank*
1 – Moderate and balanced funding	Australia, Canada, New Zealand, United Kingdom, Norway, Italy, Spain, Portugal, Czech Republic, Ireland, Estonia	16.0	22.2	22.1
2 – High business & higher education funding, lower government role	Japan, France, United States, Belgium, Slovenia, Netherlands, Denmark, Sweden, Switzerland, Germany, Finland, Iceland	12.8	15.5	10.9
3 – Balanced, stronger public sector	Austria, Israel, Estonia, Poland	28.8	32.4	24.2
4 – Lower R&D spending but higher VAE	Ireland, Slovak Republic, Hungary, Luxembourg, Portugal	23.2	33.2	30.0
5 – Lowest R&D, sometimes high GDP per capita	Chile, Mexico, Türkiye	57.3	50.7	49.7
6 – High government and public-sector spending, sometimes strong business R&D	South Korea, China	41.5	24.5	11.0

Source: Own elaboration.

Notes: Countries have been assigned to clusters based on their R&D indicators from Table 3.5, using the cluster centroids presented in Table 3.7. Cluster membership is determined by calculating multidimensional distances to cluster centroids, so not all countries fit perfectly into a single funding pattern. Averages reflect mean country ranks in the Legatum Prosperity 2023, IMD 2023, and GII 2023 indices for each R&D cluster. Lower numbers indicate better competitiveness or innovation performance. Cluster averages were calculated as arithmetic means across countries assigned to each R&D cluster.

organisations (OECD, 2023b; WIPO, 2023). What's remarkable is how consistently these countries dominate global rankings, securing average spots around 12th to 15th place across all three indices. Such high positions underscore how well this model translates into real-world competitiveness, reflecting strong capacity to transform research into marketable solutions (European Commission, 2022; Edler & Fagerberg, 2017). It's a group that shows a shared vision and strategic coherence, which is likely a major factor behind their leadership in innovation and prosperity.

Cluster 3 paints a different picture. These countries maintain a balanced mix of R&D funding but lean more heavily on the public sector. This reliance ensures stability and sustained investment in research but could also risk becoming a bottleneck if private enterprise doesn't step up to commercialise innovation and drive economic value (OECD, 2023b). On the world stage, these nations sit comfortably mid-table, with average rankings around 27th to 31st across the three indices. While not lagging far behind, this suggests they might benefit from fostering stronger public-private partnerships to move higher up the ladder (Archibugi & Filippetti, 2018).

Cluster 4 consists of countries with generally lower levels of R&D spending. Still, many remain competitive thanks to strong manufacturing sectors, which contribute significantly to their economies despite modest research budgets (OECD, 2023a; 2023b); Veugelers, 2015). However, this industrial strength risks becoming a vulnerability if technological shifts outpace the ability of traditional industries to adapt. This group averages between 28th and 30th place in global rankings, showing respectable performance but highlighting room for improvement, especially if they wish to future-proof their economies through deeper integration of R&D into industrial strategies (Edler & Fagerberg, 2017). The diversity within this cluster suggests that tailor-made solutions, rather than one-size-fits-all policies, are likely the most effective route forward.

Cluster 5 brings together nations with the lowest levels of R&D activity across all sectors. Curiously, a few of these countries still enjoy decent standards of living or significant economic size, proving that high GDP or prosperity doesn't automatically go hand-in-hand with strong research intensity (WIPO, 2023). Yet, the future competitiveness of these nations may be at risk if they fail to ramp up investment in research and technological capability (OECD, 2023b). The rankings bear this out: Cluster 5 countries sit, on average, around 46th to 55th place, placing them significantly behind other groups in terms of both competitiveness and innovation capacity. For them, creating basic research infrastructure, attracting investment, and crafting supportive policies will be crucial for keeping pace with global developments (Edler & Fagerberg, 2017).

Finally, Cluster 6 stands out for its high levels of government and public-sector spending on R&D, sometimes complemented by significant private-sector contributions. This reflects a proactive role of the state in steering strategic technologies and industrial priorities (OECD, 2023a; Edler & Fagerberg, 2017). However, a heavy public-sector focus can also bring challenges like bureaucratic rigidity or inefficiencies (Archibugi & Filippetti, 2018). Countries in this cluster achieve average positions between 17th and 25th place across the indices, signalling respectable global standing, albeit not quite matching the heights of Cluster 2. Their higher internal variability suggests diverse paths towards innovation success, with some nations managing to effectively bridge public investment with private dynamism, while others still face structural obstacles.

Taken together, these six clusters highlight that there is no single, universally optimal model for national R&D organisation. The way countries fund and structure their innovation systems varies greatly, shaped by broader economic, political, and institutional contexts. The competitiveness rankings show that while higher private-sector involvement often correlates with top-tier performance, public-sector investment can also sustain significant innovation potential – provided it's efficiently channelled and well-aligned with national priorities. For policymakers, understanding where their country sits in this landscape is crucial for designing strategies that not only promote scientific and technological progress but also secure robust economic competitiveness in a turbulent global environment (European Commission, 2022; Edler & Fagerberg, 2017). The integration of global indices into this analysis reinforces that the architecture of R&D spending is a meaningful predictor of broader national success, both economically and in terms of societal well-being.

3.2.2 CO_2 Emissions as Determinant of Strategy

Strategic planning at the state level can also be examined through the lens of environmental performance, particularly greenhouse gas emissions. CO_2 emissions have become a critical indicator of how nations balance economic development with sustainability goals. Analysing patterns in CO_2 emissions alongside socio-economic factors such as income per capita, life expectancy, population size, and recent changes in emission levels allows us to identify features of distinct state strategies and development models (World Bank, 2023; IEA, 2023).

Cluster analysis of 200 countries, based on data normalised up to 2020, reveals significant differences in how nations manage their emissions relative to economic and demographic characteristics. The results, presented in Figure 3.4, Tables 3.10, and 3.11, identify six distinct clusters that reflect not only environmental performance but also broader strategic orientations.

Cluster 1 groups countries such as China, the United States, and India, characterised by the highest total CO_2 emissions, mid-level per capita income, the largest population shares, and moderate life expectancy levels (Table 3.11). These economies exemplify nations where rapid industrialisation, large-scale manufacturing, and urbanisation remain state priorities. The sheer scale of industrial activity and population demands drives emissions upward, even as governments increasingly commit to sustainability targets (Zhang et al., 2022). Despite significant technological progress, balancing economic growth with improvements in individual welfare, as measured by indicators like life expectancy or income distribution, remains a policy challenge.

Cluster 2 gathers nations with very low total emissions, small populations, and lower life expectancy. These are often developing or least-developed countries where industrial activity is minimal and economies rely heavily on agriculture or natural resource extraction. Despite low emissions, significant challenges persist in improving socio-economic indicators such as income per capita and healthcare outcomes (UNDP, 2022). For these countries,

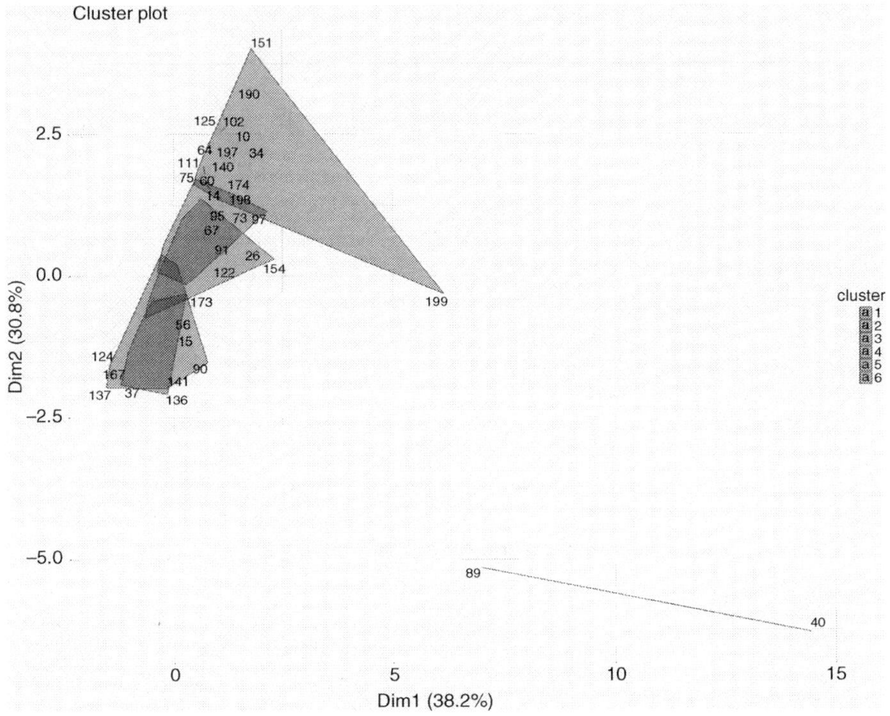

Figure 3.4 Six-Cluster Segmentation of Countries Based on Carbon Dioxide (CO_2) Emissions and Socio-Economic Indicators.

Source: Own elaboration using NbClust in R.

Notes: Each point represents a country classified into one of six clusters according to CO_2 emissions, income per capita, population size, and life expectancy. Data normalised up to 2020. The graph shows a two-dimensional projection. In such version India and China are situated in one separated cluster #1.

Table 3.10 Cluster Centres for CO_2 Emissions and Socio-Economic Variables

Cluster	*CO_2 Emissions*	*Yearly Change*	*Per Capita*	*Population*	*Life Expectancy*
1	0.621	0.332	0.124	0.968	0.641
2	0.002	0.394	0.022	0.018	0.398
3	0.001	0.324	0.009	0.016	0.170
4	0.005	0.425	0.071	0.014	0.646
5	0.011	0.290	0.142	0.015	0.849
6	0.044	0.286	0.506	0.022	0.771

Source: Own calculation using the NbClust package in R.

Notes: Values represent normalised cluster centroids obtained from k-means analysis of 200 countries. CO_2 Emissions indicate relative total national emissions. Yearly Change refers to normalised annual change in emissions. Per Capita reflects normalised GDP per person. Population and Life Expectancy are also expressed as normalised values between 0 and 1. Higher values indicate higher relative levels within the analysed dataset. Data normalised up to 2020.

Table 3.11 Clusters of Countries Based on CO_2 Emissions and Socio-Economic Indicators (2020)

Cluster	*Description*	*Example Countries (Max. 15)*
Cluster 1	High total CO_2 emissions, large populations, mid-level per capita emissions, average life expectancy. Represents the major global emitters.	China, United States, India, Russia, Japan, Germany, Brazil, Indonesia, Iran, South Korea, Saudi Arabia, South Africa, Mexico, Turkey, United Kingdom
Cluster 2	Extremely low CO_2 totals and per capita emissions, very low life expectancy, mostly poorest developing nations.	Chad, Burundi, Niger, Malawi, Lesotho, Guinea-Bissau, Central African Republic, Eritrea, Mali, Sierra Leone, Somalia, Guinea, Mozambique, Togo, Liberia
Cluster 3	Tiny emitters, very small populations, very low per capita CO_2, extremely low life expectancy. Often small island states or fragile states.	Faeroe Islands, Greenland, Western Sahara, Cook Islands, Solomon Islands, Sao Tome & Principe, Vanuatu, Tonga, Kiribati, Palau, Dominica, Saint Helena, Turks and Caicos, Timor-Leste, Samoa
Cluster 4	Small-to-medium emitters, moderate life expectancy, low-to-mid per capita CO_2. Often middle-income countries.	Costa Rica, Uruguay, Paraguay, Armenia, Jamaica, Namibia, Bhutan, Gabon, Fiji, Mauritius, Panama, Dominican Republic, Ecuador, Sri Lanka, Morocco
Cluster 5	Medium CO_2 emissions, moderate populations, highest life expectancy. Often advanced economies with strong sustainability records.	Norway, Sweden, Finland, Switzerland, Netherlands, New Zealand, Denmark, Iceland, Austria, Ireland, Luxembourg, Singapore, Israel, Australia, Belgium
Cluster 6	Medium total CO_2 but very high per capita emissions, often small rich countries with high life expectancy.	Qatar, Kuwait, United Arab Emirates, Bahrain, Oman, Saudi Arabia, Brunei, Trinidad and Tobago, Kazakhstan, Libya, Taiwan, Hong Kong, Macao, Montenegro, Luxembourg

Source: Own elaboration.

Notes: Countries were assigned to clusters based on their CO_2 emissions and socio-economic indicators from the provided dataset, using the cluster centroids in Table 3.10. Some countries lie close to the boundaries between clusters and may shift depending on which indicators are emphasised in the analysis. The numeric codes associated with each country refer to identifiers in the original dataset used for this clustering.

climate strategies focus more on adaptation and resilience-building than on large-scale emission reductions.

Cluster 3 includes very small states with extremely low emissions, low income per capita, and short life expectancy (Table 3.11). This cluster often represents vulnerable island nations or regions heavily exposed to climate risks. Although they contribute negligibly to global emissions, they face severe consequences from climate change, including sea-level rise and extreme weather events. Their strategic focus typically centres on securing international support for climate adaptation and loss-and-damage funding (IPCC, 2022).

Cluster 4 is defined by moderate CO_2 emissions, slightly higher income levels than Clusters 2 and 3, and moderate population sizes (Table 3.11). Nations in this group are often undergoing economic transitions, striving to decarbonise their energy systems while sustaining industrial competitiveness. While they may show a higher yearly change in emissions than some other groups, their life expectancy indicates reasonably effective public services and healthcare systems.

Cluster 5 comprises countries with relatively low total CO_2 emissions but higher income per capita and the highest levels of life expectancy among all groups (Table 3.11). These nations have often advanced furthest in decoupling economic growth from emissions, driven by technological innovation, strict environmental regulations, and strong societal demand for sustainable development (OECD, 2022c). Examples include many European states, where renewable energy deployment and energy efficiency improvements have significantly reduced carbon intensity. In these countries, climate strategies integrate both emission reductions and broader sustainable development goals.

Cluster 6 contains nations with moderate to significant total CO_2 emissions and the highest income per capita among the groups, coupled with high life expectancy (Table 3.11). These countries often have highly developed economies, diversified industrial bases, and significant investments in clean technologies. Although their per capita emissions can remain high due to energy-intensive industries or extensive transportation needs, they typically exhibit stable or declining annual growth rates in emissions, reflecting ongoing mitigation efforts. Policy strategies in these states focus on achieving net-zero targets while maintaining economic competitiveness (IEA, 2023). Examples include high-income, high-per-capita-emission countries such as Qatar, Kuwait, and the United Arab Emirates.

The heterogeneity within these clusters highlights those similar annual changes in CO_2 emissions can stem from fundamentally different economic structures and policy approaches. For instance, two countries showing comparable increases in emissions might differ vastly in income per capita due to factors such as economic composition, energy efficiency, or industrial specialisation. The cluster analysis based on yearly change in CO_2 emissions and income per capita (Figure 3.5) reveals a distinct group of outlier countries, especially visible in Clusters 4 and 6. In Cluster 6, there is a mix of wealthier nations – often resource-rich countries like Qatar, Kuwait, or the United Arab Emirates – that maintain high-income levels and historically high-per-capita emissions but are beginning to stabilise or slightly reduce emission growth. Conversely, other members of Cluster 6, such as Mongolia or Nigeria, are

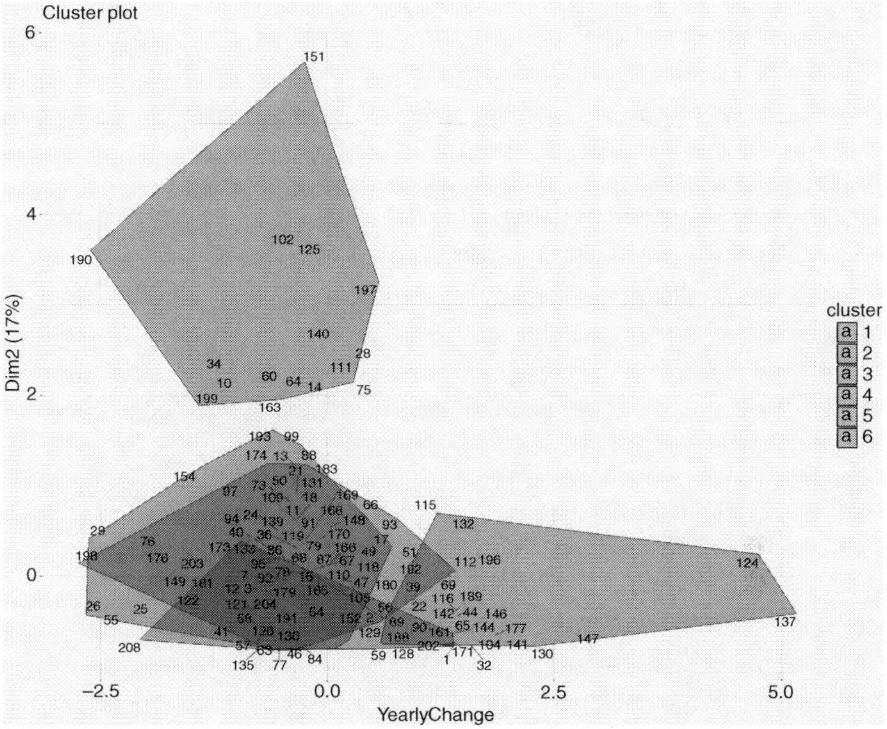

Figure 3.5 Two-Dimensional Cluster Plot of Countries by CO_2 Emission Change and Income per Capita.

Source: Own elaboration using the NbClust package in R.

Notes: Scatterplot based on two dimensions: annual change in CO_2 emissions and income per capita. The chart identifies outlier countries where rapid economic growth correlates with rising emissions, highlighting the sustainability-growth trade-off.

experiencing rapid economic expansion accompanied by rising emissions, illustrating the tension between economic development and environmental commitments. This reflects a broader dilemma faced by emerging economies striving to lift populations out of poverty while integrating into global supply chains and adhering to climate targets.

Ultimately, analysing annual changes in CO_2 emissions alongside income per capita sheds light not only on countries' environmental footprints but also on their economic philosophies, governance capacities, and development trajectories. Policymakers must confront the dual challenge of mitigating emission growth while fostering social progress and economic resilience – a balancing act increasingly central to national security, global competitiveness, and sustainability agendas (OECD, 2022c; UNDP, 2022; IEA, 2023).

3.2.3 *Happiness as an Indicator of Strategic Development*

In contemporary discussions on national development, there is increasing interest in viewing societal progress not merely through economic indicators such as GDP per capita, but rather through multidimensional well-being measures, such as happiness. This reflects the growing recognition that purely economic growth does not automatically translate into citizens' quality of life (OECD, 2023a; Helliwell et al., 2023). Using the World Happiness Report 2023, we performed a cluster analysis to group countries according to several well-being indicators: the happiness score (H), GDP per capita (GDP_pc), social support (Soc_sup), healthy life expectancy (Healthy_lexp), freedom of life choices (Free_lch), generosity (Generosity), and perception of corruption (Perc_cor). These dimensions are widely recognised in happiness research as critical drivers of subjective well-being (Helliwell et al., 2023; Easterlin, 2021).

Table 3.12 presents the centroids of the clusters identified in this analysis, based on data collected up to 2022. To improve clarity and readability, numeric values were rounded to three decimal places.

Countries like Denmark, Norway, and New Zealand fall into Cluster 1, distinguished by the highest scores across nearly all well-being dimensions except for generosity, which is slightly lower. This aligns with findings that Nordic countries consistently rank high in happiness due to robust welfare systems, social trust, and high institutional quality (Helliwell et al., 2023). By contrast, countries in Cluster 2 exhibit moderate results across most indicators but notably lower freedom of choice and generosity, paired with a higher perceived level of corruption. Countries like Greece, Türkiye, and Algeria tend to fall into this category, reflecting challenges related to economic instability and governance. Clusters 3 and 4 include nations with intermediate scores, indicating relatively balanced but not top-performing well-being systems.

Table 3.12 Cluster Centres for Happiness Indicators (2022)

No.	*H*	*GDP_pc*	*Soc_sup*	*Healthy_lexp*	*Free_lch*	*Generosity*	*Perc_cor*
1	0.886	0.887	0.909	0.831	0.911	0.425	0.706
2	0.386	0.598	0.583	0.540	0.473	0.154	0.196
3	0.680	0.743	0.820	0.732	0.708	0.197	0.106
4	0.573	0.620	0.740	0.648	0.729	0.433	0.103
5	0.381	0.368	0.439	0.354	0.515	0.392	0.162
6	0.585	0.586	0.666	0.622	0.847	0.236	0.285
7	0.262	0.397	0.220	0.442	0.757	0.385	0.451
8	0.587	0.605	0.779	0.604	0.836	0.765	0.163
9	0.731	0.829	0.837	0.785	0.761	0.249	0.337

Source: Own elaboration based on data from Helliwell et al. (2023).

Notes: H = Happiness; GDP_pc = GDP per capita; Soc_sup = Social support; Healthy_lexp = Healthy life expectancy; Free_lch = Freedom of life choices; Generosity; Perc_cor = Perception of corruption.

These countries typically achieve moderate levels of happiness and social support, though they do not reach the very high levels of economic prosperity or institutional trust seen in Cluster 1 nations. Interestingly, Cluster 5 reveals low levels across most indicators except for a moderate level of generosity, suggesting that cultural factors may sustain social solidarity even in contexts of economic hardship or weaker institutional performance. Cluster 6 groups countries with modest well-being scores but relatively high freedom of choice and slightly better perceptions of institutional integrity compared to Clusters 5 and 7. These nations may be experiencing social transitions, with some positive signs of civic engagement or governance improvements. Cluster 7 is particularly concerning, as it groups countries with low happiness, low GDP per capita, low social support, and relatively high perceived corruption. This cluster largely includes nations facing systemic political or economic difficulties, often characterised by persistent governance challenges and low institutional trust. Cluster 8 distinguishes itself through a unique combination of moderate happiness scores, mid-level economic indicators, and very high generosity levels – the highest among all clusters. This pattern suggests societies where strong cultural or religious traditions of altruism help sustain social cohesion, even when economic conditions or institutional trust are only average. Cluster 9 includes countries with high happiness levels and strong scores across most dimensions, though slightly below the absolute top levels of Cluster 1. These nations combine relatively high GDP per capita, strong social support networks, healthy life expectancy, and comparatively lower perceived corruption. While not reaching the extreme highs of the Nordic countries, Cluster 9 reflects societies with solid well-being and good institutional performance, often including prosperous small or mid-sized economies.

When we updated the analysis using the World Happiness Report 2025, the optimal number of clusters decreased to seven, indicating shifts in global well-being dynamics (Helliwell et al., 2025). The revised centroids are shown in Table 3.13. Meanwhile, Table 3.14 provides an overview of the clusters analysis of happiness indicators, summarising the key socio-economic characteristics of each group and illustrating them with example countries representative of the respective clusters.

Figures 3.6 and 3.7 visualise the cluster solutions for 2022 and 2025. This visualisation helps identify groups of countries following comparable development models or social strategies. In both years, high-performing countries (e.g., in 2025: Denmark (2), Norway (7), New Zealand (12); in 2022: Denmark (2), Norway (8), New Zealand (10)) remain grouped in clusters characterised by strong social support, economic wealth, high life expectancy, and low perceptions of corruption. Meanwhile, clusters with lower happiness scores often exhibit economic challenges, weaker institutions, and higher perceived corruption (e.g., Chile (2022: 44, 2025: 45), Panama (2022: 37, 2025: 41)).

Table 3.13 Cluster Centres for Happiness Indicators (2025)

No.	*H*	*GDP_pc*	*Soc_sup*	*Healthy_lexp*	*Free_lch*	*Generosity*	*Perc_cor*
1	0.761	0.715	0.833	0.560	0.806	0.220	0.188
2	0.872	0.897	0.893	0.882	0.867	0.482	0.750
3	0.424	0.558	0.659	0.258	0.529	0.154	0.157
4	0.824	0.797	0.861	0.785	0.856	0.477	0.317
5	0.584	0.526	0.706	0.504	0.741	0.583	0.137
6	0.447	0.397	0.419	0.347	0.631	0.386	0.249
7	0.678	0.746	0.750	0.797	0.638	0.186	0.222

Source: Own elaboration based on data from Helliwell et al. (2025).

Notes: H = Happiness; GDP_pc = GDP per capita; Soc_sup = Social support; Healthy_lexp = Healthy life expectancy; Free_lch = Freedom of life choices; Generosity; Perc_cor = Perception of corruption.

Figure 3.8 shows how 144 countries are spread out in a two-dimensional map based on Principal Component Analysis (PCA). The map takes complex data about happiness and well-being and turns it into an easier-to-read picture. Each dot represents a country, and its colour tells us which cluster it belongs to, based on similarities in things like income, health, social support, freedom, generosity, and perceptions of corruption.

We can spot some clear patterns. Countries in Cluster 1 (Table 3.14) – like Norway, Denmark, New Zealand, and Finland – sit in the top-right part of the plot. They stand out because they score high on almost every measure of well-being: people live long lives, feel supported by others, trust their institutions, and enjoy good living standards. It's no surprise these nations regularly top global happiness rankings. Cluster 2 also contains wealthy and stable countries with high levels of happiness and well-being, though sometimes with slightly lower generosity or higher perceptions of corruption than Cluster 1. Countries like France, Germany, or the Netherlands might belong here. These places still enjoy very high quality of life, even if they don't hit the absolute top on every measure. Countries in Cluster 3 – such as Greece, Türkiye, or Algeria – are more in the middle of the chart. They show average scores across happiness and well-being indicators. These are often nations where people experience decent social support and freedom, but economic or political challenges limit overall life satisfaction. Cluster 4 includes countries with lower levels of happiness and income but with some positives like moderate social support or community generosity. Many of these nations are in transition or are still developing, working to balance social progress with economic growth. Cluster 5 represents countries struggling the most. Here, happiness, income, and life expectancy are often low, and corruption may be more common. Yet, even in these countries, strong family or community ties sometimes help people stay resilient. Malawi, Tanzania, or Burkina Faso could be examples here. Finally, Cluster 6 brings together countries with mixed profiles. They may have lower incomes but show surprisingly strong scores in areas like generosity or freedom of choice. Countries like Morocco

Table 3.14 Clusters of Countries and Their Profiles Based on Happiness Indicators (2025)

Cluster	*Description*	*Example Countries (Max. 15)*
Cluster 1	Countries with moderately high happiness and solid socio-economic conditions, strong social support, good health, and considerable freedom of choice. Generosity and corruption perceptions are moderate. Generally stable, developed nations, though not the absolute top performers globally.	Austria, Australia, Belgium, Canada, Czechia, Denmark, Estonia, Finland, France, Germany, Iceland, Ireland, Lithuania, Luxembourg, Netherlands, New Zealand, Norway
Cluster 2	The global leaders in happiness and development. Very high levels of happiness, health, social support, freedom, generosity, and low perceptions of corruption. Represent the "best-off" countries worldwide.	Israel, Singapore
Cluster 3	Countries with low happiness levels, weak health and social indicators, and low GDP per capita. Freedom is more restricted, and corruption perceptions are higher. Typically developing or poorer countries, often facing economic or social challenges.	Afghanistan, Albania, Algeria, Armenia, Azerbaijan, Bangladesh, Benin, Bolivia, Bosnia and Herzegovina, Botswana, Brazil, Bulgaria, Cambodia, Cameroon, Chad
Cluster 4	Highly developed and happy countries, though not as exceptional as Cluster 2. High health, solid GDP, strong freedom, and relatively high generosity, but with higher corruption perception than Cluster 2.	Hong Kong SAR of China, Kuwait, United Arab Emirates
Cluster 5	Middle-ground countries with moderate happiness and well-being, decent health, freedom, and social support, but notably higher generosity. Positioned between developed and developing countries.	Libya, Mauritius, Republic of Moldova
Cluster 6	Countries with lower scores across most indicators, particularly health and social support, yet with somewhat higher freedom than Cluster 3. Often nations in transition or experiencing socio-economic instability.	China, Cyprus, Dominican Republic, Kosovo, Kuwait, Saudi Arabia, Serbia, Uruguay
Cluster 7	Countries with solid happiness and health levels but lower freedom and GDP than Cluster 2. Generally strong performers, though less distinguished in generosity and corruption perception.	Chile, Panama

Source: Own elaboration.

Notes: The country lists above include the group of representatives for each cluster, chosen alphabetically. Countries were assigned based on minimum Euclidean distance to cluster centres, using all seven indicators from Table 3.13.

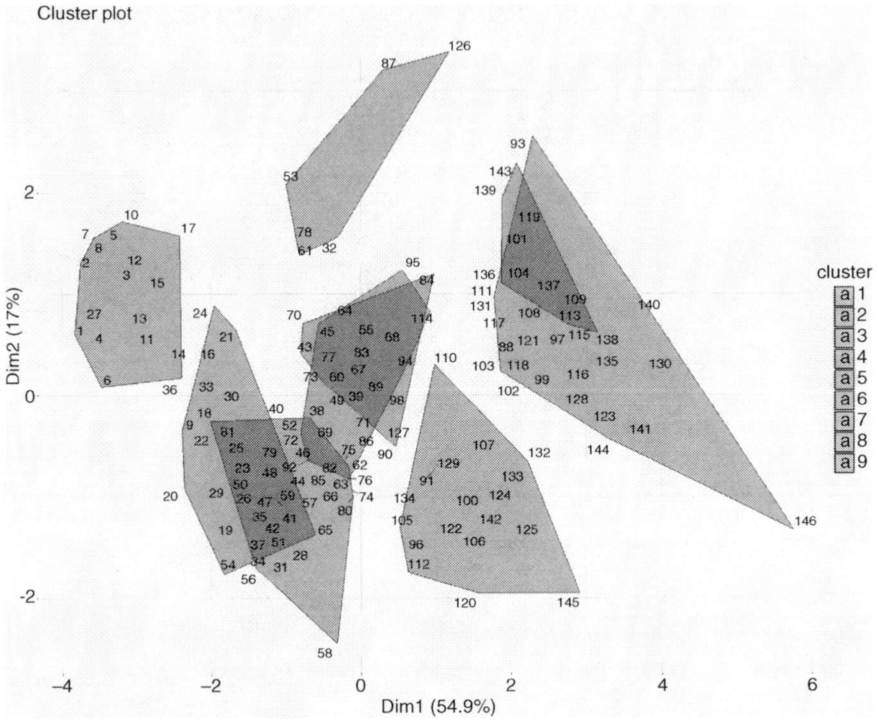

Figure 3.6 Clusters of Countries Based on Happiness Indicators (2022).

Source: Own elaboration based on data from Helliwell et al. (2023). The country numbering has been retained as in the baseline study.

Notes: One hundred and forty-six countries clustered using seven happiness-related factors. Nine clusters determined via NbClust (R). Visualisations reveal differing national well-being profiles and strategic pathways.

(2022: 100, 2025: 109) or Guatemala (2022: 39, 2025: 44) might fall into this group, showing that even with less wealth, people can maintain positive social connections that boost well-being.

Accordingly, this visualisation illustrates that while economic prosperity is an important driver of national happiness, other factors like social trust, institutional quality, and community cohesion profoundly shape well-being outcomes. Clusters overlap in some areas, emphasising that similarities in well-being profiles can emerge across regions with different economic levels. This has strategic implications, suggesting that countries grouped in similar clusters might learn from each other's policy experiences to enhance national well-being. It also reinforces the idea, central to initiatives like the OECD's "Beyond GDP", that sustainable development and strategic planning should integrate multidimensional measures of progress rather than focusing solely on economic growth (OECD, 2023a; 2023b; Helliwell et al., 2025).

Figure 3.9 provides spider charts comparing specific clusters. For instance, Clusters 3 and 5 differ sharply in generosity and perceived corruption. High

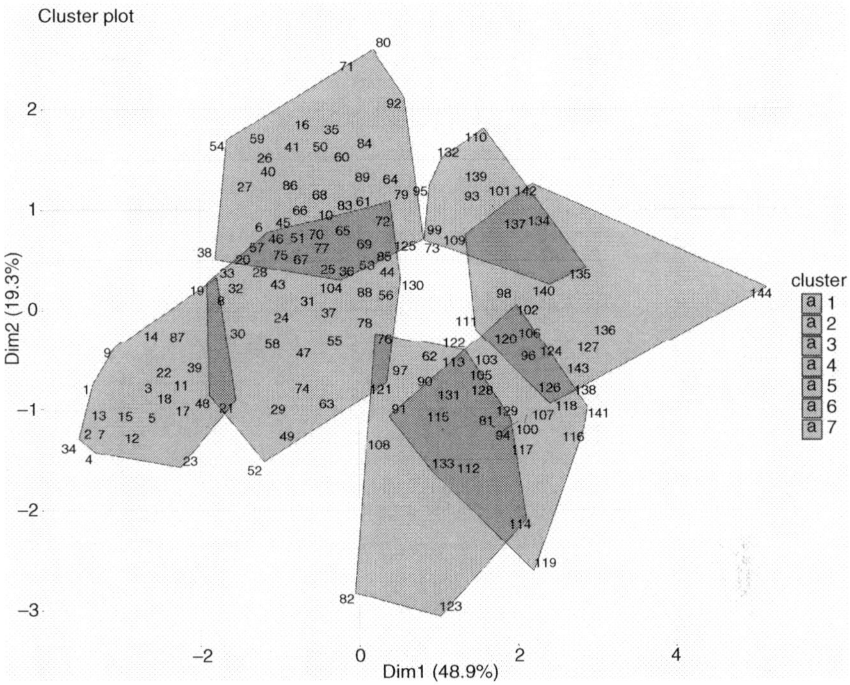

Figure 3.7 Clusters of Countries Based on Happiness Indicators (2025).

Source: Own elaboration based on data from Helliwell et al. (2025).

Notes: One hundred and forty-six countries clustered on seven happiness indicators. Seven clusters found via NbClust (R).

Visualisations reveal differing national well-being profiles and strategic pathways. The country numbering has been retained as in the baseline study.

generosity levels appear to mitigate the negative effects of lower income in some nations, consistent with research emphasising the non-monetary determinants of happiness (Dolan et al., 2008; Helliwell et al., 2023). From a broader perspective, these cluster analyses underscore those national strategies targeting well-being must consider multiple social dimensions beyond income. While economic growth remains important, institutional quality, social support, and perceived freedom critically shape subjective well-being. This aligns with the OECD's "Beyond GDP" framework, which emphasises multidimensional progress (OECD, 2023b).

3.3 Synthesis and Strategic Implications for National Competitiveness

The preceding analyses reveal how deeply interwoven geopolitical dynamics and national strategies are with the economic underpinnings of state competitiveness. Whether modelled through the confrontational lens of the Chicken Game, the collaborative potential of the Stag Hunt, or the caution

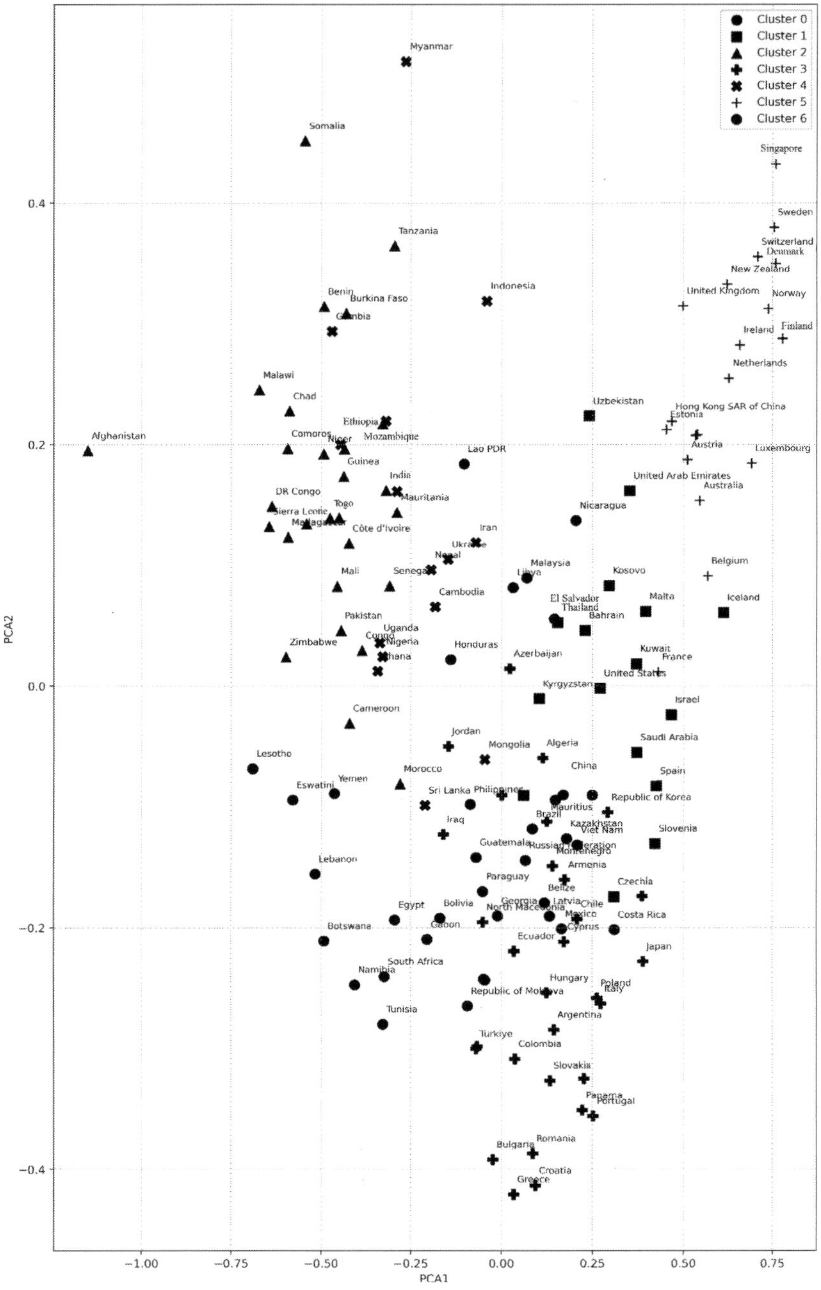

Figure 3.8 PCA Projection of Countries by Happiness-Related Indicators.

Source: Own elaboration based on data from Helliwell et al. (2025).

Notes: Principal component analysis (PCA) projection showing relative positions of 144 countries in multidimensional happiness space. Clusters derived from k-means algorithm in Python.

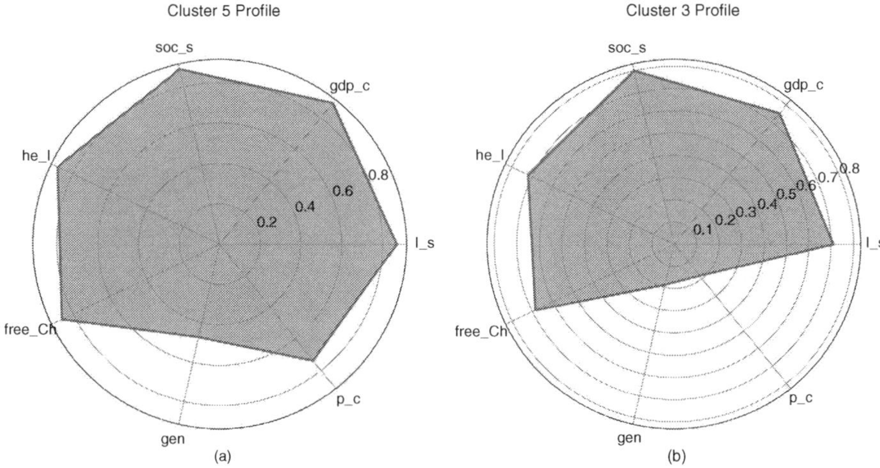

Figure 3.9 Radar Charts Comparing Happiness Profiles of Selected Clusters.

Source: Own elaboration based on data aggregated from R and Python cluster analyses.

Notes: Radar charts compare average values across key happiness indicators for selected clusters, showing differences in happiness score (H), GDP per capita (GDP_pc), and social support (Soc_sup), illustrating differences in national well-being strategies.

and mistrust inherent in the Prisoner's Dilemma, each game-theoretic framework offers unique insights into how nations navigate the complex interplay of risk, trust, and self-interest. A recurring pattern across all models is the centrality of strategic flexibility. Nations that adopt rigid, one-dimensional approaches – such as pure Tit For Tat strategies – often underperform in volatile geopolitical environments. Instead, strategies that incorporate memory, adaptive learning, and calibrated reciprocity tend to prevail over longer time horizons. This holds true whether we examine military standoffs, diplomatic negotiations, or economic competition. For instance, the emergence of the Generic Memory Two Player as a consistently top-ranking strategy underscores the advantage enjoyed by actors who balance past experiences with present circumstances, enabling nuanced responses rather than mechanical retaliation.

From a geopolitical standpoint, the strategic behaviours modelled in these games mirror the broader international system's current fragmentation. As alliances shift and rivalries deepen, countries increasingly rely on diversified strategies that enable them to hedge against multiple contingencies. China's cyclical strategies, blending periods of cooperation with deliberate, limited defections, reflect its calculated pursuit of strategic autonomy and global influence. Japan, by contrast, demonstrates a persistent orientation towards stability, technological leadership, and integration within multilateral frameworks. These strategic inclinations are also reflected in economic realities, as evidenced by the empirical analysis of optimal portfolio compositions in both China and Japan during contrasting geopolitical periods. In times of heightened geopolitical tension, China's investment strategies show strong concentration in sectors deemed critical for national security and technological self-sufficiency, such as advanced manufacturing, defence industries, and strategic infrastructure. Japan, on the other hand, channels its economic focus towards sectors enhancing quality of life, innovation capacity, and regional interconnectedness, even amid geopolitical shocks. Such portfolio allocations are not merely financial decisions; they serve as economic signatures of national strategy, revealing how each country translates its geopolitical worldview into concrete economic priorities.

A crucial implication for national competitiveness is that economic resilience is deeply intertwined with strategic clarity. Nations that maintain flexibility while safeguarding core strategic sectors are better positioned to absorb shocks and preserve long-term competitiveness. Moreover, the rising significance of technological industries, clean energy, and digital economies indicates that future competitiveness will increasingly depend on a state's capacity to innovate and integrate into global value chains – while simultaneously managing geopolitical risks. Moreover, financial markets emerge as sensitive barometers of geopolitical shifts. The sharp increases in Sharpe Ratios observed during periods of geopolitical stress, such as in early 2025, reveal heightened market concentration around national priorities and a declining tolerance for external uncertainties. This phenomenon reflects broader trends towards economic decoupling and the reconfiguration of global supply networks along geopolitical lines.

The synthesis of game theory and empirical market data underscores a critical lesson: there is no universal blueprint for national strategy. Countries must navigate an increasingly fluid geopolitical landscape by combining economic foresight, strategic adaptability, and a nuanced reading of global signals. Those capable of balancing cooperation with assertiveness – and aligning their economic structures with their geopolitical ambitions – will likely emerge as the most competitive actors in the evolving international order. These insights hold significant value not only for policymakers and strategists but also for investors, analysts, and businesses seeking to anticipate and respond to the shifting contours of global competition. As the 21st century progresses, the interplay between geopolitical tensions and economic strategy will remain a defining axis along which national fortunes rise or fall.

Shifting focus to the second part of this chapter, the analyses collectively illuminate the profound complexity inherent in shaping national strategies for the 21st century. In this broader context, strategy transcends traditional geopolitical calculations to encompass the structural determinants of competitiveness, innovation capacity, and societal resilience. The cluster analyses reveal that there is no single optimal pathway towards national competitiveness. Instead, countries pursue diverse configurations of policy and investment, each reflecting unique historical legacies, institutional structures, and socio-economic priorities. The segmentation of nations by R&D funding profiles demonstrates this vividly. Nations clustered around high private-sector involvement in R&D consistently achieve superior standings in global competitiveness and innovation indices. This underscores the strategic advantage of harnessing market dynamics and fostering close synergies between industry, academia, and public institutions. Such configurations often translate research outputs more efficiently into economic value, reinforcing a virtuous cycle of innovation and growth. However, other strategic models can also produce significant outcomes, albeit through different mechanisms. For example, high levels of government-led R&D spending – as seen in countries like China and South Korea – reflect deliberate national strategies aimed at securing technological sovereignty and steering industrial policy. These state-centric approaches can indeed be powerful instruments of competitiveness, provided they remain flexible and responsive. Still, the higher internal variability observed within this cluster signals potential tensions between centralised direction and the dynamism required for vibrant innovation ecosystems.

The environmental clusters highlight yet another dimension of strategic complexity. Nations that have succeeded in decoupling economic growth from carbon emissions show that sustainability and competitiveness can, indeed, be mutually reinforcing rather than mutually exclusive. Conversely, the challenges faced by emerging economies clustered in groups with rising emission trajectories underscore the enduring strategic dilemma between economic development and environmental stewardship. These findings point to the necessity of tailored policy instruments that support both decarbonisation and inclusive growth, particularly in contexts where industrialisation remains a critical path to prosperity.

Equally significant are insights from the happiness-based clusters, which offer a nuanced lens on the social underpinnings of competitiveness. Nations with robust social support networks, high institutional trust, and widespread perceptions of freedom tend to perform strongly not only in well-being rankings but also in broader measures of competitiveness. This highlights that factors traditionally regarded as belonging solely to the realm of social policy – such as trust, social cohesion, and citizen engagement – are, in fact, strategic assets with tangible implications for a nation's capacity to sustain innovation, absorb shocks, and maintain social stability.

Taken together, the evidence suggests that national strategy in the contemporary era must be conceived as an integrated architecture, simultaneously addressing technological progress, environmental sustainability, economic resilience, and societal well-being. Countries that succeed in aligning these dimensions are better positioned to secure sustainable competitive advantages and navigate the uncertainties of an increasingly multipolar world order. Moreover, the comparative cluster results underline the importance of contextual intelligence in strategic policymaking. Even among countries grouped in the same cluster, significant heterogeneity exists, reflecting distinct institutional frameworks, cultural factors, and geopolitical circumstances. Effective strategy, therefore, is not merely a matter of adopting best practices but of carefully adapting solutions to national realities while maintaining the agility to pivot as global conditions evolve.

In conclusion, these findings reinforce a core thesis of this book: strategy is fundamentally about choices – about recognising trade-offs, anticipating systemic risks, and orchestrating policy levers in a way that harmonises economic dynamism with social and environmental imperatives. As the data show, nations that manage to integrate innovation, sustainability, and social progress into a coherent strategic vision are those most likely to thrive in the turbulent decades ahead. This multidimensional perspective on competitiveness offers policymakers and scholars valuable tools to assess not only where nations stand today but also how they can shape their futures in an increasingly complex global landscape.

References

Archibugi, D., & Filippetti, A. (2018). *Innovation in times of crisis: National systems of innovation, structure, and policy responses*. Routledge.

Blackwill, R. D., & Harris, J. M. (2016). *War by other means: Geoeconomics and statecraft*. Harvard University Press. https://www.hup.harvard.edu/books/9780674979796

Bremmer, I. (2022). *The power of crisis: How three threats—and our response—will change the world*. Simon & Schuster.

Cabinet Office of Japan. (2024). *Annual economic and fiscal report 2024*. Government of Japan. https://www5.cao.go.jp/keizai3/whitepaper-e.html

Center for Strategic and International Studies (CSIS). (2023). *China's New Strategy for Waging the Microchip Tech War*. CSIS Reports. https://www.csis.org/analysis/chinas-new-strategy-waging-microchip-tech-war

Dolan, P., Peasgood, T., & White, M. (2008). Do we really know what makes us happy? A review of the economic literature on the factors associated with subjective well-being. *Journal of Economic Psychology, 29*(1), 94–122. https://doi.org/10.1016/j.joep.2007.09.001

Easterlin, R. A. (2021). *An economist's lessons on happiness: Farewell dismal science!*. Springer.

Easton, A. (2021, October 9). Poland stokes fears of leaving EU in 'Polexit'. *BBC News*. https://www.bbc.com/news/world-europe-58840076

Edler, J., & Fagerberg, J. (2017). Innovation policy: What, why, and how. *Oxford Review of Economic Policy, 33*(1), 2–23. https://doi.org/10.1093/oxrep/grw025

European Commission. (2022). *European innovation scoreboard 2022*. Publications Office of the European Union. https://research-and-innovation.ec.europa.eu/knowledge-publications-tools-and-data/publications/all-publications/european-innovation-scoreboard-2022_en

Friedman, G. (2023). *The storm before the calm: America's discord, the coming crisis of the 2020s, and the triumph beyond*. Doubleday.

Fukuyama, F. (2022). *Liberalism and its discontents*. Profile Books.

Helliwell, J. F., Layard, R., Sachs, J. D., De Neve, J.-E., Aknin, L. B., & Wang, S. (Eds.). (2023). *World happiness report 2023*. Sustainable Development Solutions Network. https://worldhappiness.report/ed/2023/

Helliwell, J. F., Layard, R., Sachs, J. D., De Neve, J.-E., Aknin, L. B., & Wang, S. (Eds.). (2025). *World happiness report 2025*. University of Oxford: Wellbeing Research Centre.

IMD. (2023). *IMD world competitiveness ranking 2023*. Lausanne: International Institute for Management Development. https://www.imd.org/centers/world-competitiveness-center/rankings/world-competitiveness/

International Energy Agency. (2023). *World energy outlook 2023*. IEA. https://www.iea.org/reports/world-energy-outlook-2023

IPCC. (2022). *Climate change 2022: Impacts, adaptation and vulnerability*. Cambridge University Press. https://www.ipcc.ch/report/ar6/wg2/

Ikenberry, G. J. (2018). *After victory: Institutions, strategic restraint, and the rebuilding of order after major wars* (2nd ed.). Princeton University Press.

Japan External Trade Organization (JETRO). (2023). *JETRO global trade and investment report 2023*. https://www.jetro.go.jp/en/reports/statistics.html

Kendall-Taylor, A., Frantz, E., & Wright, J. (2020). The Digital Dictators: How Technology Strengthens Autocracy. *Foreign Affairs, 99*(2), 103–115. https://pure.psu.edu/en/publications/the-digital-dictators-how-technology-strengthens-autocracy

Legatum (2023). *The Legatum prosperity index 2023*. London: Legatum Institute. https://www.prosperity.com/rankings

Li, L. (2021). Dual circulation and China's economic future. *The China Quarterly, 248*, 1084–1103. https://doi.org/10.1017/S0305741021000813

Mayer, A. (2019, March 29). Can game theory help to explain the UK's current Brexit difficulties? *Institute of Economic Affairs*. https://iea.org.uk/can-game-theory-help-to-explain-the-uks-current-brexit-difficulties/

Ministry of Economy, Trade and Industry (METI). (2022). *White paper on international economy and trade 2022*. Government of Japan. https://www.meti.go.jp/english/report/data/gIT2022maine.html

Ministry of Economy, Trade and Industry (METI). (2024). *White paper on international economy and trade 2024*. Government of Japan. https://www.meti.go.jp/english/report/pdf/0709_001a.pdf

Naughton, B. (2021). *The Chinese economy: Adaptation and growth* (2nd ed.). MIT Press.

OECD. (2021). *OECD economic outlook, volume 2021 issue* 2. OECD Publishing. https://doi.org/10.1787/39a88ab1-en

OECD. (2022a). *Main science and technology indicators (*Edition *2022/1)*. OECD. Stat. https://stats.oecd.org/Index.aspx?DataSetCode=MSTI_PUB

OECD. (2022b). *STAN industry database (Edition 2022)*. OECD.Stat. https://stats.oecd.org/Index.aspx?DataSetCode=STANINDIC

OECD. (2022c). *Green growth indicators 2022*. OECD Publishing. https://greengrowthindex.gggi.org/wp-content/uploads/2023/02/2022-Green-Growth-Index-1.pdf

OECD. (2023a). *How's life? 2023: Measuring well-being*. OECD Publishing. https://www.oecd.org/en/publications/how-s-life-2013_9789264201392-en.html

OECD. (2023b). *OECD economic outlook, volume 2023 issue* 1. OECD Publishing. https://www.oecd.org/en/publications/oecd-economic-outlook/volume-2023/issue-1_ce188438-en.html

Rolland, N. (2020). *China's vision for a new world order*. National Bureau of Asian Research. https://www.nbr.org/publication/chinas-vision-for-a-new-world-order/

Roubini, N. (2022). *MegaThreats: Ten dangerous trends that imperil our future—and how to survive them*. Little, Brown and Company.

Semiconductor Industry Association (SIA). (2022). *2022 SIA annual report*. https://www.scribd.com/document/690235150/SIA-State-of-Industry-Report-Nov-2022

United Nations Development Programme (UNDP). (2022). *Human development report 2022: Uncertain times, unsettled lives*. United Nations Development Programme. https://hdr.undp.org/

United States–China Economic and Security Review Commission. (2023). *2023 annual report to Congress*. US Government Publishing Office. https://www.uscc.gov/annual-report/2023-annual-report-congress

Veugelers, R. (2015). The role of R&D and innovation in productivity growth in Europe. *European Economy Discussion Papers*, No. 8. European Commission. https://ec.europa.eu/economy_finance/publications/eedp/pdf/dp008_en.pdf

World Bank. (2021). *Global economic prospects, June 2021*. World Bank Publications. https://openknowledge.worldbank.org/handle/10986/35647

World Bank. (2023). *World development indicators*. World Bank Data. https://databank.worldbank.org/

World Bank. (2024). *World development report 2024: Global value chains and development*. World Bank Publications. https://www.worldbank.org/en/publication/wdr2024

World Bank. (2025). *Global economic prospects, January 2025*. World Bank Publications. https://www.worldbank.org/en/publication/global-economic-prospects

World Intellectual Property Organization (WIPO). (2023). *Global innovation index 2023: Innovation in uncertain times*. WIPO. https://www.wipo.int/global_innovation_index/en/

Zhang, Y., Liu, Z., & Chen, B. (2022). Decarbonizing China's industrial emissions: Progress and challenges. *Nature Reviews Earth & Environment*, 3(7), 556–569.

Postface

This book set out to explore the profound transformations reshaping the strategic landscape of the 21st century – a world where economics, technology, and geopolitics are no longer separate spheres, but intricately interwoven elements of a single, volatile system. From the seismic shifts in global alliances to the tremors coursing through financial markets, from technological rivalries to evolving societal values, it has become increasingly evident that strategic thinking is no longer a luxury for a few specialised experts. Rather, it is a fundamental competency for any nation, institution, or individual seeking to navigate – and shape – the emerging age of global competition.

Once regarded primarily as the domain of military doctrine or corporate manoeuvring, strategy has expanded to encompass the full spectrum of national policy, technological ecosystems, social cohesion, and institutional resilience. National competitiveness today cannot be measured solely by familiar indicators like GDP growth, trade balances, or even technological output. Instead, it increasingly reflects a nation's ability to foster innovation ecosystems, integrate into global value chains without sacrificing strategic autonomy, and align economic aspirations with sustainability and societal well-being. Throughout this book, we have seen how the very fabric of strategy has become more complex and systemic. No single lever – be it military strength, financial power, or technological supremacy – is sufficient in isolation. Strategy has evolved into an architecture that requires both vision and agility. The COVID-19 pandemic, geopolitical shocks like the Russia–Ukraine war, and escalating technological rivalries have all demonstrated that the rules of the game are being rewritten in real time. The essence of modern strategy has shifted from static optimisation towards continuous recalibration – an adaptive process of anticipating shocks, managing uncertainty, and harnessing opportunities even amidst chaos.

A consistent pattern emerges from the analyses in this book: rigid strategies are increasingly inadequate in a world defined by volatility and interdependence. Nations and institutions that cling to fixed doctrines, no matter how rational under stable conditions, risk faltering when the environment shifts. Consider the insights gleaned from the Axelrod tournament framework. Pure Tit-for-Tat strategies perform well under certain conditions but

DOI: 10.4324/9781003660194-4

falter when confronted with more sophisticated opponents, unexpected defections, or evolving rules of engagement. The simulations highlight the power of strategies that incorporate memory, learning, and calibrated reciprocity. The geopolitical parallels are striking. As alliances shift and rivalries deepen, nations that combine long-term vision with tactical flexibility tend to preserve both influence and security. We see this reflected in China's blend of cyclical cooperation and selective defection, Japan's emphasis on technological leadership and multilateralism, and the European Union's evolving approach to balancing internal cohesion with external strategic autonomy. Ultimately, strategic resilience emerges not merely from planning, but from the capacity to pivot – to recognise signals early, recalibrate swiftly, and respond with nuance rather than dogma.

Yet perhaps the most significant conclusion emerging from this work is that the very idea of competitiveness itself is undergoing a transformation. Economic strength today is inseparable from technological leadership, environmental stewardship, social trust, and institutional adaptability. At the heart of this shift lies the concept of econothinking – a strategic mindset that views economic decisions as profoundly interconnected with geopolitical realities, technological pathways, and the institutional fabric of societies. It is not merely a method of analysis but a lens through which strategists can perceive systemic dynamics that transcend narrow financial metrics. Adopting econothinking means recognising that investing in green technology is simultaneously an economic opportunity, a geopolitical statement, and a moral commitment to future generations. It means understanding that R&D spending is not merely budget allocation but a determinant of national resilience and influence in global power structures. It means seeing national strategy as a dynamic architecture rather than a static blueprint. Throughout our chapters, we have seen how countries practicing econothinking – those integrating technological innovation, sustainability, and social cohesion – often secure more durable competitive advantages. The cluster analyses of R&D investments, environmental policy, and happiness-based social indicators all converge on this insight: future competitiveness belongs to those who understand that economic choices shape – and are shaped by – the broader geopolitical and societal context.

The empirical studies in this book reveal how financial markets act as both barometers and amplifiers of geopolitical tensions, technological shifts, and social transformations. During the pandemic years of 2020–2023, financial markets mirrored society's sudden prioritisation of health, digital connectivity, and technological solutions. In periods of geopolitical tension, markets shifted capital towards strategic industries such as semiconductors, energy infrastructure, and defence sectors. Emerging markets in regions like Central and Eastern Europe and South America stand at a crossroads. They exhibit enormous potential yet remain exposed to vulnerabilities such as concentration risk and institutional fragility. The convergence of these markets with global standards, as shown through applications of the Fama–French model and machine learning techniques, is a promising sign – but significant structural gaps remain. Moreover, the rise of algorithmic trading and AI-driven investment strategies adds a new layer of complexity. Markets now respond in milliseconds to geopolitical events, creating feedback loops that amplify volatility. Policymakers and strategists must recognise that financial markets are not only economic mechanisms but also increasingly strategic ecosystems capable of influencing geopolitical realities.

Strategic thinking today demands navigating paradoxes and trade-offs. Short-term competitive manoeuvres – such as protectionist tariffs, technological decoupling, or currency interventions – can yield immediate advantages. Yet these actions often carry unintended consequences, including the erosion of global cooperation, economic inefficiencies, and vulnerabilities in supply chains. Nations face difficult questions: how can they protect critical industries without isolating themselves from global innovation networks? How can environmental goals be pursued without undermining economic development in emerging economies? How can societies embrace technological change without exacerbating inequality or social fragmentation? This book makes clear that there is no universal blueprint for national strategy. What works for one country, given its institutional heritage and geopolitical circumstances, may fail elsewhere. Effective strategy requires contextual intelligence – the ability to tailor solutions to unique national realities while maintaining agility to pivot as conditions evolve.

Yet as this book has shown, strategy is not purely technical or mechanical. At first glance, strategic thinking might seem daunting. It demands an understanding of the environment, insight into competitors, and an honest assessment of one's own strengths and limitations. Sometimes, as the fable of the frog and the scorpion reminds us, even rational actors behave unpredictably. Modern computational tools like AI offer extraordinary assistance. Even modest programming skills can unlock analytical power that, in the past, was reserved for elite experts. Tools like Axelrod's tournament, the Fama–French model, and clustering algorithms allow us to simulate, stress-test, and explore strategic choices with unprecedented depth and speed. Yet beyond technical proficiency lies a deeper truth: strategy remains profoundly human. AI can detect hidden patterns, model complex systems, and run countless simulations. But it cannot answer questions like: who am I in this world? What legacy will I leave? What is the destiny of my state or my company? These are questions of identity, values, and purpose – questions rooted in culture, history, and the human longing for meaning.

AI is, as we've argued, a mirror and a lens. It reflects the inputs we give it and magnifies patterns we might otherwise miss. But it cannot substitute for human moral judgement, empathy, or imagination. Strategy without values is aimless. Values without strategy risk ineffectiveness. Humans and AI must collaborate – AI as an analytical lens, humans as the keepers of purpose and meaning.

Accordingly, several practical implications arise for policymakers, business leaders, and scholars alike.

- Strategic thinking must remain multidisciplinary. The future demands integrated insights from economics, political science, technology, and behavioural sciences – all bound together by econothinking.
- Data-driven tools are indispensable – but incomplete. Neural networks, agent-based models, and econophysical simulations offer invaluable insights, yet they must be paired with human judgement, ethical consideration, and contextual awareness.
- Competitiveness requires balancing national resilience with interdependence. Nations must define critical domains where autonomy is vital, while also recognising areas where cooperation yields shared benefits.
- Institutional trust and social cohesion are strategic assets. Societies characterised by trust, transparency, and inclusive governance are better positioned to innovate, weather shocks, and maintain sustainable competitiveness.
- Environmental sustainability is now inseparable from economic strategy. Nations seeking to decouple economic growth from carbon emissions not only protect the planet but also position themselves as leaders in emerging green industries.
- Geopolitical foresight must inform economic planning. As illustrated through examples like China's strategic cycles and Japan's steadfast technological focus, nations must anticipate how economic choices ripple through alliances and rivalries.

In the final analysis, this book argues that econothinking emerges as an indispensable compass for navigating the turbulence of the 21st century. It bridges the world of numbers and narratives, connecting empirical models with human purpose. It reminds us that strategy is not just about predicting markets or modelling alliances – but about aligning actions with values, ethics, and long-term visions. This book is not merely an academic exercise. It is a call to action for those who wish to engage with a world where technology, geopolitics, and economics collide at ever-increasing speed and complexity. The tools and insights presented here are meant not only to analyse but also to empower readers to anticipate change, shape strategy, and pursue goals that reflect both competitive advantage and human values.

We close this book with the conviction that the future will belong to those who can combine strategic clarity with adaptive capacity – and who understand that true competitiveness lies not simply in gaining advantage, but in building systems resilient enough to endure and flourish amid continuous change. Above all, we believe that econothinking will remain an essential compass for anyone seeking to navigate – and shape – the turbulent currents of the 21st-century global order. We thank the reader for accompanying us on this journey through the intertwined worlds of strategy, economics, technology, and geopolitics. May the insights shared in these pages serve both as a compass and as inspiration for thriving in the age of global competition.

Index